T
CHALLENGE

THE DIVINE CHALLENGE

on

Matter, Mind, Math, and Meaning

John Byl

THE BANNER OF TRUTH TRUST

THE BANNER OF TRUTH TRUST
3 Murrayfield Road, Edinburgh EH12 6EL, UK
P O Box 621, Carlisle, PA 17013, USA

*

*

Typeset in 11/14 pt Sabon by
Initial Typesetting Services
Edinburgh EH13 9PH

*

Printed in Great Britain by
The Cromwell Press Ltd.,
Trowbridge,
Wilts.

Contents

Preface   xiii
List of Diagrams   xii

1. THE CHALLENGE FRAMED   1

Is God Dead?   4
The Mysterious Trio – Matter, Mind and Math   7

2. WORLDVIEW WARS   12

Worldview Questions   13
We Need Assumptions   15
Worldviews in Conflict:
    Theism, Naturalism, Relativism   17
Judging Worldviews   19
Science and Common Sense   21
    Basics of Common Sense   22
    Basics of Science   23
Logic and Truth
    Contradictions of Absurdity   24
    Refuting Oneself   25
    What Is Truth?   26
    Everything Has a Reason   27
Conclusions   28
Appendix: A Brief Primer on Logic   28

3. NATURALISM   32

The Days of Myth and Magic   33
The Impact of Christianity   35
The Scientific Revolution   36
Basics of Naturalism
    Nature Is the Ultimate Reality   40
    Nature Is a Closed System   41
    Man Is a Mere Machine   41
    Only Sense Knowledge Counts   42
    Man Sets the Standards   42
    History Has No Purpose   42
Conclusions   42

4. MYSTERIES OF MATTER   44

Why Does the World Exist   45
Why Is the World Orderly?   48
Why Is the World Uniform?   51
Why Can We Understand the World?   53
How Can Math Make Matter?   57
How Does the One Relate to the Many?   59
Conclusions   61

5. CHANCE, CAUSE AND CHAOS   63

The Puzzle of Gravity   64
Causes of Chaos   66
The Strange World of Atoms   68
    Predicting Uncertainty   71
    Is Chance a Cause?   72
    Does Everything Have a Cause?   73
Making Sense of the Atomic World
    An Unknowable World   74
    A Determined World   75

Mind Makes Reality   77
Many Worlds   78
Taking Your Pick   78
Mind over Matter?   80
Conclusions   81

6. FROM MATTER TO MIND   82

Making Matter Come Alive   84
The Complexity of Life   84
The Tale of the Selfish Genes   87
Implications of Information   90
Detecting Design   91
Does Life Have a Purpose?   93
Turning Matter into Mind   95
Mysteries of Mind   96
What Are Thoughts about?   97
Is Mind More than Brain?   98
Emerging Mind   98
Dismissing the Mind   100
Are You for Real?   101
Meme Machine Minds   103
Can You Believe Your Beliefs?   106
Thoughts about Thoughts   106
Turning Thought into Action   108
Conclusions   109

7. FROM MIND TO MATH   111

Let's Be Reasonable   112
Who Knows?   112
Can You Trust Your Mind?
Survival or Truth?   113
Physics or Purpose?   115

Justifying Truth
    Where in the World Is Truth?   116
    A Question of Logic   117
    Math Is Ideal   118
    Are There Absolutes?   118
    Where Are the Standards?   121
How Do You Know?   122
    Is Non-Science Nonsense?   123
    Making Sense of Sense   124
    The Ideal Connection   125
    The Gift of the Gab   126
    Beauty and the Naturalist Beast   129
Conclusions   131

8. MYSTERIES OF MATHEMATICS   133

The Classical View on Math   134
    Math in an Ideal World   135
    Math in the Mind of God   136
Removing God from Math   137
Putting Math on Its Feet   138
Math in Crisis   140
Man-made Math   144
Evolution-made Math   147
Are Numbers Real?   149
Conclusions   153

9. BEYOND NATURALISM   155

Naturalism's Failures   156
    The Magic of Emergence   157
    The Dangers of Self-Refutation   159
The Post-Modern Backlash   160
    The Loss of Truth   160

Playing with Words	160
Power Makes Truth	162
Post-Modern Post-Mortem	163
The Ghost of Naturalism	166
What Does a Worldview Need?	167
Creating a Natural God	168
Do Atoms Have Feelings?	170
Finding Firm Ground	171
Appendix: How to Refute Scepticism	173
Testing Assumptions	173
Trying out the System	174
An Impossible Life	175

10. THE CHRISTIAN WORLDVIEW	178
Basics of the Christian Worldview	
God Is the Ultimate Reality	179
The Universe Totally Depends on God	183
Man Was Created to Be God's Steward	185
God Created Man to Know	187
God Sets the Standards	189
History Unfolds God's Plan	190
Examining the Christian Worldview	190
A Total Worldview	190
Justifying Worldview Tests	191
The Test of Experience	191
The Test of Scripture	192
The Test of Consistency	193
The Test of Livability	193
The Danger of Compromise	194
Conclusions	195

11. GOD AND THE PHYSICAL WORLD   196

God's Creation   197
    Why We Can Understand the Universe   197
God's Providence   198
    God Uses Secondary Causes   199
    Miracles Happen   199
Does God Play with Dice?   201
    Providence and Chance   202
    Does God Limit Himself?   204
    Knowing an Uncertain Future   206
    Butterflies and Storms   208
Conclusions   208

12. FREE WILL AND RESPONSIBILITY   210

What Is Human Free Will?   212
    Two Views on Free Will   213
Freedom within Uncertainty   214
    The Need for Chance   214
    A Missing Proof   215
    Freedom Shackled   216
    Limiting God   216
    God's Knowledge of Our Choices   218
    Where Does It Lead?   220
Freedom within Reason   221
    More than Physics   222
    Forming Your Fate   223
    Do You Really Have a Choice?   224
    Who Is Responsible?   226
The Bible and Responsibility   227
The Problem of Evil   231
Conclusions   235

13. BODY AND SOUL   237

What Is the Soul?   239
Body and Soul in the Bible   240
  Human Souls Survive Death   241
Body, Mind and Common Sense   243
Do You Need a Soul?   244
Probing an Immaterial Mind   245
  How Do Minds Operate?   246
  Minding Energy   248
  Where Is Your Mind?   250
  Who Made Your Soul?   251
Conclusions   253

14. A CHRISTIAN VIEW OF MATHEMATICS   254

God and Math   256
God and Logic   257
God and Number
  Infinity   258
  The Trinity   259
  Connecting the One to the Many   261
God and Necessary Truths   262
How Do We Learn Math?   265
  Our Inborn Abilities   265
  The Rule of Logic   267
  The Leaps of Intuition   267
How Can We Justify Math?   269
  A Bible-based Math?   269
  Classical Math and God   270
  Some Simple Set Theory   271
  Counting beyond Infinity   273
  The Axiom of Choice   274
  Justifying Math as a Whole   276
Conclusions   277

15. THE CHALLENGE SETTLED   279

Brief Summary
   The Nature of Worldviews   280
   Naturalism and Relativism   281
   The Christian Worldview   282
   Assessing Christianity   283
Defending the Faith   284
Why (Post-) Modernists Reject Christianity   286
World Stories: Human and Divine   289
The Return of the Pagans   291
Finale   293

Bibliography   299
Index   311

DIAGRAMS

Figure 1.1: Three Worlds and Three Mysteries   9
Figure 4.1: Some Simple Mathematical Shapes
            in Nature   50
Figure 5.1: The Double Slit Experiment   69
Figure 6.1: The Simple Cell   86
Figure 6.2: The DNA Molecule   88
Figure 8.1: The Mandelbrot Set   150

Preface

This book is about the war between God and fallen man. It concerns the double challenge, from God to man and from man to God, to establish who will rule. The war will be addressed at the level of competing worldviews and their ability to explain reality and assign meaning. The battleground will range over the realms of matter, mind and math.

The prime purpose of this book is the apologetic one of showing the superiority of the Christian worldview over its main competitors. The main thesis is that only Christianity offers a coherent, meaningful worldview. The challenges of modern naturalism and post-modern relativism ultimately self-destruct.

This book is addressed to the intelligent non-expert. Although the discussion will range over various issues in science, math, philosophy and theology, no prior knowledge of these disciplines is assumed. The aim is to convey the basic thrust of the arguments in non-technical language, as simply as possible. Nevertheless, some of these issues are very subtle, requiring the reader's close attention.

I thank Trinity Western University for a sabbatical leave, in which most of this book was written. I am grateful also to Shane Beazley for his critique of various chapters.

Earlier versions of several portions of this book have appeared previously in various publications. Portions of Chapters 6, 7 and 15 appeared in 'Naturalism, Theism and Objective Knowledge' in

Journal of Interdisciplinary Studies, XIV (2002): 69–90. Part of Chapter 14 appeared in 'Theism and Mathematical Realism', Association of Christians in the Mathematical Sciences Conference Proceedings (2001): 33–48. Parts of Chapters 5, 11 and 12 appeared in 'Indeterminism, Divine Action and Human Freedom', *Science & Christian Belief,* 15 (2003):101–116.

JOHN BYL
August 2004

The Challenge Framed

I cannot conceive of a God who rewards and punishes his creatures, or has a will of the type of which we are conscious in ourselves. An individual who should survive his physical death is also beyond my comprehension, nor do I wish it otherwise; such notions are for the fears or absurd egoism of feeble souls. In their struggle for the ethical good, teachers of religion must have the stature to give up the doctrine of a personal God, that is, give up that source of fear and hope which in the past placed such vast power in the hands of priests . . . The further the spiritual evolution of mankind advances, the more certain it seems to me that the path to genuine religiosity does not lie through the fear of life, and the fear of death, and blind faith, but through striving after rational knowledge.

ALBERT EINSTEIN (*The World as I See It* 1999:5; *Ideas and Opinions* 1954:48–49)

* * * * *

For the preaching of the cross is to them that perish foolishness; but unto us which are saved it is the power of God. For it is written, I will destroy the wisdom of the wise, and will bring to nothing the understanding of the prudent. Where is the wise? . . . hath not God made foolish the wisdom of this world? For after that in the wisdom of God the world by wisdom knew not God, it pleased God by the foolishness of preaching to save them that believe . . . Because the foolishness of God is wiser than men; And the weakness of God is stronger than men . . . God hath chosen the foolish things of the world to confound the wise; and God hath chosen the weak things of the world to confound the mighty.

1 CORINTHIANS 1:18–27

No one wants to be taken for a fool. We prefer to be considered wise. But how is wisdom to be distinguished from folly?

Albert Einstein (1879–1955), one of the founders of modern physics, is widely considered to have been the greatest scientist of the 20th century, if not of all time. Although most scientists tend to be poor philosophers, Einstein's philosophical writings are generally well respected. In many ways, his thoughts reflect those of the modern era. Little wonder, then, that Albert Einstein is acclaimed as a great, wise man.

And, undoubtedly, he was – by *worldly* standards, that is. However, judged by *biblical* standards, a rather different assessment emerges. Einstein openly rejected belief in a personal, transcendent God. He did not claim to be an atheist; he professed that his scientific work was motivated by a 'cosmic religious feeling'. This feeling consisted, however, of only a deep conviction of the rationality of the universe. Einstein's God was no more than an impersonal abstraction, seen in the mathematical structure of the universe. Accordingly, Einstein sought his religion through the human path of rational inquiry and scientific knowledge. The above quote reveals his scorn for the God of the Bible and for the salvation that he offers us within its pages. Thus, in this most important matter, Einstein was, by biblical standards, no wiser than the fool who said in his heart, 'There is no God' (*Psa.* 14:1).

Wisdom and folly thus depend on the yardstick we adopt to measure our choices. Should norms for wisdom be determined by God or man? That is the prime question addressed in this book.

The divine challenge to which the title of this book refers is closely linked to wisdom and knowledge. It is a double challenge.

First, it concerns man's challenge to God's supremacy. This challenge is as old as man:

> And the serpent said unto the woman, Ye shall not surely die: For God doth know that in the day ye eat thereof, then your eyes shall be opened, and ye shall be as gods, knowing good and evil. And when the woman saw that the tree was good for food, and that it was pleasant to the eyes, and a tree to be desired to make one wise, she took of the fruit thereof, and did eat, and gave also unto her husband with her; and he did eat. And the eyes of them both were opened, and they knew that they were naked; and they sewed fig leaves together, and made themselves aprons (*Gen.* 3:4–7).

Our first parents, Adam and Eve, were enticed to sin through their desire to be wise, to be 'as gods, knowing good and evil'. Thereafter, fallen humanity 'changed the truth of God into a lie, and worshipped and served the creature more than the Creator' (*Rom.* 1:25).

The human challenge to God is based on pride and envy. It deeply concerns knowledge, and the power knowledge brings. Man strives to dethrone the biblical God and to replace him with gods of his own making. Man seeks to reinterpret the universe according to his own standards, assigning it new meaning and transforming it to suit his own purposes.

In response, God issues forth his own challenge to sinful man. Here, too, knowledge plays a key role. Through his prophet Isaiah, God puts the question to man:

> Produce your cause, saith the LORD; bring forth your strong reasons, saith the King of Jacob. Let them bring them forth and shew us what shall happen: let them shew the former things, what they be, that we may consider them, and know the latter end of them; or declare us the things to come. Shew us the things that are to come hereafter, that we may know that ye are gods: yea, do good, or do evil, that we may be dismayed, and behold it together (*Isa.* 41:21–23).

The divine challenge to man's pretensions of knowledge can be found also in the latter chapters of the book of Job. The Lord answered Job out of the whirlwind, saying:

Who is this that darkeneth counsel by words without knowledge? Gird up now thy loins like a man; for I will demand of thee, and answer thou me. Where wast thou when I laid the foundations of the earth? declare, if thou hast understanding . . . Knowest thou the ordinances of heaven? canst thou set the dominion thereof in the earth? . . . Canst thou send lightnings, that they may go, and say unto thee, Here we are? Who hath put wisdom in the inward parts? or who hath given understanding to the heart? Who can number the clouds in wisdom? (*Job* 38:1–4, 33-37).

God is determined to destroy the wisdom of the worldly wise, to unmask it for the foolishness it really is.

Yet, modern scientific man, in his arrogance, believes that he can take up the divine challenge. He believes that he has far surpassed previous, pre-modern generations. He believes that he can now answer many of the questions God posed to Job. Armed with scientific knowledge and technological power, modern man is ready to seize God's throne.

Indeed, modern man believes that his rational wisdom has made foolish the biblical wisdom, with its tall tales of a personal God, of life after death, and of heaven and hell. 'Such notions', Einstein declared, 'are for the fears or absurd egoism of feeble souls.' Modern man believes himself to have outgrown the need for God.

Is God Dead?

Whither is God? . . . I will tell you. We have killed him – you and I . . . Do we hear nothing as yet of the noise of the gravediggers who are burying God? Do we smell nothing as yet of the divine decomposition? Gods, too, decompose. God is dead. God remains dead. And we have killed him.

Thus spoke the madman in Friedrich Nietzsche's book, *The Gay Science* (1882, section 125). Of course, Nietzsche (1844–1900), the famous German philosopher, did not believe that God had literally died. That would imply that God had once been alive. How could the omnipotent God of Christianity possibly die? Rather, Nietzsche was referring to the belief in the Christian God, which he considered to be no more than a fiction. In a later edition of his book he elaborated, 'The greatest recent event – that God is dead, that the belief in the Christian God has become un-believable – already casts its first shadows over Europe' (2nd ed. section 343).

Nietzsche believed that modern, rational society, particularly its science, had made belief in the Christian God untenable. Modern society thought itself to have progressed beyond the need for God. In pre-modern days God had stood in the centre of knowledge, meaning and life. Now God was pushed aside. God had become irrelevant to Western European culture. In the heart of modern man, God is dead, killed by science.

How did science 'kill' God? Modern man believes his science to have proven that miracles are impossible. The Bible stories can no longer be accepted as true. Further, modern man believes that his science can fully explain reality without having to resort to the supernatural. Hence, modern man has dispensed with the need for God, the very notion of God being now dismissed as a naive, pre-scientific myth. He is confident that, by the strength of his superior reasoning ability and technological prowess, he can answer all questions and solve all problems. Nothing, man boasts, is beyond his grasp.

Christian clashes with modernist views are often depicted as confrontations of mythical, subjective, irrational religion versus factual, objective, rational science. This is the myth of scientific neutrality, still strongly promoted in the secular press and academic institutions. Viewed in such terms, it is a foregone con-clusion that 'religion' must always give way to 'science'.

Yet, ironically, man's reason, when applied to science, has now revealed that science has its own share of problems. It has become increasingly clear that science and religion have much more in common than was once thought. It is nowadays generally granted that modern science itself has highly subjective aspects. Consider, for example, the speculative nature of scientific theories. It has become evident that scientific theories do not simply flow from what we observe. Rather, theories involve a large measure of imagination and invention. The same observations can often be explained by a host of competing theories. How, then, are we to choose the correct theory? We may prefer theories that are simple or beautiful. But this raises the question of why simple or beautiful theories are more likely to be true. Answering this question takes us beyond the observed data into the realm of philosophy. Ultimately, we choose scientific theories that best fit in with our most basic beliefs about what the world is like.

Such considerations have led many scholars to abandon modernity for post-modernity. Post-modern man stresses that science cannot operate without various assumptions about reality, including the assumption of the reliability of human reasoning. These assumptions cannot be rationally proven; they must be accepted on faith. For post-modern man, truth has lost its objectivity and has become entirely subjective. Whereas modern man was confident he could discover all truth, post-modernity is sceptical about even the actual existence of truth. Post-modern man argues that truth cannot be found, but must rather be created by ourselves.

Much of this Nietzsche foresaw. He clearly discerned the inherent shortcomings of modernity. Nietzsche declared that modern science had killed more than God. It had also killed *truth*. The dismissal of God destroyed the possibility of absolute norms. If God is dead then everything is permissible. In reaction to modernity, Nietzsche advocated a return to a more comprehensive view of life, to a pre-modern view that placed more stress on faith rather than reason. He felt that myth and its child, art, could convey a more ambiguous view of life – a metaphorical view that better expressed its complexities and harsh realities. Through such means, humanity must create its own meaning and cultural values, replacing those of the dead God. Nietzsche welcomed the 'death' of God as a necessary step towards the development of a new, great, fully human culture.

Now, more than a century after Nietzsche's death, his thoughts have become ever more popular. Nietzsche's critique of both

Christianity and modernity is widely acclaimed. Nietzsche has become the prophet of post-modernity. Society, at the beginning of a new millennium, seems poised for change along the directions sketched out by Nietzsche.

Modernity is still, however, a powerful force. Science, for example, remains predominantly modernist. Moreover, most post-moderns, however sceptical they may profess to be of truth claims elsewhere, still accept the naturalist, evolutionary view of origins.

Currently, then, in the Western world, the challenge between God and man is played out in the struggle of Christianity versus naturalistic modernity and relativistic post-modernity. We shall therefore examine these three worldviews to assess the wisdom and knowledge they entail. How well can they explain reality, provide meaning, and guide our lives to worthwhile ends?

The Mysterious Trio – Matter, Mind and Math

In order to explain reality, we must first ask: What is reality? What elements or substances make up reality?

The eminent Nobel prize-winning biologist Sir Francis Crick opened his book *The Astonishing Hypothesis* with the shocking statement:

> The Astonishing Hypothesis is that 'You', your joys and your sorrows, your memories and your ambitions, your sense of personal identity and free will, are in fact no more than the behaviour of a vast assembly of nerve cells and their associated molecules (1994:3).

According to Sir Francis, the real 'you' is just an illusion caused by physical processes in your brain. Many of his fellow scientists concur.

How did Sir Francis arrive at such a drastic hypothesis? His reasoning was actually quite simple. Sir Francis was a materialist. He believed that matter is the ultimate reality. Hence everything – even the human mind – must somehow be explained in terms of matter. Since feelings and thoughts cannot be reduced to matter, he dismissed these as mere illusions.

The question of how matter and mind interact is an ancient puzzle that has baffled scientists and philosophers. How does the objective physical world of flowers, wine and thorns relate to our subjective inner experiences of beauty, joy and pain?

The mystery deepens when we add a third component: the world of timeless truths. This concerns such things as knowledge, understanding, wisdom, and their underlying norms. Typical of this abstract world are such simple truths as '2 + 2 = 4'. I shall refer to this third world as that of mathematics. How do we gain entry into this mathematical world? How does mathematics interact with the worlds of matter and mind? These are among the most profound questions confronting humanity.

The physicist Roger Penrose concludes a lengthy book on this topic by noting three main mysteries (1994:413–414). These are illustrated in Figure 1.1. The first mystery is why mathematical laws play such a large role in the physical universe. The physical universe seems to emerge mysteriously from the mathematical realm. Note, however, that only a small portion of the mathematical world is actualized into concrete material form. The second mystery is how the physical world of matter can produce perceiving minds. Note, again, that only some matter (that is, brain cells) produces mind. The final mystery, which brings us full circle, is how a perceiving mind can create mathematical concepts. Once again, only a portion of the mind produces mathematics.

How can these mysteries be resolved? Many founders of modern science appealed to a Christian worldview. Kepler, Galileo, and Newton all believed that the God of the Bible created the universe according to a rational plan, that God created man in his image, and hence, that man is able to discern the rational structure of the universe. God provided the coherence between matter, human minds, and mathematics. Yet, over the last two centuries, most scientists have come to reject Christianity. Instead, they prefer naturalism, which holds that all of reality can be explained in terms of purely natural processes.

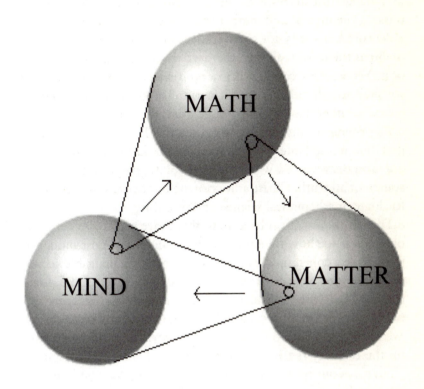

Figure 1.1: Three Worlds and Three Mysteries. Roger Penrose's mysteries are how the three worlds interact (based on Penrose, *Shadows of the Mind*, London: Vintage, 1994, p. 414).

The most dominant form of naturalism is *materialism*, the notion that everything in the universe derives from matter/energy. As we shall see, materialism has great difficulty explaining the mere existence of mind, let alone its rationality. It has no place for non-physical things such as logic, mathematics, or abstract knowledge. It can 'resolve' Penrose's three mysteries only by dismissing the mental and mathematical worlds as illusions.

Penrose himself is not a materialist. He takes the mathematical realm as the most real, the other two worlds being mere shadows of it. Yet, Penrose comes no closer to resolving his mysteries. Nor, we shall see, do other forms of naturalism or post-modernity.

On the other hand, we shall argue that the Christian worldview does provide a fully consistent account of Penrose's three worlds and their mutual interactions. It can justify knowledge by grounding it on the revealed Word of the absolute, tri-personal God, the source of all truth. Christianity can yield the necessary grounding for logic, mathematics, science and morality.

This book aims to substantiate the above claims. Accordingly, one goal is to show the failure of naturalism and post-modernity to provide a coherent worldview that can yield a plausible account of the various aspects of our experienced lives. A second goal is to show that the biblical worldview *does* give coherent explanations of the mysteries raised by matter, mind and mathematics. We shall argue that only a Christian worldview, squarely based on the truth of the Bible and the comprehensive sovereignty of God, gives our lives coherence, meaning, purpose and hope.

In brief, our agenda is as follows. In the next chapter we shall discuss the general nature of worldviews, the need for presuppositions, and how to assess competing worldviews. In the following six chapters we shall examine naturalism as it relates to matter, mind and mathematics. This is followed by a chapter assessing naturalism and some of its post-modern alternatives. In Chapter 10 we lay the basis for a Christian worldview. The following chapters discuss God's action in the physical world, human free will and responsibility, the biblical view on body and soul, and, finally, God and mathematics. The last chapter sums up our main conclusions and makes a few closing remarks.

In short, this book is about wisdom and folly regarding basic issues about the universe. Our prime thesis concerns the foolishness, not of God, but of boastful man, who vainly attempts to usurp God's rightful place. We shall argue that worldly wisdom is folly, even by its own standards, and that the alleged folly of the gospel is the only feasible gateway to genuine wisdom.

2

Worldview Wars

CROSSFIRE

We want to stand upon our own feet and look fair and square at the world – its good facts, its bad facts, its beauties, and its ugliness; see the world as it is and be not afraid of it. Conquer the world by intelligence and not merely by being slavishly subdued by the terror that comes from it. The whole conception of God is a conception derived from the ancient Oriental despotisms. It is a conception quite unworthy of free men. When you hear people in church debasing themselves and saying that they are miserable sinners, and all the rest of it, it seems contemptible and not worthy of self-respecting human beings . . . A good world needs knowledge, kindliness, and courage; it does not need a regretful hankering after the past or a fettering of the free intelligence by the words uttered long ago by ignorant men.

BERTRAND RUSSELL (*Why I Am Not a Christian* 1957:23)

* * * * *

Beware lest any man spoil you through philosophy and vain deceit, after the tradition of men, after the rudiments of the world, and not after Christ. For in him dwelleth all the fullness of the Godhead bodily. And ye are complete in him, which is the head of all principality and power.

COLOSSIANS 2:8–10

The clash between worldly and biblical wisdom is an all-encompassing one. At bottom it is based on radically differing views on the nature of man and God. Bertrand Russell (1872–1970), a prominent philosopher of the last century, makes it crystal clear that his philosophy is grounded in the freedom, intelligence, and self-respect of man. His contempt of God, and the notion of sin, is reminiscent of Einstein's remarks noted in the previous chapter. It was of this kind of philosophy that the Apostle Paul warns Christians, in the above quotation. Paul urges us to build our philosophy on the solid foundation of Christ, rather than on the shaky pretensions of worldly wisdom.

In this chapter we shall discuss the nature of worldviews, the presuppositions entailed in worldviews, and the rational assessment of competing worldviews.

Worldview Questions

The world of our experiences has a manifold richness. Consider, first, the variety of shapes, colours, sounds and smells encountered by our senses. These are impressed upon us by physical things outside us, by objects such as mountains, birds and flowers. Second, there is our inner life of thoughts, beliefs, emotions and desires. These seem to come from within ourselves. Third, there are laws of logic, mathematics and morals. The universal validity of these abstract norms implies they transcend our individual human minds. These three worlds of our experiences – we shall simply refer to them as the worlds of matter, mind and mathematics – seem distinct and yet intricately inter-connected.

Reflecting upon our experiences, weighty questions inevitably arise. What connects our numerous diverse experiences into a unified whole? This is the *problem of the one and the many*, a major issue in ancient Greek philosophy. Why does the world, or anything in it, exist? This was Aristotle's prime question. How did the three different worlds originate? How do they interact? These are questions raised by Penrose. What can we know? What should we do? What can we hope for? Immanuel Kant (1724–

1804) considered these to be the three most important questions in life.

These profound questions are among the deepest in philosophy. Our answers to such questions – and even the type of questions we may ask – are largely determined by our *worldview*. Our worldview consists of our most basic faith commitments, through which we interpret the world we experience and by which we live. Our worldview is the pair of spectacles through which we view the world and make sense of it. Everyone has one, although not everyone may be fully aware of their worldview or able to express it precisely. *Philosophy* is our attempt to articulate our worldview as a coherent system of basic beliefs, in terms of which all our experiences, beliefs, desires and hopes can be rationally explained and interpreted.

The main worldview questions that will concern us are the following:

1. What is the *ultimate* reality? This is basically a question of *religion*, defined in its broadest sense, as that to which we subject everything else. This could be the Christian God, nature, or man himself.

2. What is the *nature* of the world? This is a question of *metaphysics*. It concerns the substances that constitute reality. These could be matter, mind, abstract norms, spirits, and so on. A related question is how these various substances interact.

3. What is man? This is a question of *anthropology*. Is man a creature made in God's image, for a specific purpose, or merely a complex machine, formed through purposeless accidents?

4. How do we know? This is a question of *epistemology*. It concerns how we acquire knowledge, what we can know, and how we can justify our beliefs.

5. How can we distinguish right from wrong? This is a question of *rationality* and *ethics*. It concerns the question of the existence of universal norms that should guide our reasoning and conduct.

6. What happens at death? Is there life after death? If so, is the quality of that life related to our actions in this life? These are questions of *eschatology*, the doctrine of the last things.

7. What is the purpose of life? This is a question of *teleology*, which is closely linked with eschatology.

These questions are very similar to those found in James Sire's *The Universe Next Door* and Ronald Nash's *Life's Ultimate Questions*, two excellent books that deal with worldviews in general.

We Need Assumptions

A worldview, we noted, is a way of looking at the world and making sense of it. It forms the basis by which we explain reality and guide our lives. Our worldview consists of our most basic beliefs, the things that we take for granted concerning God, the world, and ourselves.

These basic beliefs have the nature of initial assumptions or *presuppositions*. They themselves are not supported by other beliefs or arguments. Rather, they form the means by which we assess other beliefs. They are reached when 'why?' questions must be stopped with a 'that's just the way it is'. They mark the end of our rational chain of explanations. The network of worldview presuppositions forms the foundation by which other propositions are either proven or disproven. We explain reality in terms of our presuppositions, but the presuppositions themselves must be accepted on faith.

Worldview presuppositions are like axioms in geometry. In geometry we start off with a set of axioms that are assumed to be true. From these we can derive a vast number of theorems. Changing the axioms can cause many changes in the consequent theorems. Likewise, our network of worldview presuppositions largely determines our conclusions about reality. A small change in our presuppositions can lead to significant changes in how we view the world.

Worldview presuppositions form the spectacles through which we see the world. They control the colour and sharpness of what we see. Everyone wears worldview spectacles. One might object that one's worldview must be based on proper evidence and that the evidence itself will lead to an objective worldview, without any need of presuppositions. But this cannot be done. One cannot move from mere observation to explanation without making some assumptions about reality. We need such assumptions if we are to decide which of our many experiences are more significant, to decide on a course of action, and so on. Evidence does not become evidence for anything until it is viewed through the spectacles of a worldview. Evidence, by itself, leads nowhere. Even our very standards of what it means to be rational or objective depend on our worldview.

Worldview presuppositions are unavoidable. In worldview disputes it is never a case of a worldview based on presuppositions versus one based solely on facts. *Everyone* starts with presuppositions.

However, disputes *are* often between those who explicitly acknowledge their presuppositions and those who do not. Unfortunately, as Phillip Johnson (1995: 67) notes, metaphysical assumptions are most powerful when they are unconscious, in which case they do not come to the surface because they are taken for granted. One thing we usually do not see through our world-view spectacles are the spectacles themselves! When not looking in the mirror of self-contemplation, it is easy to forget that we are in fact wearing spectacles.

Many people hold their worldviews implicitly, without having deeply reflected on what they believe and why they believe it. They may not even realize that they have a worldview. Consequently, they may unwittingly hold beliefs that are mutually contradictory. The first task in inter-worldview dialogue is to challenge opponents to reflect on where they stand on the major issues. What are their priorities in life? What are their worldview presuppositions? Once worldview presuppositions have been made explicit, their implications can be examined.

A worldview consists of an interconnected network of beliefs. However, we do not attach the same importance to all the presuppositions. Our most basic beliefs, as we have already noted, concern God and our relationship to him. Secondary, less important, beliefs might be about how we know things, how things originated, the relation between matter and mind, and so on. If you were to become convinced that your worldview is untenable, the simplest remedy might be to modify your network of worldview beliefs by changing one or more *secondary* beliefs, leaving the more basic ones intact. The clash between opposing worldviews often boils down to the clash between two basic beliefs, usually of a religious nature.

Worldviews in Conflict

Although a wide variety of worldviews exist, we shall focus on the three worldviews most prevalent in the Western world. These are theism, naturalism, and relativism. These will be discussed in detail in later chapters. Brief summaries of these three worldviews are as follows:

(a) THEISM

Under theism we shall limit ourselves to orthodox Christianity. Central to the Christian worldview is the notion of a sovereign, all-knowing, tri-personal God who has revealed himself through the Bible. This God is the creator of everything, even logical and moral absolutes. Everything that happens unfolds according to God's eternal plan. In this plan man, who was created in God's image, plays a major role, glorifying and enjoying God. Man was created good but, through his own choice, fell into sin. Through God's grace, man is redeemed in Christ. After physical death, our soul lives on, to be re-united with a renewed body on the Day of Judgment, at the Second Coming of Christ. Thereafter we shall receive our eternal reward.

(b) NATURALISM

Naturalism seeks to explain all of reality in terms of purely natural processes and entities. As such, it almost always incorporates an evolutionary process wherein everything in the universe – even man – evolved from primitive, purposeless matter/energy. Consequently, man is viewed as a complex machine that ceases to exist once his material body dies. Rational norms and ethical standards are considered to be mere human inventions, with no objective authority.

One form of naturalism, popular among scientists, is materialism. Biologist Edward Wilson, for example, believes that all truth can ultimately be acquired through science. Wilson asserts that all our knowledge, as well as our appreciation of beauty and perception of right and wrong, can in principle be reduced to the laws of physics (Wilson 1998:266). This view is similar to that of Sir Francis Crick. Crick was quoted in the previous chapter as asserting that our beliefs, our sense of personal identity, purpose and free will, are mere illusions caused by our brain neurons. Such materialism stresses the physical world at the expense of robbing our mental world of any genuine content.

(c) RELATIVISM

Some philosophers, partly in reaction to radical naturalist claims, go to the other extreme. They deny that there can be such a thing as objective knowledge. This is known as *relativism*. It stresses the *subjective self* at the expense of *objective knowledge*. Some forms of relativism are quite drastic. Thus, for example, the Scottish philosopher David Hume (1711–1776), denied almost all knowledge of the external world beyond the senses, including knowledge of our self. More recently, philosopher Richard Rorty contends that there is no objective knowledge at all, only linguistic constructs that have no connection with truth (1991:60). Rorty wants to drop the distinction between knowledge and opinion, as well as the notion that truth should correspond with reality (1991:25). Likewise, literature professor Barbara Smith defends the view that truth, knowledge, and reason are mere creations of human minds and as such, differ from mind to mind (Smith

1997:86). Such radical relativistic views deny that we can know anything objective about reality. Hence, one cannot be certain about even the possible existence of universal truths. In effect, radical relativism gives up on explaining reality.

Although relativism has become popular in the humanities, in the sciences naturalism still reigns supreme. Most of the leading scientists are naturalists. Historian Edward Larson and journalist Larry Witham (1999) note that over 90% of members of the (U.S.) National Academy of Sciences reject belief in supernatural theism. The relativism in non-scientific fields merely adds weight to the notion that only scientific knowledge counts as valid knowledge. Accordingly, our prime focus in the following chapters shall be to examine the viability of naturalism.

Judging Worldviews

How are we to judge between two opposing worldviews? Can we ever hope to convince someone with a different worldview that ours is better? At first sight this seems impossible. After all, a clash between worldviews is a clash between two opposing systems of thought, between two rival sets of presuppositions. Each side, in terms of its own presuppositions, will judge the other side's presuppositions (and subsequent conclusions) to be wrong.

If one's worldview reflects one's most basic faith commitments, how can we hope to rationally convince an opponent that any particular belief of theirs is false? To put it another way, if worldviews are like spectacles through which we view the world, how are we to convince someone wearing yellow-tinted spectacles that there are blue flowers? He won't be able to see blue until he exchanges his yellow spectacles for a pair that enable him to see a wider range of colours. But that amounts to a radical conversion, a major switch in faith commitment. A first step in that direction is to convince the person that he *is* wearing spectacles. The next step is to persuade the person that his spectacles are defective.

We may hope to show that one worldview is superior in terms of various criteria, such as consistency, comprehensiveness or

simplicity. However, these rules themselves are worldview dependent. Different worldviews may have different standards for what
makes a worldview acceptable and what defines rationality. Each
worldview will establish its own criteria for worldviews in terms
of its worldview presuppositions. For example, the Christian
worldview, unlike naturalism, will rate faithfulness to the Bible
as an important worldview criterion.

No one is neutral. Everyone is influenced by one's own worldview. Since everyone assesses worldviews in terms of one's own
criteria, how can we ever attain an objective assessment of rival
worldviews? How can we ever convince someone that his worldview is deficient?

This would seem to require the application of some very basic
criteria that must be used by any feasible worldview. Which
criteria qualify? A worldview, by definition, serves to explain our
experiences and guide our lives. As such, we should expect it to
be *consistent* with our actual *experiences* and, also, to be of *practical* value as we face the various choices of daily life. This suggests
that any viable worldview should fulfil the criteria of (1) consistency, (2) experience and (3) livability. Let's consider these in
more detail.

(1) CONSISTENCY.

This concerns not just a proper fit between our worldview and
our experiences, but also the *internal* coherence of a worldview.
[The essential role of logic will be discussed later.] Any set of
presuppositions that leads to contradictions must be rejected as
false. At least one of its presuppositions will then have to be
suitably modified. Also, consistency should apply to one's criteria
for assessing worldviews, in that any worldview should satisfy its
own criteria as to what constitutes a viable worldview. Moreover,
a worldview should be able to justify its criteria in terms of its
own worldview presuppositions. In this regard, later chapters will
show that naturalism, unlike Christianity, has difficulty fulfilling
its own criteria for rationality.

(2) Experience.

The presuppositions should not entail consequences that contradict our experiences. For example, a radical form of materialism that denies the existence of our conscious inner life must be rejected as inadequate. Further, the scope of our worldview should be such that it can address the basic worldview questions. Otherwise, our set of worldview presuppositions may have to be suitably expanded. Thus, for example, we must deem as incomplete any worldview that does not account for subjective thoughts and emotions.

(3) Livability.

The pragmatic test of a worldview is whether it can be consistently lived out. One may well doubt the credibility of any philosophy that cannot be coherently upheld in daily life. For example, any worldview that denies the validity of logic cannot be consistently lived, since logical reasoning is an essential part of our daily lives.

Science and Common Sense

The livability of a worldview includes, among other things, its ability to account for the actual activities of scientists and philosophers.

Of particular importance is the question of whether one's *defence* of one's worldview contradicts the *contents* of that worldview. Suppose, for example, that you believe that language cannot convey any truth. You cannot assert this belief – say, by writing or lecturing – without implicitly assuming the opposite. Hence, your very defence of this belief is itself the *reductio ad absurdum* of that belief.

Clearly, the defence of one's worldview must be consistent with, and indeed, justifiable in terms of, the premises of that worldview. What, then, does the defence of a worldview entail? It presumes a number of very basic, common sense notions that we all intuitively know to be true.

BASICS OF COMMON SENSE

First, for me to think about defending my worldview requires that I exist as a conscious, reflecting, purposeful *self*. If I am conscious of anything at all, it is surely this. For me to think *rationally* entails that there are such things as logical laws, truth, and objective rational standards. Next, to express my thoughts my mind must be able to cause my fingers to type the appropriate words. To expect *others* to learn my thoughts from the typed words presumes that there is a real world outside of myself in which there exist other people with minds similar to myself. Further, this assumes that we have a common, objective language and that human senses – and minds – generally work reliably.

These are all common sense things that we assume constantly in our daily lives. To sum up briefly, any meaningful talk presumes the following things:

1. a conscious, reflecting, purposeful self

2. truth and the laws of logic

3. objective rational standards

4. the ability of our mind to affect our body

5. an objective, physical world

6. other minds similar to our own

7. objective language

8. the reliability of our senses and mind

Any worldview that denies one or more of these elements cannot be rationally defended. Any defence of such a worldview is self-contradictory and therefore, irrational. As we shall presently see, various widely held worldviews are incoherent in the sense that their rational defence necessarily presupposes concepts that are explicitly denied by that worldview. This applies particularly to relativism and materialism.

BASICS OF SCIENCE

A further pragmatic test concerns the activities of scientists. Naturalism, in particular, has a high regard for scientific knowledge. What presuppositions does science entail?

Science is the systematic study of the natural world. Through observation and reason, scientists seek to acquire knowledge of the physical universe. Science is grounded in detailed experiments and observations of natural events. These are then analysed for patterns and regularities. This presumes that the universe has an underlying order and that this order is comprehensible to humans.

Observational data gives us direct information only about that portion of the universe that we have actually observed. One of the prime goals of science is to *extend* this knowledge to the (as yet) unobserved parts of the world – to the future, the distant past, and far away corners of the universe. This can be done only by making a number of assumptions (or theories) regarding the nature of the universe. The most important assumption is that of *uniformity*. Scientists assume that the physical laws observed here and now are valid everywhere and always.

As we shall see, mathematics plays a large role in science, particularly in physics and astronomy. Mathematics is essential in describing observational regularities, in deriving laws from general principles, and in making predictions. The scientist must presume that mathematics is applicable to the universe, and that numbers exist. Scientific theories are formulated also to *explain* physical reality. The observations are explained in terms of physical laws, the laws in terms of more basic principles, and so on. There is, however, a large gap between the observational data and the theories that are constructed by scientists to extrapolate and explain the data. Theories have a strongly subjective aspect and many of them can extend and explain the same set of observations.

We must make value judgments in deciding which theory is best. We tend to choose those theories that best fit in with our worldview. Value judgments are needed also to weed out dishonest research, to assess the reliability of data, to make ethical applications, and so on.

In short, all scientific activity is based on a number of crucial presuppositions. In addition to the ones needed for rational discourse, we must add the following:

9. the orderliness and comprehensibility of the world

10. the uniformity of nature

11. the applicability of mathematics and the existence of numbers

12. the existence of values, regarding knowledge, ethics, aesthetics, and method

The necessity of these is discussed in greater detail by the Christian philosopher J. P. Moreland (1989:109–133).

These, then, are the twelve basic assumptions that must be accounted for by any viable worldview.

Logic and Truth

In assessing worldviews, one of the most basic notions needed is that of *consistency*, which relates to logic. Logic and truth play such an essential role in worldviews that they warrant further discussion at this point. The laws of logic, referred to below, are briefly discussed in an appendix at the end of this chapter.

CONTRADICTIONS OF ABSURDITY

A contradiction in a worldview has drastic consequences. Why? Suppose that a proposition *A* implies both another proposition *B* and its direct opposite, *not B*. If both *B* and *not B* are true we have a contradiction, which, by the *Law of Non-contradiction*, is false. Since the consequence of *A* is false, it follows that *A* itself must also be false.

For example, suppose that a scientific theory (A) predicts both that gravity always travels at the speed of light (B) and that gravity does not always do so (*not B*). These predictions are contradictory and cannot both be true. Since theory (A) thus makes at least one false prediction, it cannot be a valid theory.

Any proposition leading to a contradiction must be false. Hence, a powerful means of falsifying a proposition – or a set of pro-positions – is to show that it leads to a contradiction. Any world-view leading to a contradiction is likewise falsified. In an inconsistent worldview, each part of the picture, or each individual presupposition of the worldview, may look fine when considered by itself. Yet the total picture is impossible.

The effect of a contradiction in a worldview extends far beyond itself. If a worldview *W* contains a contradiction, then any pro-position – no matter how absurd – can be derived from *W*. We can prove 'the Moon is made of green cheese', 'unicorns exist', and even 'worldview *W* is false'. There are various rigorous logical proofs of this. A simple way of looking at this is to note that if *B* and *not B* are both true then the *law of non-contradiction* no longer applies. Truth is then indistinguishable from falsity. The laws of logic are thus no longer relevant. Since no proposition, then, has any definitive truth value, all meaning is lost. Therefore, any worldview containing a contradiction leads to absurdity. A worldview containing a contradiction is said to be *incoherent*.

Reducing an argument or worldview to an absurdity is known as *reductio ad absurdum*. One means of doing so is to show that it is incoherent. Another way is to show that the argument, or worldview, entails a consequence that contradicts one of our core common sense beliefs, listed in the previous section. *Reductio ad absurdum* arguments can be very effective means of defeating a worldview.

REFUTING ONESELF

An argument or statement is *self-refuting* if it is inconsistent with what it asserts. For example, the statement 'this sentence is not written in English' *is* written in English, and so refutes itself. Self-refuting arguments frequently occur in relation to worldview issues. Consider the claim 'all truth is relative', which, if taken to be absolutely true, refutes itself. Or take the statement 'language cannot convey meaning', which itself makes a meaningful assertion. Or the statement 'only material things exist', which expresses a (non-material) thought.

The rational defence of any worldview is self-refuting if that worldview denies any of the common sense assumptions that are implicit in any rational argument. For example, we cannot rationally defend a worldview that denies the laws of logic since our very defence requires us to apply logic. The assertion of any statement, even the statement that the laws of logic are unnecessary, aims to convey a particular meaning, rather than its opposite. But this presumes the law of non-contradiction. Thus any attempt to refute logical laws is self-refuting, since we must use logic to argue against them.

What is Truth?

Logic is very closely tied to truth. Logical propositions are either true or false. What do we mean when we say a statement is *true*? By this is generally meant that it corresponds to what really is the case. Thus, for example, the statement 'it is now raining' is true if, and only if, it is in fact now raining. This is known as the *correspondence* theory of truth. The correspondence theory links a proposition to the reality it aims to describe. Since the proposition and the link are non-physical, this theory does not fit well within a materialist worldview.

Further difficulties for materialism arise when we make truth claims about non-physical objects. Consider, for example, the mathematical equation '$2 + 2 = 4$'. If we hold this to be a true statement then, according to the correspondence theory, it must really be the case that '$2 + 2 = 4$'. This means that the numbers 2 and 4 must really exist, with the properties reflected in this equation.

Since the correspondence theory of truth requires non-material abstractions, it is not easy to reconcile with materialist worldviews. Hence other definitions of truth have been devised. One alternative standard of truth is that of *coherence*. For something to be true it should *cohere* with other propositions that we know to be true. However, the mere fact that a proposition coheres with other truths is not sufficient to establish that it does, in fact, correspond with reality. For example, 'my car is green' may well cohere with all other truths about my car, even though my car may in fact be blue.

Another standard of truth is *pragmatism*, which equates truth with usefulness. Yet, the mere fact that a belief has useful results is not enough to establish its truthfulness. For example, Newtonian mechanics is a very useful theory that is now generally considered to be false. Further, to take an example from everyday life, although lies may at times seem to serve useful purposes, that does not transform them into truths.

Yet another standard of truth is *relativism*, which defines truth subjectively in terms of what a person or a society might believe. It denies the existence of objective standards of truth. Note, however, that the assertion 'all truth is relative' is itself a non-relative truth claim and is therefore self-refuting!

Everything Has a Reason

One of the goals of worldview philosophy is to answer questions of 'why?' This quest presumes the basic notion that, in an intelligible universe, all that exists has a reason for existing and for existing in the way it does. This is known as the *principle of sufficient reason*. In a logical sense, this principle affirms that any proposition is true if it is validly derived from true axioms. In a deeper sense, this principle further affirms that the basic axioms, as well as the laws of logic, have a sufficient reason for their existence.

Closely related to the principle of sufficient reason is the *principle of causality*, which affirms that all events can be completely explained in terms of causes. Nothing happens without a sufficient cause.

Conclusions

Worldviews were the main concern of this chapter. Everybody has a worldview, which interprets their experiences and guides their lives. Each worldview is based on presuppositions that are rarely made explicit.

Worldviews can be assessed in terms of the criteria of consistency, experience and livability. Any viable worldview should, at the very least, be able to account for such activities as normal conversation and scientific work. Hence, a worldview must accommodate the core common sense assumptions needed for these activities. These include the laws of logic, the correspondence notion of truth, and the principle of sufficient reason.

Further, since one of the tasks of a worldview is to account for our experiences, it must also be able to account for the existence of logic and truth. If a worldview is to justify its rationality, it must start off by justifying logic and truth, as well as the principle of sufficient reason.

Finally, we note that, even if we could convince someone that their worldview falls short, this in itself rarely causes that person to exchange their worldview for ours. Conversion is usually stiffly resisted. More often, the opponent will try to save his most basic worldview beliefs by modifying one or more secondary premises. For example, a demonstration of the incoherence of materialistic naturalism might cause the adherent to modify his metaphysics by allowing for the existence of mind while still retaining his naturalism. Or he might simply prefer to live with an inconsistent worldview rather than opt for a more distasteful alternative.

* * * * *

Appendix: A Brief Primer on Logic

LAWS OF LOGIC

The soundness of our reasoning depends on the validity of logic, the science of correct reasoning. A valid argument must obey the laws of deductive logic. Without such laws meaningful speech is impossible.

Consider, for example, the most basic law of logic:

1. *The law of non-contradiction*: Not (*A* and *not A*).

This law asserts that a meaningful proposition cannot be both true and false. *A* and its logical opposite, *not A* cannot both be true. More precisely, no meaningful proposition can assert of the same subject, in the same respect, an attribute and its opposite. Thus, for example, a plane geometric figure cannot be triangular and square at the same time. The statement 'all even numbers are the sum of two primes' cannot be true and false at the same time.

When we make a statement we generally intend to convey a particular thought, rather than its opposite. To assert that a particular proposition is true, rather than false, is to apply the *law of non-contradiction*. Aristotle, the first great logician, proved in *Metaphysica* that the law of non-contradiction is basic to all purposeful language (Aristotle 1952:525). Without it there can be no distinction between true and false. It is also a necessary law of *being*: *A* cannot be *B* and *not B* in the same sense at the same time.

Other basic logical laws include:

2. *The law of identity*: *A* is *A*.

Anything is identical to itself.

3. *The law of excluded middle*: Either *A* or *not A* is true.

A meaningful proposition is either true or false. There is no third option. For example, the proposition 'the number of prime numbers is infinite' is either true or false. Hence, if we can prove it is not false then we can conclude it must be true.

4. *Rational inference* (*modus ponens*): If *A* implies *B*, and *A*, then *B*.

An example of this rule is: if rain implies there are clouds overhead and if it is in fact raining, then there must be clouds overhead.

Closely related to *modus ponens* is

5. *Law of contrapositive* (*modus tollens*): If *A* implies *B*, and *not B*, then *not A*.

In other words, if *A* implies *B* and *B* is false, then so is *A*. Thus, in the above example, if rain implies clouds and there are no clouds, then there can be no rain.

Common Fallacies

A fallacy is a flaw in reasoning. Two common logical fallacies concern the concept '*A* implies *B*'. Here *A* is called the *antecedent* (that which comes first) and *B* is called the *consequent* (that which results or follows).

The first fallacy is called *affirming the consequent*. It is of the form:

1. *Fallacy of affirming the consequent*: If *A* implies *B*, and *B*, then *A*.

This is a fallacious form of *modus ponens*. For example, if rain implies clouds and if there are clouds, then we cannot conclude that there must be rain. A cloudy day may be dry. Or, to take another example, if Newtonian physics predicts a solar eclipse, and the solar eclipse occurs as predicted, this does not prove Newtonian physics to be true. Some other theory, such as general relativity, may have predicted the same result. Although, by *modus tollens*, false predictions can falsify a scientific model, true predictions cannot prove it to be true.

A closely related fallacy is that of *denying the antecedent*. It is of the form:

2. *Fallacy of denying the antecedent*: If *A* implies *B*, and *not A*, then *not B*.

For example, if rain implies clouds, and if there is no rain, it does not necessarily follow that there are no clouds. There might well be clouds that bring no rain.

3

Naturalism

CROSSFIRE

Make no mistake about the power of scientific materialism. It presents the human mind with an alternative mythology that until now has always, point for point in zones of conflict, defeated traditional religion . . . Every part of existence is considered to be obedient to physical laws requiring no external control. The scientist's devotion to parsimony in explanation excludes the divine spirit and other extraneous agents. Most importantly . . . the final decisive edge enjoyed by scientific naturalism will come from its capacity to explain traditional religion, its chief competitor, as a wholly material phenomenon. Theology is not likely to survive as an independent intellectual discipline.

EDWARD WILSON (*On Human Nature* 1979:200–201)

* * * * *

For the invisible things of him from the creation of the world are clearly seen, being understood by the things that are made, even his eternal power and Godhead; so that they are without excuse. Because that, when they knew God, they glorified him not as God, neither were thankful; but became vain in their imaginations, and their foolish heart was darkened. Professing themselves to be wise, they became fools, and changed the glory of the uncorruptible God into an image made like to corruptible man.

ROMANS 1:20–23

The first worldview we shall examine in detail is naturalism. What is naturalism? Why does it present a challenge to Christianity? Naturalist biologist Edward Wilson, in the above quote, makes it clear that naturalism is a comprehensive worldview. It aims to explain every aspect of life, even religion, in purely naturalistic terms. The main underlying theme of naturalism is that nature is self-sufficient. Nature, it is alleged, exists by itself, deriving all meaning and purpose from itself. It needs nothing outside of itself to explain it.

In the Western world, over the last few centuries, naturalism has been the major competitor to Christianity. It is still the ruling philosophy of modern culture. Naturalism is particularly popular among scientists and philosophers. It has a variety of names: the *modern scientific worldview*, *modernity*, *materialistic naturalism*, *materialism*, or simply *naturalism*. Even many people who generally consider themselves post-modern or relativistic still embrace naturalism with respect to science, particularly regarding origins.

In order to understand the thinking behind naturalism, we shall first briefly sketch the historical developments leading up to the naturalism of today.

The Days of Myth and Magic

The idea of the self-sufficiency of nature is hardly new. It dates back to ancient *paganism*. Many forms of paganism maintained that the 'world-all' (the entire cosmos, both visible and invisible) is one totality that is its own origin and which evolved according to its own potentiality (see Molnar 1995: 29). Outside the universe there is nothing. There is no divine creator or director of the universe. Denying the absolute God, paganism deemed the world itself to be sacred, in its entirety and in its parts. The world is self-explicating and divine. All things are united and possess self-fuelled power. Paganism aimed at increasing the power and divinity of man.

Some forms of paganism, such as Hinduism and Buddhism, are pantheistic. They equate the universe with God. Usually such religions believe time to be cyclic. The universe goes through endless cycles. The individual soul is reincarnated in various human or animal forms. The aim of the ascetic elite is to surmount the evil of personal existence and to be re-absorbed into the world-all. This is achieved through initiation into secret doctrine and purification via detachment from the senses, worldly involvement and intellectual stimulation (Molnar 1987: 28). One loses oneself to be become one with the Absolute. The soul is just a particle of the Absolute. The real world is denied and becomes an illusion. The Absolute does not think; only the pagan sage does, while still in his fallen individualized state. He must seek to rid himself of all thoughts, which are also illusions, to reach the perfection of nothingness.

Many of the ancient religions were polytheistic, worshipping many gods. But the gods of the Greeks or Babylonians were never ultimate. They themselves were subject to cosmic law and fate. These gods personified certain aspects of nature, over which they were said to exercise control.

Ancient paganism is closely associated with *myth*. A myth is a story manifesting some aspect of the cosmic order. It uses religious symbols and metaphors to express profound truths, not easily conveyed using purely rational reasoning. Myths offer us ways to order our experiences, to tell us about ourselves, and to guide our actions. Myths are often expressed in rituals and symbolic acts. Myths serve to help us surmount insecurity by promoting social solidarity and group identity.

Paganism is also closely linked to *magic* and the *occult*. Magic is the art of controlling the forces of nature by supernatural means, such as by charms and rituals. The occult has to do with mysterious, hidden arts such *astrology* (relating heavenly motions to

human destiny) and *alchemy* (concerning the magical transformation of matter). By gaining expertise in these arts one hoped
to control one's life and one's enemies.

Paganism came in many forms. Of these, particularly *gnosticism*
and *hermeticism* were troublesome for Christianity. Gnosticism,
a mixture of Christianity and paganism, was very prevalent in
the first few centuries of the Christian era. Hermeticism was present throughout Christian history. It is named after Hermes
Trismegistes (the 'thrice-great'), the reputed author (*circa* 3rd
century B.C., or earlier) of secret doctrine on occult practices. He
was thought to be of Egyptian or Eastern origin. Much of
hermeticism was pure magic and aimed at the manipulation of
natural forces. It made use of allegories and symbols; it placed
confidence in charms and incantations, which were thought to
invoke power and control. The underlying belief of hermeticism
was a living cosmos and the magical use of its operative powers.
The ultimate objective was the spiritualization of matter. In both
hermeticism and gnosticism man strives to know himself, to realize
the divine spark in his intimate being while rejecting his material
aspect.

The Impact of Christianity

The biblical worldview was always strongly opposed to paganism.
The Bible taught that only God, who was distinct from his creation,
ought to be worshipped. Instead of myth, the biblical worldview
was grounded in the concrete history of Genesis. Instead of magic,
the Bible upheld the unlimited power of God. Indeed, the Bible
denounced divination, sorcery, witchcraft, necromancy, and such
like (*Deut.* 18:10–12).

Before the coming of Christ, the clash with paganism was local-
ized. It was an evil influence that the Israelites, God's covenantal
people, were to repel. With the advent of Christianity the
battlefield was considerably enlarged. The New Testament gospel
was to be preached to the entire world. Christianity thus challenged paganism on a worldwide front. This included numerous

battles regarding idolatry, myth and magic. For example, the church at Ephesus, under the leadership of the Apostle Paul, burned occult books valued at fifty thousand pieces of silver (*Acts* 19:19).

Christianity sought to cleanse society of myth and magic, replacing it with a new worldview. The medieval Christian worldview was one wherein God, the world, and man were harmoniously related. God had created the world according to his eternal plan; man had been created in God's image to be God's steward in the world. The world reflected God's wisdom in the perfect order it displayed. Everything had its proper place in one huge hierarchical structure.

The biblical worldview is rich in symbolism, poetic imagery and repeated patterns. This comes out very strongly in such biblical books as Psalms, Isaiah, and Revelation. Many aspects of the physical world serve as signs and symbols for deeper spiritual truths. The cosmos reflects the spiritual reality – God and his agents – that exists beyond it. As Reformed theologian James Jordan notes, 'The world and all that it contains were made, in part, as pointers to God . . . in some sense they "symbolize" God's attributes to us' (1999:17). With the modern era, much of this symbolism has been forgotten, becoming foreign even to many Christians.

It was an era when truth was determined by tradition and by the authority of Scripture. The Reformation of the early 16th century challenged the role of church tradition but kept that of biblical authority.

The Scientific Revolution

The rational system built on Christian foundations, replacing myth and magic, formed the basis for the modern scientific worldview. Various factors in the Christian worldview encouraged the development of science:

1. The biblical conception of an omniscient and omnipotent personal God, who made everything in accordance with a rational

plan and purpose, contributed to the notion that nature had a rational structure.

2. The notion of a transcendent God, who exists separate from his creation, served to counter the notion that the physical world, or any part of it, is sacred. Since the entire physical world is a mere creation, it was thus a fit object of study and transformation.

3. Since man was made in the image of God (*Gen.* 1:26), which included rationality and creativity, it was deemed possible that man could discern the rational structure of the physical universe that God had made.

4. The cultural mandate, which appointed man to be God's steward over creation (*Gen.* 1:28), provided the motivation for studying nature and applying that study towards practical ends, at the same glorifying God for his wisdom and goodness.

Such considerations strongly motivated Copernicus, Kepler, Galileo, Boyle, Newton and many other founders of science. They believed that in their scientific work they were uncovering the deeper handiwork of the Creator. They deemed observation and theoretical analysis to be the chief means to knowledge of God's creation.

Nevertheless, the break with magic was not as clear-cut as is sometimes thought. Magic was not so easily overcome by either Christianity or science. Many giants of the scientific revolution were still influenced, to some degree, by hermeticism. The German astronomer Johannes Kepler (1571–1630) dabbled in astrology. Similarly, the great British physicist Isaac Newton (1642–1727) was intrigued by alchemy. Thus Newton, often considered to be the first truly modern scientist, has been called also 'the last of the magicians'. Although, with the new scientific mindset, hermeticism lost much of its popularity, it never became extinct.

In philosophy, the Frenchman René Descartes (1596–1650) is considered to have ushered in the modern era by insisting that truth be established by evidence and argument. Descartes looked for an indubitable basis on which to build knowledge. He concluded that the only thing he knew for certain was that he was thinking. Hence his famous *'cogito ergo sum'* (i.e., 'I think therefore I am'). As theologian John Feinberg notes, with Descartes the starting point of philosophy is transferred from God to human consciousness. It is now man, rather than God, who becomes the source of reality and intelligibility (2001: 86). Human consciousness will now determine what is true.

This new approach presumed that human reason and human senses were generally reliable means to truth. Descartes was a *rationalist*, who asserted that knowledge was to be constructed primarily on the basis of the self-evident beliefs of human reason. On the other hand, the philosophers John Locke (1632–1704), David Hume and Immanuel Kant were *empiricists*, who stressed that knowledge should be based on observational sense data. Modernity came to deem as valid knowledge only those beliefs that could ultimately be justified in terms of either logic or sense data.

Modernity followed Christianity in its belief of an objective reality beyond our experiences. The world exists independently of our experiences of it. Our statements about the world are true if they correspond to the actual state of affairs in the world. Science, with its reliance on observational data and logic, was viewed as the best means of acquiring truth about the objective world.

By the late 17th century science had become very successful. Through Newtonian mechanics, the world came to be seen as a huge machine, predictably ticking along by means of fixed physical laws. Although most of the scientists in the Scientific Revolution were Christians, their successors gradually came to see God as unnecessary. It seemed that the world-machine could run by itself, with no need for any outside input or adjustment.

The success of science had implications also for man's soul. Descartes had viewed man as a duality, consisting of a physical body controlled by an immaterial mind or soul. As to the question of how an immaterial soul could interact with a physical body, Descartes asserted that God brought about this interaction in a way analogous to that in which God, who is spirit, creates and upholds the physical world by his Word.

However, as God was removed from the world, man's immaterial soul was left hanging, with nothing to empower it. Man's soul, unlike his body, was not subject to scientific investigation. Consequently, with the success of the sciences, the soul came to be regarded as merely a property of the physical body. This materialist view of man was reinforced by Darwin's theory of evolution, which postulated that all of life had evolved from non-living matter.

The result of these developments was that many scientists and scholars accepted the natural sciences as the only means of acquiring truth about the world. Religion, ethics and metaphysics were widely thought to be void of any real content. Everything was to be explained in terms of purely natural processes. God was either denied outright or banished to insignificance.

Now, at the beginning of the twenty-first century, this view is still popular among scientists. Typical of this sentiment is the statement by Edward Wilson, quoted at the beginning of this chapter. Consider, for example, the reflections of materialist historian of science, William Provine:

> Evolutionary biology . . . tells us . . . that nature has no detectable purposive forces of any kind . . . Modern science directly implies that the world is organized strictly in accordance with deterministic principles or chance . . . There are no purposeful principles whatsoever in nature. There are no gods and no designing forces that are rationally detectable . . . Second, modern science directly implies that there are no inherent moral or ethical laws . . . Third, human beings are marvellously complex machines. The individual human becomes an ethical person by means of only two mechanisms: deterministic heredity interacting with deterministic environmental influences. That is all there is. Fourth, we must conclude that when we die, we die and that is the end of us . . . There is no hope of everlasting life . . . Free will, as traditionally conceived, the freedom

to make uncoerced and unpredictable choices among alternative possible courses of action, simply does not exist . . . the evolutionary process cannot produce a being that is truly free to make choices . . . The universe cares nothing for us . . . There is no ultimate meaning for humans. (Provine 1988:64–70)

Such is the sombre creed of materialism.

Basics of Naturalism

In terms of our basic worldview questions, naturalism's answer to these can be summarized as follows.

1. NATURE IS THE ULTIMATE REALITY

To this *religious* question of where we place our ultimate trust, naturalism responds that nature itself is the ultimate reality in terms of which everything is to be explained. Naturalists believe that everything is derived from elementary particles and their interactions. Naturalists are *realists*, in the sense that they believe there is an objective reality that exists independent of one's opinion about it.

Most naturalists are *materialists*. We shall use the word *matter* to denote all physical entities such as particles, light, and energy. Materialism is the belief that everything – even consciousness and mind – is just a form of matter. It assumes that there exists only one substance – matter – and that everything in the universe is ultimately explicable in terms of material properties and interactions. Materialists assert that the ultimate reality is matter, which is self-existing and not created by any external agent. Materialism rules out the existence of a supernatural, non-physical God.

Materialism has a very long history. It was defended already by Democritus of Abdera (*circa* 460–370 B.C.). Democritus held that the world consisted only of atoms, emptiness and motion. Everything else was formed through random interactions between the atoms moving through infinite empty space. Asserting that the universe had existed since eternity, he tried to banish both creator and designer.

A minority of naturalists believes in *pan-psychism,* which holds that all entities, even atoms, consist of both material and mental aspects. Pan-psychism will be discussed in a later chapter.

2. NATURE IS A CLOSED SYSTEM

How do naturalists view the *nature* of the universe? If, as naturalists believe, the cosmos is itself the ultimate reality, then all events in our universe should be explicable in terms of purely natural causes and effects. There are no external, super-natural forces. The physical cosmos is a closed, entirely self-contained system.

It follows that God, if he exists at all, can be ignored. He plays no significant role in the universe. Naturalists reject the notion that a supernatural being can intervene in the physical world. They claim to have neither need nor room for miracles. Some naturalists deny that God exists; others contend that we cannot know that God exists. Either way, God is superfluous.

By rejecting miracles, naturalists must uphold some form of naturalistic evolution as the only acceptable explanation for origins. They presume that man naturally evolved from lesser animals and ultimately from non-living matter. This entails that all human characteristics, including consciousness, mind, and purpose, are all derived from elementary physical entities. Everything that exists must have arisen from purposeless matter.

Many naturalists adhere to *physics-ism,* the belief that all of reality can be explained in terms of the most basic physical particles and their interactions, so that everything is ultimately explicable in terms of the laws of physics. Other naturalists believe that higher levels of complexity require explanations in terms of higher-level laws.

3. MAN IS A MERE MACHINE

To the *anthropological* question as to the nature of man, naturalists answer that man is just an accident of evolution. If he has evolved solely from matter, then he can be no more than a complex, material machine. His thoughts are then no more than the interaction of brain neurons. Man can have no immaterial soul. When he dies, he dies and that is the end of him.

4. ONLY SENSE KNOWLEDGE COUNTS

To the *epistemological* questions of how and what we know, naturalists respond that our knowledge is limited to what we learn through our physical senses, which are stimulated only by *physical* events. This is called *empiricism*. It follows from the prior notion that all causes are *physical* causes. Empiricism rules out all non-sensory experience, such as innate knowledge, intuition, extra-sensory perception, or divine revelation.

5. MAN SETS THE STANDARDS

If the ultimate reality is matter then there is no place for such things as non-physical, universal norms. There can be no absolute standards of true or false reasoning, right or wrong mathematics, or good or evil morals. Even if there were, empiricism denies that we can acquire knowledge of such norms. After all, we can only observe what *is*, not what *ought to be*. Hence, naturalism must postulate that all norms – whether rational, mathematical, or moral – are purely human inventions. Truth and falsity, right and wrong, and good and evil are thus reduced to mere human opinion or convention.

6. HISTORY HAS NO PURPOSE

If the ultimate reality were mindless matter then we would hardly expect the universe to have a purpose. Accordingly, materialists deny purpose and meaning to the universe. History is thus reduced to a chaotic stream of accidents. In the words of Macbeth, life is then 'a tale told by an idiot, full of sound and fury, signifying nothing'.

Conclusions

Naturalism is thus strongly opposed to Christianity. It rejects any notion of divine miraculous activity, any divine source of knowledge, or spiritual experiences. Naturalist Robert Segal, stipulates that naturalism must seek to explain even religion itself as having 'a naturalistic rather than divine origin' (Segal 1989:19).

It would seem, at first sight, that the defence of naturalism as a total worldview is no easy task. How is one to show that *everything* – including life, mind, mathematics, and morals – can be derived from lifeless matter? How is one to prove that purpose can come from non-purpose, mind from non-mind, 'ought' from 'is'? This seems to require, to say the least, great feats of ingenuity.

The naturalist quest becomes even more difficult when we recall the constraints that naturalism imposes on itself. The only valid knowledge, according to naturalism, is empirical scientific knowledge. The only valid method for confirming hypotheses is through empirical tests.

Yet naturalism is itself a *philosophical* doctrine. As such, it is not an empirical scientific hypothesis whose truth can be tested in a laboratory. No naturalist devises experiments to test naturalism. Rather, the truth of naturalism is assumed from the start as a basic presupposition. The claim that empirical scientific method is the only valid source of knowledge is thus self-refuting, since the claim itself is non-empirical. Moreover, the notion that only scientific knowledge is valid knowledge is itself *extra*-scientific, for science cannot prove that it alone can provide knowledge about reality.

In the next few chapters we shall examine the ability of naturalism to answer worldview-type questions. Particular attention will be paid to interactions between matter, mind and mathematics. A prime question is whether naturalism can account for human rationality and knowledge. A second closely related question concerns self-refutation. As we noted in Chapter 2, the rational defence of any worldview is self-refuting if that defence presumes certain common sense items (such as effective minds and rational norms) that are denied by the worldview that is being defended. Can naturalism avoid the charge of self-refutation?

4

Mysteries of Matter

CROSSFIRE

There is of course one big, cosmically big, seemingly real question: Where did it all come from? . . . Religion adopts the adipose answer: God made it – for reasons that will forever remain inscrutable until, perhaps, we become one with Him (that is, until we are dead). Such an answer, while intrinsically absurd and evil in its implications, appears to satisfy those for whom God is a significant part of their existence . . . There is, of course, no beyond-the-grave except in the minds of those who cannot come to terms with the prospect of their own annihilation . . . Science, in contrast, is steadily and strenuously working toward a comprehensible explanation . . . Though difficult, and still incomplete, there is no reason to believe that the great problem, how the universe came into being, and what it is, will not be solved; we can safely presume that the solution will be comprehensible to human minds. Moreover, that understanding will be achieved this side of the grave. In short, whereas religion scorns the power of human comprehension, science, the nobler pursuit, respects it.

PETER ATKINS (*Awesome versus Adipose* 1998)

* * * * *

Who hath measured the waters in the hollow of his hand, and meted out heaven with a span, and comprehended the dust of the earth in a measure, and weighed the mountains on scales, and the hills in a balance? . . . To whom will you liken me, or shall I be equal? saith the Holy One. Lift up your eyes on high, and behold who created these things, that bringeth out their host by number.

Isaiah 40:12–26

O ur universe is a very mysterious thing. Two of the biggest questions are: Where did it come from? And why does it exist?

The Oxford chemist, Peter Atkins, is confident that human reason, relying on materialistic science, can and will provide naturalistic answers to these questions. He believes the universe came into being without any help from a supernatural being. According to Atkins, the world came into existence by itself, from a mathematical set of points.

There are further intriguing questions about the material world. Why does it have the high degree of order that we can discern? Why is it uniform? Why does it have a mathematical structure? Why is its structure comprehensible to humans? How are the unity and the diversity of the universe to be related?

Such questions form the subject of this chapter. In particular, at this time, we shall address these issues in terms of the naturalist worldview. Naturalism aims to explain *everything* in terms of purely natural causes. How well can naturalism solve the above mysteries?

In a later chapter we shall return to these mysteries, this time from a Christian point of view. For our present purposes we shall define the universe to be the physical universe, consisting of the sum total of all the matter and energy in the world.

Why Does the World Exist?

The first mystery is why the material universe exists at all. It seems quite possible that there could have been no material universe. So, why is there something rather than nothing? And why does the universe continue in its existence? The principle of sufficient reason affirms that there must be a reason for everything. Surely, then, there should be a reason for the existence of the physical universe.

Naturalism is often tied to big-bang cosmology, which traces the origin of our physical universe to an immense explosion, from virtually nothing, a finite time ago. The reason for the existence of the universe could then be reduced to the reason for the big bang. The big bang is sometimes said to have been caused by a chance event in a pre-existing quantum field. Such a proposal, however, merely shifts the question of existence to the quantum field. What caused this field to exist? Or did it always exist?

One interesting proposal comes from Peter Atkins, who conjectures that everything that exists ultimately came into being by itself, from absolutely nothing. Atkins writes,

> In the beginning there was nothing. Absolute void, not merely empty space. There was no space; nor was there time, for this was before time. The universe was without form and void. By chance there was a fluctuation, and a set of points, emerging from nothing and taking their existence from the pattern they formed, defined a time. The chance formation of a pattern resulted in the emergence of time from coalesced opposites, its emergence from nothing. From absolute nothing, absolutely without intervention, there came into being rudimentary existence (Atkins 1994:149).

These initial points were supposedly purely mathematical points (1994:128). Because numbers can be defined in terms of the empty set (*i.e.*, a collection of objects that contains nothing), which Atkins equates with 'nothing', he believes that numbers can simply emerge from the empty set (Atkins 1994:115). Everything else then emerges from these mathematical points:

> The deep structure of the universe may be a globally self-consistent assemblage of the empty set. We, like mathematics, and like it or not, are elegant, self-consistent, reorganizations of nothing (Atkins 1994:115).

One difficulty here is that what Atkins terms as 'absolute nothing' is actually something (the empty set) with very specific properties. A second problem is how nothing can fluctuate. As noted by theologian Keith Ward (1996:39), also from Oxford, this seems to require a background space-time in which fluctuations can occur. A third question is, what caused the fluctuation? A further puzzle is, how can mathematical points give rise to material objects? These considerations indicate that Atkins has not solved the problem of how the universe came into existence.

If the physical universe started to exist at some time then we must look for some cause beyond the universe for its reason of existence. The notion that the universe just sprang into existence, without any cause, is not very satisfactory. However, since naturalism by definition limits itself to explanations within the natural universe, it can give no reason why the universe should begin to exist.

To get around this, some naturalists have proposed that the universe had no beginning. If matter is the ultimate reality then its existence must be accepted as a brute fact; there can then be no time at which matter did not exist. Perhaps, it might be argued, our present physical universe originated from a previous one, which originated from another universe, and so on, *ad infinitum*. A number of such 'beginningless' cosmologies are discussed in Byl (2001).

Yet even an eternal universe must have a reason for its existence. If the universe is the ultimate reality – the presupposition of naturalism – then the reason for its existence must be found within itself. This would be the case if the universe were a *necessary* being, like God. The reason that a necessary being exists is that it is impossible for it not to exist. The non-existence of a necessary being is inconceivable. The universe, however, seems to be *contingent*, rather than necessary. By contingent, we mean that it could have been different. For example, we can conceive that the universe could just have consisted of one galaxy, or one planet, or one rock, or one speck of dust . . . or nothing at all. For any contingent object we can ask, why is it the way it is and, indeed, why does it exist at all?

Philosopher Richard Taylor argues that anything that is contingent must depend on something else for its existence (1974:110). Ultimately, all contingent beings must derive their existence from something that necessarily exists, something that exists by its own nature, independent of anything else. This conclusion fits in well with theism, which asserts that God, a necessary Being, is the cause of the physical universe. Naturalism, on the other hand, cannot account for the existence of our contingent universe. Naturalism lacks a necessary being that alone can provide the ultimate sufficient cause of our universe.

To avoid this conclusion, some naturalists deny that the principle of sufficient reason applies to the universe as a whole. For example, naturalist philosopher J. L. Mackie argues that this principle is not necessary, as it is just based on our experiences. Further, he contends, even if it did hold *within* the world, this is no reason to expect it to hold *for* the world as a whole or for its basic laws (Mackie 1982:85).

However, the principle of sufficient reason is a basic presupposition of scientific and philosophical enquiry. Indeed, one of the aims of philosophy is to show that one's worldview can account for this principle. To deny its general validity is to allow for some things to exist or happen for no reason at all. This undermines rational enquiry. Moreover, if one were to restrict the principle of sufficient reason, this should itself be done for sufficient reasons. Otherwise, its denial in special cases is purely arbitrary. The burden of proof is therefore on Mackie to demonstrate the limited nature of the principle of sufficient reason. He must show that the principle of sufficient reason is over-ruled by some yet deeper principle. But what would such a profound principle be? It is hard to imagine what it could be . . . other than the naturalist presupposition that nothing exists beyond nature.

Why Is the World Orderly?

A second mystery concerns the orderly nature of our world. Our world is not a chaos. Rather, it is an intricately ordered and harmonious whole. There is much evidence of regularity, symmetry and other simple mathematical patterns. These can be seen in such diverse things as spiral galaxies, snowflakes, and flowers (see Figure 4.1).

Where does this order come from? Why does the world contain all the order it does? Did the world initially contain all the order we now see? or did order enter the world later? If order was there from the start then its origin could not, of course, be explained in terms of prior material influences. Thus an initial order can have no naturalist explanation.

Could the universe have started out relatively unstructured, becoming more ordered as time went by? This naturalist option also faces difficulties. It is our general experience that order is transformed into disorder, not the other way around. An elaborately designed sand castle, resplendent with its crenulated towers, when abandoned on the seashore soon decays into a nondescript mound of sand. The opposite never happens. This tendency towards increasing disorder is known as the *second law of thermodynamics*. Since the universe is currently highly structured, this implies that its initial order must have been even greater than that currently observed. Where did all this initial order come from? Physicist Paul Davies writes,

> The conundrum is this. If the universe is simply an accident, the odds against it containing any appreciable order are ludicrously small. If the big bang was just a random event, then the probability seems *overwhelming* (a colossal understatement) that the emerging cosmic material would be in thermodynamic equilibrium . . . As this was clearly not the case, it appears hard to escape the conclusion that the actual state of the universe has been 'chosen' or selected somehow from the huge number of available states, all but an infinitesimal fraction of which are totally disordered. And if such an exceedingly improbable initial state was selected, there surely had to be a *selector* or *designer* to 'choose' it (1983:168).

The naturalist, who is constrained to explain all things in terms of nature itself, has no recourse but to simply accept the initial

Figure 4.1: Some Simple Mathematical Shapes in Nature.
(Horn, spiral galaxy, shells, snowflake, hurricane off Florida,
cone flower.)

order as an inexplicable brute fact. He cannot appeal to anything beyond the universe that could impose order either initially or with the passage of time.

Why Is the World Uniform?

A closely related problem is that of *uniformity*. The universe usually appears to behave in regular, predictable ways. One of the main assumptions needed in science is that the physical laws, observed to work here and now, are the same everywhere and always. But why should that be the case? Why should the universe behave in a regular manner?

This brings us to the *problem of induction*. Jumping from a finite number of observations to conclusions of universal validity is called *inductive* reasoning. To conclude, having observed that every swan we have seen is white, that *all* swans, everywhere, are white, is an example of inductive reasoning. We expect similar causes to always produce similar effects. But why should this be true? Ever since it was first discussed by David Hume (1711–76), the problem of justifying induction has perplexed naturalist philosophers of science. No satisfactory naturalist justification of induction has yet been found. Nor is it likely that one will ever be forthcoming.

Why not? The difficulty is that all our predictions concerning *unexperienced* events are based on our past *experiences*. We assume that the unexperienced parts of the universe resemble the experienced parts. *Logically*, however, this resemblance need not exist. We could just as well conceive of, let us say, red swans. Since the possible existence of red swans cannot be disproved by logic alone, it follows that induction cannot be justified by mere logic.

But neither can it be proven through our *experiences*. By definition, unexperienced events lie outside our range of experience. No matter how regular nature may have been in our past experience, that by itself does not prove that it has been so elsewhere. Our past experience can give direct and certain information only of those precise events that we have experienced. Laws of nature are not *prescriptive* of what *must* happen, but only *descriptive* of what *has* thus far been observed to happen.

In short, all 'proofs' of the alleged uniformity of nature presuppose, hidden away as it might be, the very thing that they are supposed to demonstrate. The atheist philosopher, Bertrand Russell, gives an entertaining illustration of the uncertainty of induction (1959:63). A chicken is fed well every day. Applying induction, it expects this to continue forever. Each passing day strengthens its confidence in the validity of induction. Yet, there comes a day when the farmer chops off the chicken's head, thereby showing that a more refined view of induction would have been in order for the chicken. Likewise, our own confidence in the uniformity of nature may well suffer a similar fate.

Naturalism generally assumes that all valid knowledge is empirical. Since induction goes beyond our experiences, it follows that naturalism cannot justify induction. Of course, the lack of proof for induction need not stop anyone from using it. After all, unjustified extrapolations are better than no extrapolations at all. Indeed, our daily lives would be well-nigh impossible if we were to ban induction. In practice, induction is indispensable. The function of a worldview, however, is to explain and justify all our claims in terms of our worldview presuppositions. Thus, to the extent that naturalism cannot justify induction, induction must be adopted as an additional basic presupposition of naturalism.

The impossibility of proving induction leaves open the possibility of miracles or other naturally inexplicable irregularities. Yet Hume, having concluded that laws of nature are not necessarily uniform, nevertheless argues strongly against miracles. Hume contends,

> A miracle is a violation of the laws of nature; and as a firm and unalterable experience has established these laws, the proof against a miracle . . . is as entire as any argument from experience can possibly be imagined (Hume 1957:126).

According to Hume, we have a uniform experience against every miraculous event, which amounts to a full proof against the existence of any miracle (1957:127).

One can hardly deny that, if human experience were completely uniform, then no miracles could have occurred. But has human experience been completely uniform? In fact, there have been numerous reports of miracles, both in the Bible and elsewhere. Hence, to hold that human experience has been completely uniform, all such reports must be rejected as false. But how do we know they are false? Only if we know that miracles have not occurred. Thus Hume is arguing in a circle. Naturalism can rule out miracles only by assumption.

Why Can We Understand the World?

A further puzzle concerns the *comprehensibility* of the universe. Why is it that the universe is comprehensible to *humans*? Although, as we saw in Chapter 1, Albert Einstein rejected a personal God, he nevertheless marvelled at the unexpected and inexplicable comprehensibility of the universe. Einstein, in a letter to a friend, writes:

> You may find it surprising that I think of the comprehensibility of the world . . . as a miracle or an eternal mystery. But surely, *a priori*, one should expect the world to be chaotic, not to be grasped by thought in any way. One might (indeed one *should*) expect that the world evidence itself as lawful only so far as we grasp it in an orderly fashion . . . Even if the axioms of the theory are posited by man, the success of such a procedure supposes in the objective world a high degree of order which we are in no way entitled to expect *a priori*. Therein lies the 'miracle' which becomes more and more evident as our knowledge develops . . . And here is the weak point of positivists and of professional atheists, who feel happy because they think that they have not only pre-empted the world of the divine, but also of the miraculous. Curiously, we have to be resigned to recognizing the 'miracle' without having any legitimate way of getting any further (1956:114–15).

Einstein considered the comprehensibility of the world to be a miracle, an eternal mystery, which atheists have no hope of explaining.

The world's astonishing comprehensibility is best illustrated in physics. We have already noted that many objects in the world have a distinct mathematical shape. Actually, the mathematical structure of the universe runs much deeper than this. It is remarkable that a wide range of physical phenomena can be understood in terms of a very small number of physical principles and theories. For example, general relativity can be used to describe the behaviour of objects ranging from billiard balls and bicycles to rockets and planets. Maxwell's equations allow us to account for everything involving electricity and magnetism. Quantum mechanics provides the basis for chemistry.

These physical theories are of a highly *mathematical* nature. Physics has been a highly successful science primarily because its basic principles can be readily translated into precise mathematical equations. Further mathematical manipulations then lead to very specific predictions. These, in turn, lend themselves to many useful technological applications.

In 1960 Eugene Wigner, a Nobel-prize winner in physics, gave a famous lecture on *The Unreasonable Effectiveness of Mathematics in the Natural Sciences*. He concluded that the amazing applicability of mathematics to the physical world is a mysterious, undeserved and inexplicable gift.

Part of the mystery is due to the fact that, sometimes, mathematics developed for purely mathematical purposes, later turns out to have unexpected physical applications. For example, in 1609 the astronomer Johannes Kepler found that planetary orbits are best described in terms of *ellipses*, mathematical curves that had been studied two thousand years earlier by Greek mathematicians. Another example concerns the mathematical speciality known as *group theory*. Group theory was developed in the early 1800s by Evariste Galois, a French mathematician. He used group theory to study high-order algebraic equations. Much later, around 1960, group theory was found to have just the right structure to apply to the properties of elementary particles in physics. Group theory, thus applied, led to the prediction of a new particle, which was in fact subsequently discovered a few years later.

Steven Weinberg, another Nobel-prize winner in physics, remarks:

> Physicists generally find the ability of mathematicians to anticipate the mathematics needed in the theories of physics quite uncanny. It is as if Neil Armstrong in 1969, when he first set foot on the surface of the moon, had found in the lunar dust the footprints of Jules Verne (1992:157).

Philosopher Mark Steiner (1998) notes that Wigner's 'mystery' is open to various objections. First, Wigner ignores the failures, those instances where appropriate mathematical descriptions could not be found. Also, many mathematical concepts have not yet been shown to have any practical applications. Further, Wigner deals only with individual cases.

Nevertheless, Steiner believes that Wigner is on to something. He contends that the applicability of mathematics concerns not just a few isolated successes in physics. Rather, it pertains to the much broader applicability of mathematics as a global research strategy. Physicists, from Kepler and Galileo onwards, have been gripped by the conviction that mathematics is the ultimate language of the universe. Physicists probe nature with an eye for mathematical structures and analogies.

But such a mathematical research strategy for making discoveries is essentially an *anthropocentric* (that is, man-centred) strategy. It presumes that humans have a special place in nature. This is because mathematics relies on human standards such as simplicity, elegance, beauty and convenience. Anthropocentrism is most blatant in those cases where even the *notation* of mathematics plays a major role in scientific discovery.

Steiner gives various historical examples. One of these is physicist Paul Dirac's discovery of a new type of particle. In 1930, Dirac wanted to apply quantum mechanics and special relativity to electrons. He ended up with a quadratic polynomial that had to be factored. When real and complex numbers did not work,

Dirac factored the equation by introducing higher-dimensional number-like objects (4 dimensional matrices). This factoring resulted in several extra solutions, in addition to that corresponding to the electron. One of these solutions suggested the existence of a particle similar to the electron but with an opposite charge.

Two years later the existence of such particles – called *positrons* – was confirmed experimentally. Thus a mere mathematical trick, invented for computational convenience, resulted in a major physical discovery. Remarkably, the mathematical method Dirac applied (known as *Clifford algebra*) had been developed already in the 1800s for entirely different, purely mathematical, purposes.

Quantum mechanics, which deals with the structure of the atom, involves further mysteries. Most quantum physicists hold that we cannot adequately picture or model what goes on inside the atom. This leaves only the *formalisms* of the mathematical equations themselves. How can mere formalisms explain the great success of quantum mechanics? Steiner comments:

> The success of the formalism of quantum mechanics in predicting the properties of helium should have no bearing on its probable success with uranium . . . to say that a connection is 'formal' is just another way of saying that the connection is mediated by nothing more than notation. And a connection mediated by notation, I have been arguing, is anthropocentric . . . I have no quarrel with a physicist who is happy with the status quo, and works with quantum mechanics as a mere formalism. My only claim is that such a 'happy' physicist has no right to be a naturalist (Steiner 1998:145–6).

So the philosophical problem is not just the applicability of mathematics to our *descriptions* of physical reality but, even more, the major role of *human* mathematics in the *discovery* of new phenomena.

Steiner concludes that our universe appears to be intellectually 'user friendly' to humans. It is amazingly accessible to human research. This presents naturalism with a perplexing problem. Naturalists consider humans to be mere accidents in a purposeless world of matter. As such, they cannot expect the universe to reflect our standards of beauty and convenience. How, then, are naturalists to account for the fact that the universe's mathematical structure is just simple enough for *humans* to discern? Is this to be shrugged off as merely a lucky coincidence?

Steiner's examples of the amazing use of mathematics, in both scientific description and discovery, argue strongly against the notion that mathematics is merely a human invention. Rather, it favours the realist view that mathematics exists in a realm of its own, beyond human minds and material objects. Both the physical world and our human minds somehow reflect aspects of that mathematical realm.

How Can Math Make Matter?

Why should precise and profoundly *mathematical* laws play such an important role in the behaviour of the *physical* world? This, you may recall from Chapter 1, was Roger Penrose's first mystery (Penrose 1994:413). According to Penrose, the concrete world of physical reality seems to mysteriously emerge out of the ideal world of mathematics. Penrose views the mathematical world as the primary, real world, whereas the two other worlds – the physical and mental worlds – are only ethereal shadows of the mathematical world (Penrose 1994: 417).

Other scientists have made similar remarks. We recall, for example, the conjecture by Peter Atkins that physical reality is really mathematics, and that the universe originated from a mathematical set of points (Atkins 1994:128).

The views of Penrose and Atkins illustrate a danger facing scientists, particularly mathematical physicists. This peril is what Keith Ward calls 'the fallacy of misplaced concreteness' (Ward 1996:28). The hazard is that we become so impressed by the beauty and predictive power of our mathematical model of reality that we come to see our model as the true reality. The fallacy is to mistake our *abstract model* for the *concrete reality*. Our actual concrete experiences, upon which our model must ultimately be based, are then relegated to the realm of mere subjective illusion.

On the contrary, we must never forget the proper limits of our mathematical models. Models of the universe function like maps of landscapes. A map is just an *abstract representation* of the landscape and, as such, should never be mistaken for the real thing.

There is a further difficulty in identifying the world of mathematics with physical reality. These worlds are actually quite distinct. The mathematical world consists of necessary, timeless, abstract, universal truths. This is an ideal realm of pure thought. The physical world, on the other hand, consists of contingent, temporal, concrete particulars.

The mystery is how abstract, necessary universals can produce concrete, contingent, physical facts. How is it possible to *actualize* a physical world from a mere mathematical abstraction? Abstractions are of themselves inert. The famous physicist Stephen Hawking, after trying to show that the world is self-contained, needing no Creator, nevertheless concludes his book *A Brief History of Time* with the apt words,

> Even if there is just one possible unified theory, it is just a set of rules and equations. What is it that breathes fire into the equations and makes a universe for them to describe? The usual approach of science of constructing a mathematical model cannot answer the questions of why there should be a universe for the model to describe. Why does the universe go to all the bother of existing? Is the unified theory so compelling that it brings about its own existence? Or does it need a creator, and, if so, does he have any other effect on the universe? And who created him? (1988:174).

The move from mathematical abstraction to physical world seems to require an active being who can bridge the gap between necessity and contingency.

Further, out of an infinity of possible physical worlds, what caused precisely *this* particular universe to be chosen? Why not a universe that was slightly different? The principle of sufficient reason implies that there must be some reason for this. Again, naturalism has no ready answer.

Naturalism has great difficulty dealing with mathematical objects. Mathematical objects are abstract ideas. How can matter ever evolve into ideas? How can ideas exist other than in some mind? Naturalism alleges that mind evolved from matter. How, then, did mathematics exist before mind evolved? If the answer is that mathematics did not exist before the appearance of man, how are we to account for the mathematical structure of the laws of physics, which are assumed to have held from the start? If mathematical truths are universal and eternal, this seems to require the existence of a universal, eternal Mind. Yet, if mathematics exists objectively, beyond the human mind and physical world, how can man gain access to it? These questions will be examined more closely in later chapters.

How Does the One Relate to the Many?

A closely related question concerns the unity and the diversity of the universe. On the one hand, the universe is full of many different things and events. Each instant of time brings changes. Our bodies are not the same as they were when we were children. On the other hand, there is an underlying unity to our manifold experiences. Many phenomena, such as the motions of planets, follow a systematic pattern. We experience a sense of continuity between our present selves and our past. Flowers, although continually growing and decaying, exhibit a constancy of *flower-likeness* that never seems to change.

The question of how *the One* (that is, the underlying unity of the universe) is related to *the Many* (that is, the multitude of concrete individual things) is one of the oldest philosophical problems. Which is ultimate: *the One*, referring to the unity of the universe, or *the Many*, referring to its diversity? The universe is full of particular, individual things. Is the truth concerning them inherent in their individuality or in their basic oneness? What links the One to the Many? Such questions were extensively debated by the ancient Greek philosophers.

One of the most ancient of such debates was between Heraclitus of Ephesus (*circa* 540–475 BC) and Parmenides of Elea (*circa* 504–456 BC). Heraclitus argued that everything is in flux; nature has no stability or rest. He advocated the primacy of the Many over the One. Heraclitus stressed plurality and motion. Parmenides, on the other hand, held that the real is the totally unchanging, that which is beyond change and time. The real is that which is grasped by reason, in contradiction to the appearances presented to the senses. He emphasized the supremacy of the One over the illusions of the Many, which exist only as expressions of the One.

A similar opposition of the One to the Many can be found in modern naturalism. On the one hand, naturalism stresses the primacy of particular things. This is evident first of all in its empiricism, which takes knowledge to consist of sensual experiences. Knowledge, thus defined, is reduced to a steady stream of sense data. This dissolves the world into a chaos of unrelated and meaningless facts, without any unifying laws.

On the other hand, a prime aim of philosophy and science is to reduce the multiplicity of things to unity by finding underlying laws and principles. Materialism holds that all the things we experience are unified in that they all share the same material substance. This unity is of rather limited value, however, since materialism still places ultimate reality in particular material things themselves, rather than in such non-physical things as scientific laws or philosophical principles. What materialism fails to account for, as we shall shortly see, is how and why there can be any abstract, universal principles.

Penrose stresses the primacy of a unifying mathematical structure. However, as we saw, he leaves unresolved the question of how a specific mathematical structure can be physically actualised into concrete particulars. The search for a unifying *theory of everything* likewise elevates the One, in this case the supposed all-encompassing laws of nature, over the particulars that actually exist in the physical world. This quest ignores the importance of such contingencies as initial conditions and personal choices.

Much Far Eastern thought, such as Hinduism and Buddhism, also resolves the problem in favour of the One. The ultimate goal of being, even for the individual human, is to be absorbed into the One. Consequently, as noted by the Reformed scholar R. J. Rushdoony (1978:5), any particularity – including the human self – is considered to be unreal or illusory.

Modern scientific theories offer further, more specific examples of the inability to satisfactorily link the One to the Many. For example, quantum field theory treats the universe as a seamless whole, devoid of discrete objects. This renders scientific data illusory and subjective. The Copenhagen view of quantum mechanics takes waves and particles to be *complementary* descriptions of reality. There are two equally ultimate, independent principles, without any unifying factor. This solution to the One and Many problem produces an uneasy tension that provides no final coherence.

None of these proposed solutions provide a satisfactory account of how the One and the Many can peacefully co-exist in mutual harmony.

Conclusions

We have seen that naturalism has great difficulty answering basic questions about the material universe:

Naturalism cannot explain why the universe exists or why it is what it is.

Naturalism cannot explain why the universe contains all the order that we observe.

Naturalism cannot explain why nature is uniform.

Naturalism cannot justify induction.

Naturalism cannot explain why the universe has a mathematical structure or how a particular mathematical structure came to be actualized in our physical world.

Naturalism cannot explain why the universe happens to be so mathematically comprehensible to humans. A prime mystery of matter is its intimate relation to human mathematics.

Finally, naturalism cannot resolve the tension between the unity and the diversity of the universe.

5

Chance, Cause and Chaos

Indeterminism was the first example of quantum weirdness. It implied the existence of physical events that were forever unknowable and unpredictable. Not only must human experience give up ever knowing when a particular atom is going to radiate . . . but these events are even unknown in the perfect mind of God. Physicists, irrespective of their belief, may invoke God when they feel issues of principle are at stake because the God of the physicists is cosmic order . . . Even God can give you only the odds for some events to occur, not certainty.

HEINZ PAGELS (*The Cosmic Code* 1982: 83)

* * * * *

I am God, and there is none like me, Declaring the end from the beginning, and from ancient times the things that are not yet done, saying, My counsel shall stand, and I will do all my pleasure: Calling a ravenous bird from the east, the man that executeth my counsel from a far country: yea, I have spoken it, I will also bring it to pass; I have purposed it, I will also do it. Hearken unto me, ye stouthearted, that are far from righteousness.

ISAIAH 46:9–12

A basic, perhaps the most basic, assumption of science is that everything has a cause. Nowadays, however, many scientists believe that some things – in the atomic world – happen by *chance*. By chance they mean that atomic events are not fully caused. Thus the physicist Heinz Pagels asserts that not even God, whom Pagels equates with the cosmic order, can predict when a radium atom will decay.

The previous chapter brought to light some very general mysteries relating to the physical universe. These concerned its order and mathematical structure. In this chapter we shall uncover some more problems associated with particular modern physical concepts and theories.

The main issue we shall examine has to do with *causes*. What causes physical events to happen? Are all physical events fully predictable? Do some things happen without a cause? Is there such a thing as genuine chance? How well founded is the notion that events in the atomic world are truly chance-like? Such questions form the focus of this chapter.

The Puzzle of Gravity

First, we shall ask a rather simple question: How can one physical object affect another one? In our daily life we have much experience of interaction between objects in terms of direct contact. We push open a door, we pick up a piece of paper, we kick a ball, and so on. Affecting an object without any direct contact, or a chain of such contacts, smacks of magic.

What, then, causes the planets to move in their orbits? They don't seem to be in contact with anything. Aristotle thought the planets were embedded in solid, but invisible, glasslike spheres, moved by intelligent, spiritual agents. Some of the medieval scholastics explained unusual physical events in terms of occult qualities such as sympathy, affinity and attraction.

René Descartes, in his *Principles of Philosophy* (1644), imposed more stringent rules on natural explanation. He banished all occult qualities. Instead, Descartes insisted that all physical events should be explained in terms of the direct impact of one physical object on another. This 'mechanical' philosophy worked well for such things as a baseball hit by a bat or a collision between billiard balls. However, regarding gravity, where objects seemed to influence each other at a distance, greater ingenuity was needed. Descartes explained the motion of the planets in terms of the flow of an invisible celestial fluid, which carried the planets along like bits of wood in a whirlpool.

Descartes' solution was soon displaced by Isaac Newton's theory of gravity, which involved action at a distance. This counter-intuitive aspect of Newtonian gravity was initially a strong factor against its ready acceptance. Newton's arch-rival, the great philosopher-scientist Gottfried Leibniz (1646–1716), mocked Newtonian gravity as black magic. Indeed, it was admittedly a mystery to Newton himself, who was unable to find a mechanistic explanation for gravity. In a letter to Richard Bentley, 25 February 1693, Newton wrote:

> That Gravity should be innate, inherent, and essential to matter, so that one body may act upon another at a distance through a vacuum, without the mediation of anything else, by and through which their action and force may be conveyed from one to another, is to me so great an absurdity that I believe no man who has in philosophical matters a competent faculty of thinking can ever fall into it. Gravity must be caused by an agent acting constantly according to certain laws; but whether this agent be material or immaterial I have left to the consideration of my readers (Cohen 1978: 302).

Newton believed that gravity, unlike size or shape, was not an essential property of matter. On the contrary, gravity was a special property added on to matter by God. Newton accepted that God's power was such that, if he so willed it, God could create bodies capable of acting upon one another across distances. Yet, although God was the primary cause of gravity, Newton freely admitted that he did not know the secondary cause. He did not even know whether it was material or immaterial. Newton concluded that God had denied man ultimate insight into this mystery of his creation. It is noteworthy that Newton was greatly interested in alchemy, the ancient quest for the mythical philosopher's stone that allegedly possessed various magical powers, including the ability to change lead into gold. Some scholars assert that it was precisely Newton's openness to magic that led him to propose the notion of action-at-a-distance.

There is no logical necessity that requires the earth to exert a gravitational force on the moon. Science merely describes *how* it does so, in terms of the inverse-square law of gravity. The actual reason *why* material objects generate gravitational forces remains unexplained. Similar considerations hold for electromagnetic forces. In the smaller quantum world of atomic interactions, things are even more mysterious, as we shall soon see.

However, it is not only indirect causes that are puzzling. Philosophers such as John Locke and David Hume have pointed out that even direct interactions between physical objects are mysterious. There is no logical reason why a given physical cause should produce a given effect. For example, we could imagine that two billiard balls, upon meeting, simply pass through each other, rather than rebounding. On the basis of such considerations, Locke and Hume concluded that physical cause-effect correlations are deduced primarily from *empirical* observations. Physical laws are thus *descriptive* of what we observe rather than *prescriptive* of what must happen. This conclusion is closely related to the naturalists' inability to prove induction (the presumed uniformity of nature), discussed in the previous chapter.

Causes of Chaos

Assuming that physical laws are uniformly valid, how well do they enable us to predict the future? Newtonian mechanics can be applied to a wide range of objects. Its predictions are generally quite accurate, as long as the speeds are small with respect to the speed of light, so that relativistic effects can be ignored.

Newtonian mechanics is completely *deterministic*. By this we mean that, given the initial positions and speeds of a system of particles, their subsequent development can be completely predicted. In the nineteenth century the famous French scientist Pierre Simon de Laplace (1749–1827) asserted that, given the positions and speeds of all particles in the universe at any single instant of time, an infinite intelligence could fully predict all subsequent events. This assumes, of course, a full-blooded materialism in which everything – even human choices – can be reduced to purely physical interactions.

Since then, several developments in modern physics have raised doubts about such Newtonian determinism, even if the world were completely material. One such factor is the discovery of *chaos*. It has been found that, in many cases, what happens to a system of physical objects depends very critically on the precise initial conditions. A tiny change in the position or speed of a particle can cause drastic changes to the system at later times. Such systems are said to be *chaotic*. Chaos seems to be widespread in our physical world.

For a simple example, consider a pencil balanced point-down on a desk. We can predict that a very small vibration will cause it to fall. But in which direction will it fall? That is virtually impossible for us to predict.

Consider now a more pertinent example. Why is it that scientists, some of whom presume to tell us what happened millions of years ago, cannot accurately predict the weather one week from now? The reason is quite simple. The physical processes governing the weather are chaotic. Small changes in the physical circumstances can result in drastic changes in the weather. Thus, for example, a small draft of air due to a fluttering butterfly can set off a chain of events culminating in a tornado five days later. This is known as the 'butterfly effect'.

To predict the weather in the distant future we would have to know the positions and speeds of all air particles of the atmosphere, of all butterflies, birds and other possible influences on the atmosphere. Some of these influences, such as disturbances caused by aircraft, are due to human decisions that seem humanly unpredictable. Further, the quantities needed would have to be known to *infinite* precision. Hence, the calculation of predictions would require a computer of infinite capacity. In principle, then, we can never accurately predict the weather beyond a few days.

Due to its sensitivity to initial conditions, chaos has been proposed as a means by which the mind can influence the brain. One concern about actions of mind on matter is how the non-physical mind can apply energy to the physical brain. Biologist Alfred Lotka suggested in 1924 that the brain might be a chaotic system. In that case, the brain could amplify very weak signals. Hence the mind would have to control only a tiny amount of energy (Herbert 1993:248).

In short, even in a purely deterministic world, the presence of chaos puts a severe limitation on human ability to predict the future. An all-knowing God can, of course, know the initial conditions to the infinite accuracy required. From his perspective a chaotic universe thus remains fully predictable. Chaos therefore challenges determinism only in the sense that it undermines accurate human predictions, particularly in the long-term. Only *human* knowledge of the future is hampered. At heart, chaos still presumes a fully deterministic universe.

The Strange World of Atoms

A much more serious challenge to determinism is posed by quantum physics. Quantum physics deals with the properties of matter on the smallest scales. It is concerned with such things as atoms and photons (that is, units of light).

Strange things happen in the quantum world. The first mystery is that of light. Does light consist of particles, as argued by Isaac Newton? Or does it consist of waves, as suggested by the Dutch physicist Christiaan Huygens (1629–95)? The double slit experiment (Figure 5.1) of Thomas Young (in 1801), with its pronounced interference patterns, seemed to prove that light was a wave. Other experiments, however, showed that light also had properties associated with particles.

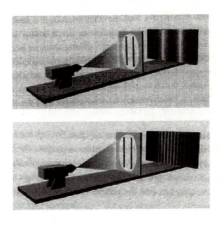

Figure 5.1: The Double Slit Experiment. The top figure shows what we would expect to see if light were not a wave. The lower figure shows the observed interference wave effect. (From www.users. totalise.co.uk; permission to reproduce requested.)

Such odd wave-particle behaviour is exhibited not only by light. The same dual properties are observed also for matter. When the electron was first discovered, in 1897, it seemed to be a particle. Later it was found that when electrons are shot through a double slit they, too, form an interference pattern. This is the case even when the electrons are shot through the slit one at a time. Electrons, too, have wave properties.

Indeed, it is evident that many entities – electrons, atoms, photons and so on – have both particle and wave properties. We can set up experiments to study either of these properties but not both at the same time. This is very mysterious. Waves and particles are quite distinct. Waves are continuous; they spread out over a large area and cause interference patterns. Particles, on the other hand, are discrete, confined to a small area, and travel in straight paths. It is hard to imagine how one entity can have both, seemingly contradictory, properties.

One result of wave/particle duality is that, at any instant, we can measure accurately either the position or the speed of an object, but not both at once. This is known as the *Heisenberg uncertainty principle*, named after the German physicist Werner Heisenberg (1901–76), one of the founders of quantum mechanics. Another consequence is that we cannot predict exactly where an individual photon, after passing through a slit, will hit a photographic plate. Nor can we tell exactly when a particular radium atom will decay. However, we can calculate accurate probabilities of what will happen. Hence, even though we cannot predict exactly what will happen in each individual case, in the long run we *can* predict precise patterns for large numbers of events.

In mathematical terms, quantum mechanics represents a quantum entity, say an electron, using a *wave function*. The wave function is a mathematical formula that computes the probability of the electron being in any particular spot. Since the wave function effectively spreads out over all of space, the unseen electron seems to be everywhere, although the probability is largest near the position where it was last observed. On the other hand, we cannot say precisely where the electron actually is between observations. The electron seems to be everywhere and nowhere at the same time.

The wave function's change in time can be calculated using Schrödinger's wave equation. This equation is completely deterministic. From any initial conditions we can precisely predict the future behaviour of the wave function. However, as we noted, the wave function yields only a set of possibilities. To find out which possibility actually happens in an experiment, one has to make a measurement. When a particular measurement is made, the electron will be found to be in one precise location. The wave function, with all its infinite possibilities, is then reduced to one particular outcome. This is called the 'collapse of the wave function' or the 'quantum jump'. Quantum theory predicts, not the exact outcome of any particular measurement, but only the statistical distribution of many measurements.

PREDICTING UNCERTAINTY

The mathematical equations of quantum mechanics work extremely well. They can account for all quantum experimental results. Thus, on a practical level, quantum mechanics is a great success. On the explanatory level, however, many questions remain. Quantum mechanics does not explain *how* the wave function collapses to a particular value, how that value is chosen, or what the electron actually does between observations. Answers to such questions depend very much on how one *interprets* quantum mechanics.

Does quantum uncertainty just reflect limited human knowledge, due to our inability to accurately measure the very small quantum events? Or does it mean that nature itself behaves in a random fashion? That is a very important question. Many physicists believe, with Heisenberg, that quantum events are genuinely random. We shall call this the *Heisenberg interpretation* of quantum uncertainty.

Such a view of quantum mechanics raises deep questions. No longer is the course of the universe determined by its initial conditions. The randomness of quantum events makes the universe *indeterministic*, by which we mean inherently unpredictable. Consider a radium atom, about to decay. In any given instant it will either decay or not. What makes the choice? In a *deterministic* universe the choice fully depends – although perhaps in a very complicated way – on the present state of the universe. But what makes the choice in an *indeterministic* universe?

IS CHANCE A CAUSE?

Often it is said that the quantum choice is made by *chance*. This raises the question: What is *chance*? The word chance can be used in various senses. Often, we use chance in the sense of accidental or unplanned. For example, by chance I met an old friend on the bus yesterday. In quantum mechanics, however, chance is meant in a different sense. It refers now to the notion of *indeterminism*. Chance, in this sense means, as defined by statistician D. J. Bartholomew (1984:67), that there is more than one possible outcome for an event and one cannot predict, with certainty, which outcome will occur.

It is important to note that chance, thus defined, is not a *cause*. Chance is not an agent that can do anything. Rather, chance indicates the *absence* of a *sufficient* cause for an event. It means that there is *no* reason why a particular outcome occurs. Hence, Keith Ward (1996:21) asserts that no reason can be given why a particular radium atom decays at a particular time, rather than at some other time. He argues that quantum events are not sufficiently determined by their physical causes.

Not all physicists are happy with such a strange conclusion. For example, physicist Henry Stapp, an expert on quantum mechanics, comments:

> Many physicists of today claim to believe that it is perfectly possible, and also satisfactory, for there to be choices that simply come out of nowhere at all . . . The claim that the choice comes out of nowhere

at all should be regarded as an admission of contemporary ignorance, not as a satisfactory final word (Stapp 1993: 216).

Elsewhere he remarks, 'Chance is an idea useful for dealing with a world partly unknown to us. But it has no rational place among ultimate constituents of nature' (Stapp 1993:91).

Earlier we noted that a basic principle of rational enquiry is that everything has a sufficient reason. This *principle of sufficient reason* implies the *principle of causality*, which affirms that every event has a cause. To say that a quantum choice is made by chance is to say that *nothing* makes and actuates the choice. This contradicts the principle of sufficient reason. To say that an event has no cause is to give up on science and to invoke magic, in this case magic without even a magician.

Stanley Jaki (1989:142–5) notes that the great philosophers, including Plato, Aristotle, Aquinas, and even Hume, asserted that there was no such thing as 'chance'. David Hume, for example, commented, 'It is universally allowed that nothing exists without a cause of its existence, and that chance, when strictly examined, is a mere negative word, and means not any real power which has anywhere a being in nature' (Hume 1777:104). Rather, he considered that what we call 'chance' is just a name for our ignorance of the actual cause.

DOES EVERYTHING HAVE A CAUSE?

The irrational nature of the suggestion that quantum events are not fully caused leads us to ask: how well established is the claim that quantum events have no sufficient cause?

First, can we be certain that there is no sufficient *physical* cause? To eliminate all possible physical causes one must show that a quantum event is not fully determined by the present state of the universe and/or the internal state of the quantum particle. But neither of these is completely known – or even knowable – to human investigation. Humans, unlike God, are not omniscient. How, then, can we be sure that there exists no inherent determinism at a deeper physical level, as yet hidden from the human observer? It follows we cannot definitely rule out the possibility that all quantum events *do* have sufficient physical causes.

Suppose, for the sake of the argument, that one *could* establish the definite absence of a full *physical* cause in quantum events. This still leaves open the possibility of *non-physical* causes. These might be human minds, spiritual beings such as angels or demons, or even the direct action of God himself. Such non-physical causes are, by definition, beyond scientific enquiry. Thus it is scientifically unwarranted to assert that the absence of *physical* cause entails the absence of *any* cause. That conclusion requires the metaphysical assumption that there are no non-physical causes.

Note that the absence of a sufficient natural cause for quantum events, if true, presents naturalism with a problem. The basic presupposition of naturalism, the reader will recall, is that the universe is entirely explicable in terms of natural causes. Hence, if quantum events were to lack sufficient natural causes, this would serve to contradict the main tenet of naturalism.

Making Sense of the Atomic World

The lack of proof for the indeterminist Heisenberg interpretation of quantum mechanics raises the question of whether one could interpret quantum mechanics differently. Several alternative interpretations have indeed been proposed.

AN UNKNOWABLE WORLD

One possibility is to simply refrain from speculating about what happens in the unobserved quantum realm. This is the *Copenhagen Interpretation*, due to the Danish physicist, Niels Bohr (1885–1962), one of the founding fathers of quantum physics. This view is still the dominant view of quantum mechanics. It holds that humans cannot know the quantum world in itself. We can only probe it via various experiments. On this view, science does not describe nature as it is, but only how it responds to our methods of observation. This interpretation is essentially *positivistic*, in that it limits genuine knowledge to that which we can observe. As such, it stresses the limits of human knowledge and considers as unknowable whatever may happen beyond the observations.

A Determined World

Not all scientists are happy with such a positivist view of quantum mechanics. Scientists are usually realists, in the sense that they believe scientists should try to find out what is really going on in the hidden world beyond our observations. Some scientists believe that it should be possible to construct a hypothetical model of the quantum world along deterministic lines. Such a theory will involve what are called 'hidden variables', quantities that do away with quantum uncertainty but which cannot themselves be measured directly. Albert Einstein, one of the founders of quantum mechanics, believed, in opposition to Bohr, that quantum mechanics should ultimately be explicable in terms of hidden variables.

Favouring hidden variables is the fact that quantum events are not *entirely* random. Quantum choices are, in practice, constrained to be within a very limited range, following a well-defined formula. We can predict very accurately what pattern will emerge after a long series of observations. This suggests that quantum choices are perhaps not genuinely random but, rather, are fully determined by precise laws at some deeper, sub-quantum level.

Consider, for example, a roulette wheel. Here any individual event seems to be due to chance, although the outcomes are quite limited and predictable when averaged over a long series of events. Yet, in actuality, any individual outcome is precisely fixed by the initial conditions. That the outcome of the roulette wheel may have the *appearance* of chance is due only to our ignorance of the initial conditions and our inability to calculate the end result from the initial conditions. Might the situation not be exactly the same for quantum effects? It seems prudent to allow for possible determinist sub-quantum mechanisms.

One such prospective mechanism is the pilot-wave model of the physicist David Bohm. This theory interprets quantum mechanics in terms of well-defined deterministic laws. In Bohm's model each particle always has both a precise location and a precise speed. However, the force on each particle depends on the precise locations, at that instant, of all other particles in the universe. Each particle has its own private *pilot wave,* which senses the location of all other particles in the universe, much like a radar beam. The pilot wave guides its own particle by supplying pertinent information to it. This model allows us to hold on to the realist notion that particles do exist objectively between observations. Bohm's model is thus often classified as *neo-realism.*

One objection raised against Bohm's model is that the pilot waves are in principle unobservable. Another difficulty is that the pilot waves transmit information faster than light. The force on a particle depends on the precise locations, at that instant, of all other particles in the universe. This violates *locality*, the property of physical theories that forbids distant causes to have instantaneous nearby effects.

However, such non-locality has in fact been confirmed in recent quantum experiments. These experiments, which demonstrate that hidden-variable theories *must* violate locality, have put significant constraints on such theories. Thus, non-locality, rather than being a weakness, is actually a strength in Bohm's model.

In Bohm's model a particle always has both a precise position and speed. In practice, however, our knowledge of these is inevitably limited. We cannot measure precisely the initial conditions of the particle. Nor can we fully know the present configuration of the rest of the universe and how this influences the particle. Thus, although the underlying quantum world is held to be deterministic, human ignorance still restricts our ability to make precise predictions. God's knowledge is, of course, not thus limited. In Bohm's model God can predict exactly the future states of the physical world. Thus, in this interpretation of quantum mechanics, the indeterminism of quantum mechanics reflects only human ignorance rather than any actual uncertainty inherent in nature.

MIND MAKES REALITY

Although the work of David Bohm and his colleagues shows that quantum mechanics can be interpreted within a determinist framework, only a small minority of modern quantum theorists support hidden-variable models. Most dismiss such models, due to the strange features they entail, such as mysterious pilot-waves and non-locality.

Nevertheless, alternative interpretations are no less weird. Quantum mechanics is unavoidably different from classical (*i.e.*, Newtonian) physics. Hence, it contradicts our normal intuitions. The question is which feature, if any, of the classical realm an interpretation should retain.

Let us briefly survey some of the more popular interpretations of quantum mechanics that have been presented. We shall consider first, the proposal of mathematician John von Neumann (1903–57) that consciousness is needed to collapse the wave function. He thought that, since the experimental apparatus is itself physical, it too must be described in terms of a wave function. Indeed, the entire physical world exists as a huge wave function. This wave function can be collapsed into a particular observation only by something that is *non*-physical and, hence, independent of the wave function. This non-physical entity is, von Neumann claimed, consciousness. Von Neumann considered the entire physical world to exist in a state of pure possibility, except in those limited regions where some conscious mind collapses it into an actual existence. Consciousness thus creates reality.

In this view, mind exerts its power over matter by selecting which quantum outcome actually occurs. It is not clear, however, how human observers can actually do such selecting. Although experiments have been performed to test the possible influence of human conscious intention on quantum events, no deviations from chance have ever been observed (see Herbert 1993:225).

Further, this interpretation raises obvious difficulties for a materialist view of origins. If consciousness is needed to create reality, how did the universe exist before consciousness arrived? It implies that consciousness existed before the material world did. Where did this consciousness come from? It could not have come from matter, as naturalists would have it, since, by hypothesis, consciousness is non-material and, in any case, matter had no real existence until created by consciousness. In demanding the existence of a non-material mind, as well as in making matter dependent on mind, this theory clearly contradicts materialism.

MANY WORLDS

Another radical interpretation is due to physicist Hugh Everett. His 'many-worlds' interpretation asserts that, whenever an observation is made, the wave function does not collapse into *one particular* state but into *all possible* states. The universe splits into a set of new universes, each containing one particular state. Thereafter, these varied universes exist separately, with no further interaction. Quantum theory then gives for the observer the probability that he will find himself, after making the observation, in one particular universe rather than another.

One problem with this interpretation is that, when an observation takes place, there are generally not merely two or three possible outcomes. Rather, there is a whole continuum of possibilities. This means that the universe must split, at each observation, into an infinity of new universes. This seems implausible. Further, since none of the other universes are observable to us, this theory is beyond observational proof or disproof.

Taking Your Pick

There are other interpretations of quantum mechanics. Physicist Nick Herbert cites eight different views of quantum reality. How is one to choose among these? Herbert writes:

> The quantum reality problem is, strictly speaking, not a physics question at all, but a problem in metaphysics, concerned as it is not

with explaining phenomena but with speculating about what kind of reality lies behind and supports the phenomena . . . Each of these eight realities from Bohm's neo-realist particle-plus-wave model to von Neumann's consciousness-created world is perfectly compatible with the same quantum facts. We cannot use experiments – or at least experiments of the usual kind – to decide among these conflicting pictures of what lies behind the phenomenal world (Herbert 1993:160).

The choice of how one interprets quantum mechanics must thus be made in terms of extra-scientific, metaphysical considerations.

It seems prudent to concur with Bohr that quantum mechanics surely puts a limit on *human* knowledge about the sub-quantum world. We can only speculate as to what exists beyond what we can observe. Here we must be guided by our basic philosophical convictions.

What philosophical guidelines should we appeal to? Physicist-turned-theologian John Polkinghorne justifies an indeterminist view of quantum mechanics on the grounds that we should try to maximize the correlation between our knowledge and our belief about reality (Polkinghorne 1998:53). According to him, our conjectures about reality should be guided by our epistemology (*i.e.*, our theory of knowledge). Hence, since we cannot fully know quantum causes, he argues that quantum events are not fully caused.

It seems strange, however, that our beliefs about reality should be governed by human ignorance. Why should objective reality be limited to what can be humanly measured? It seems more prudent to refrain from speculating about what exists beyond human horizons. Although Polkinghorne professes to be a theist, his truncated view of reality must surely be rejected by any serious Christian. Theistic views on reality must be driven by what God can do, not by what humans cannot do.

A further factor to keep in mind is the *fallacy of misplaced concreteness*, discussed in the previous chapter. The quantum wave function is just an abstract, mathematical representation of reality, not reality itself. Indeed, strictly speaking, it represents, not even reality, but only our limited *knowledge* of reality. The mathematical formulation of quantum mechanics yields only the probabilities of various outcomes of a given experiment. We must thus be careful not to confuse the wave function with the real world, for then the real world is demoted to a mere probabilistic shadow, until collapsed into concrete form by an observation. Rather, we must discard any interpretation that treats the wave function as a real entity rather than as a mere mathematical tool.

A further appropriate guide is the principle of sufficient reason, which is essential to scientific enquiry. This entails that *any* causal explanation of an event, no matter how unlikely or implausible, is rationally preferable to postulating *no* cause at all. Therefore, the belief that quantum events are fully caused is rationally superior to the hypothesis that they have no sufficient cause. This cause may well be explicable in terms of Bohm's pilot-wave model, some other (as yet) unknown physical mechanism or by some non-physical force.

In short, quantum mechanics limits our human ability to know what goes in the quantum world. Nevertheless, it gives us no valid grounds for doubting the inherent determinism of the physical world.

MIND OVER MATTER?

In quantum mechanics the observer is closely connected to what he observes. The mere act of making a measurement introduces changes into the quantum world. Many of the interpretations of quantum mechanics give a large role to human consciousness. For example, the Copenhagen Interpretation rests on the notion that the aim of quantum theory is merely to describe certain connections between human experiences, rather than to describe a physical world existing independently of us.

Many scientists and philosophers believe that matter and mind are closely related through quantum mechanics. Some believe that quantum mechanics provides a mechanism by which the mind can control the brain. The idea is that the mind somehow influences a particular quantum outcome. Although such an effect would be extremely small, an appropriate chaotic device in the brain could amplify it sufficiently to activate the required bodily action. Thus for example, if I want to raise my arm, my wind causes a quantum change in a neuron, which triggers a chain of neural reactions resulting in a suitable message to my arm muscles. There is, however, no actual evidence that the mind can actually influence the outcome of any quantum event.

Conclusions

To sum up, many physical events are mysterious. Gravity, electromagnetism, and atomic forces all operate at a distance. Although we can describe well *how* they act, explaining *why* they do so is much more difficult. Both chaos and quantum events place severe restrictions on the human ability to predict future physical events. Quantum mechanics has a strong mathematical basis and again illustrates the intricate connection between matter and mathematics.

There are many different interpretations of quantum mechanics. Since these use the same mathematical equations and make the same predictions, the choice of interpretation must be made on the basis of philosophical preferences. Although many quantum interpretations place much emphasis on consciousness, the actual connection between quantum events and the human mind is not very clear.

The notion that quantum events lack sufficient causes is contrary to the principle of sufficient cause. A better approach is to consider quantum 'chance' as merely an expression of human ignorance of the actual cause. Interpretations of quantum mechanics that do not require indeterminism are therefore rationally preferable. These conclusions regarding chance and determinism will be of great relevance regarding questions of God's sovereignty and human free will, to be discussed in later chapters.

6

From Matter to Mind

CROSSFIRE

The universe we observe has precisely the properties we should expect if there is, at bottom, no design, no purpose, no evil and no good, nothing but blind, pitiless indifference. As that unhappy poet A. E. Housman put it: 'For Nature, heartless Nature will neither care nor know.' DNA neither knows nor cares. DNA just is. And we dance to its music.

RICHARD DAWKINS (*River Out of Eden* 1995:133)

* * * * *

For thou hast possessed my reins: thou hast covered me in my mother's womb. I will praise thee; for I am fearfully and wonderfully made: marvellous are thy works; and that my soul knoweth right well. My substance was not hid from thee, when I was made in secret, and curiously wrought in the lowest parts of the earth. Thine eyes did see my substance, yet being unperfect; and in thy book all my members were written, which in continuance were fashioned, when as yet there was none of them.

PSALM 139:13–16

Thus far we have examined some very general mysteries of the universe and its laws, primarily from the viewpoint of physics. Naturalist explanations were found to fall short. We now move on to even more difficult ground. How well can naturalism account for the enigmas surrounding life?

Life is a great mystery. What defines life? How did it start? How did it become so astonishingly diverse? How did the various forms of life adapt so well to each other and to the earthly environment? How did simple life give rise to consciousness and mind? Such questions will be our primary concern in this chapter.

Oxford evolutionary biologist Richard Dawkins, sees no difficulties for naturalism. He claims that naturalism can explain everything, including life. Unhappily, that explanation does not come cheap. Dawkins is prepared to give up design, purpose, goodness and even his own freedom. Does Dawkins' solution work? And is it worth the price?

It was long thought that the existence of living creatures provided clear proof for an intelligent cause – the divine Creator. Life was considered to be so complex and mysterious that it seemed impossible that it could have originated other than by a direct act of God.

This put naturalists in an awkward position. It seemed clear that life, particularly conscious life, had not always existed on earth. There must then have been a time when only inanimate matter existed. If only natural causes exist, as the naturalists assumed, then life must have somehow developed from non-living matter. Naturalism, to account for the origin and subsequent proliferation of life, must thus rely on some form of natural evolution. But what materialist mechanism would do the trick?

An answer was provided by Charles Darwin (1809–82). In his influential book, *On the Origin of the Species* (1859), he presented his theory of evolution. Darwin's mechanism for evolution consisted of combining random changes with natural selection. Random interactions of molecules allegedly produced a simple cell that could reproduce itself. Thereafter, random mutations (*e.g.*, changes in the cell caused by radiation or errors in reproduction) resulted in the production of slightly modified daughter cells. Natural selection then ensured that the fittest of the offspring survived to produce the most successors. Eventually, this process is alleged to have led to the generation of ever more complicated living organisms. Over time this continual combination of random mutation and natural selection supposedly yielded all the forms of life we presently observe.

Darwin's theory was eagerly embraced by the naturalists of his day. It seemed to provide the long-awaited alternative to divine creation. According to Richard Dawkins, Darwinian evolution 'made it possible to be an intellectually fulfilled atheist' (1991:6). Whether Darwin's theory is indeed as successful as it is claimed to be will be examined shortly. First, we shall look more closely at the nature of life.

Making Matter Come Alive

What *is* life? It is easy to identify life when we see it. But just what is it that makes life so different from non-life? This is very difficult to pin down exactly. One characteristic of living things is that they reproduce and grow. However, so do many non-living things such as stars and crystals. And some living things, such as mules, or angels, do not reproduce at all. Many other properties of living things can be found also in non-living things.

What, then, characterizes life? The answer is found in a combination of unusual properties. One significant feature of living things is their high degree of complexity, which is much greater than that of non-living things. Moreover, this complexity is highly organized. Any living thing functions as an integrated unit, a whole. A dog, for example, consists of a large number of complex components such as eyes, brain, liver and heart. Yet these all cooperate harmoniously. Further, living things develop and behave in a very ordered and purposeful way.

THE COMPLEXITY OF LIFE

We consider first the amazing *complexity* of even the simplest living things – cells. All living things on earth consist of cells. Cells are very small. They are specialized for particular functions. There are skin cells, bone cells, blood cells, and so on. An organ may contain many different cell types, all working together harmoniously. Cells regulate themselves, with the help of other cells and organs. Each cell reproduces by dividing itself.

Each cell contains smaller structures, known as *organelles*, which perform various tasks within the cell (see Figure 6.1). Edward Wilson describes the cell as a huge factory. The *nucleus* acts as the cell's computer or control centre. It decodes and passes on the instructions for cell development. The *mitochondrion* acts as the cell's power-plant. The *cell membrane* is the gatekeeper; it decides what enters and leaves the cell. The *endoplasmic reticulum* is the construction team. The *golgi apparatus* is the packing department. And so on. Wilson notes that the cell uses very modern technology involving digital logic, analogue-digital conversion and signal integration. The cell's amazing complexity, says Wilson (1998:93), exceeds that of super-computers and spacecraft.

Yet, according to Darwin, this astounding complexity is due solely to blind, random mutations and natural selection. Paul Davies exclaims:

> How can an incredibly complex organism, so harmoniously organized into an integrated functioning unit, perhaps endowed with exceedingly intricate and efficient organs such as eyes and ears, be the product of a series of pure accidents? (Davies 1988:108).

It seems incredible that mere accidents can give rise to highly complex, purposeful entities.

Recent developments in biology have underscored the crucial role played by *information*. As an organism develops it seems to follow a detailed blueprint, which tells it how to assemble itself. The genetic information contained in that blueprint is thought to be stored in the DNA of the original fertilized egg.

DNA (*deoxyribonucleic acid*) is a complex, giant molecule that contains, in chemically coded form, all the information needed to build and control a living organism (see Figure 6.2). It forms the

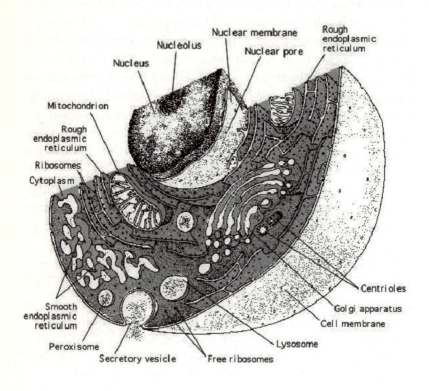

Figure 6.1: The Simple Cell. This diagram shows only a quarter of the cell. (Based on figure in H. Curtis, *Biology*, New York: Worth Publishers, 1983; permission to reproduce requested.)

basis for inheritance in all organisms, except for a few viruses. It is organized into *chromosomes*, which are contained in the cell nucleus. Each chromosome consists of a very long strand of DNA, more than a metre in length and containing millions of molecules. Each chromosome can be divided into various units called *genes*, each of which refers to one unit of inherited material, such as eye colour or nose shape. Each normal human cell contains 46 chromosomes.

The detailed structure of the DNA molecules contains the information needed to assemble each unique organism. The amount of information in each cell nucleus is fantastic. According to Richard Dawkins,

> Each nucleus . . . contains a digitally coded database larger, in information content, than all thirty volumes of the Encyclopaedia Britannica put together. And this figure is for each cell, not all the cells of the body put together. (1991:2–3)

How is that vast store of information extracted and applied? The whole assembly process is very mysterious. Each part of an organism contains the same DNA molecules. How, then, does each piece know which component of the organism it is to become? How does the tiny human egg turn information into actual growth, so that it eventually becomes a mature person?

The Tale of the Selfish Genes

Richard Dawkins sees evolution as primarily a story about competing *genes*. Somehow, so the story goes, due to time and chance, a set of lifeless molecules came to be organized into a simple gene, a basic organism that could reproduce itself. Its reproduction brought forth a host of genes. Some of them made mistakes in copying their genetic code, resulting in different genes. Genes gradually acquired bodies, whose purpose was to help the genes to reproduce. Natural selection favoured those genes whose bodies were most fit for survival. Over time, this led to the formation of all the variations of life we see today, including ourselves. Dawkins writes, 'We are survival machines – robot vehicles programmed

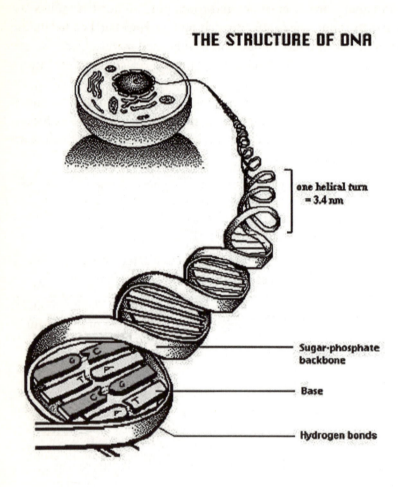

Figure 6.2: The DNA Molecule. Note the double-helical structure of this huge molecule, found in the nucleus of a cell. (From www.acessexcellence.org; permission to reproduce requested.)

to preserve the selfish molecules known as genes' (Dawkins 1976: v).

Not all naturalists are persuaded that evolution can be adequately described as the heroic saga of the relentless genes and their glorious deeds. Harvard biologist Richard Lewontin, for example, scathingly remarks:

> Molecular biology is now a religion, and molecular biologists are its prophets . . . In the words of a popular bard of the legend, genes 'have created us body and mind' . . . How is it that a mere molecule can have both the power of self-reproduction and self-action, being the cause of itself and the cause of all other things? . . . The problem with (the) story is that although it is correct in its detailed molecular description, it is wrong in what it claims to explain. First, DNA is not self-reproducing, second, it makes nothing, and, third, organisms are not determined by it. DNA is a dead molecule, among the most non-reactive, chemically inert molecules in the living world (Lewontin 1992).

Life, then, requires more than DNA and its information. That information must also be interpreted and suitably acted upon.

This, however, introduces a further level of complexity. Douglas Hofstadter comments on the perplexing problem of the origin of life:

> A natural and fundamental question to ask, on learning of these incredibly intricately interlocking pieces of software and hardware is: 'How did they ever get started in the first place?' It is a truly baffling thing . . . a bootstrap from simple molecules to entire cells is almost beyond one's power to imagine. There are various theories of life. They all run aground on this most central of all central questions: 'How did the Genetic Code, along with the mechanisms for its translation, originate?' For the moment, we shall have to content ourselves with a sense of wonder and awe, rather than with an answer (1979:548).

Now, more than two decades later, the awe remains. We are no closer to solving this central mystery.

IMPLICATIONS OF INFORMATION

Mystery surrounds also the formation of higher forms of life. According to Darwinian evolution, random errors in copying DNA led to new forms of life. Natural selection then favoured those forms that are the fittest. This is contrary to what we experience when we make errors in copying a blueprint of, say, a car or a computer. Such errors usually cause trouble. Biological experiments likewise show that most mutations are harmful. Random disturbances generally have the effect of *reducing* information, rather than increasing it. Randomness leads to chaos, not order.

Yet, if advanced forms of life developed from simple cells, their greater complexity would require a greater quantity of information to specify them. Where did this information come from? Evolutionist John Maynard-Smith sees the steady accumulation of complexity as a major difficulty for evolution. He comments, 'there is nothing in neo-Darwinism which enables us to predict a long-term increase in complexity' (1969:82).

Further difficulties arise when we consider the deeper implications of the transmission of information. After all, the concept of *information* is mainly a mathematical abstraction. It concerns the meaningful content of a transmitted message. The transmission of information requires the proper functioning of the organism at a variety of different levels. German information specialist Werner Gitt (2001:56) describes five aspects of information: (1) *statistics* concerns the actual transmitted signal, (2) *syntax* concerns the arrangement of the symbols of the code used, (3) *semantics* concerns the intended meaning of the message, (4) *pragmatics* concerns the expected action taken as a result of the message and (5) *apobetics* concerns the intended purpose of the information. All of these aspects are intricately involved in any transmission of information.

Above all, for a pattern to be accepted as information it must be meaningful and purposeful. Information cannot arise from random noise. This implies that all information has an intelligent, mental source. Although information may be stored and transmitted by matter, information as such, conveying a meaningful message, cannot be a property of matter. Further, since any living entity receives, decodes and *acts* upon information, life must be more than mere information. As Gitt (2001:81) notes, matter and information are essential for life, yet life cannot be reduced to these.

DETECTING DESIGN

How can complex information arise? There seem to be only three possibilities: by an unintelligent law-like process, by accident, or by intelligent design. How can we tell which of these is more plausible?

Imagine, for example, that we receive signals from space, in the form of pulses of light. If these pulses are generated by the first option (*e.g.*, by a binary star), then we would expect the signal to be quite regular but carrying very little information. In the second case (*e.g.*, the twinkling of star light due to fluctuations in the earth's atmosphere) we would expect a more random pattern, but again with little meaningful information content. Only in the last case (*e.g.*, signals from an intelligent source) would we expect to receive high information content.

William Dembski argues that we can rule out the first two cases if the signal is *contingent, complex and specified* (Dembski 1999:128). *Contingency,* which means that the signal could have been different, ensures that the signal is not caused by a mechanistic, unintelligent process that had no choice in its production. *Complexity* ensures that the object is not so simple that it could have arisen by accident. *Specified,* in the sense of being nonrandom, ensures that the object has the type of pattern characteristic of intelligence. For example, a long sequence of signals yielding the first ten prime numbers would qualify as being contingent and having specified complexity.

How can complex specified information (*CSI*, for short) be generated? Not by rigid algorithms or deterministic laws. A fixed set of rules allows for no contingency and thus cannot generate information. Any apparent information generated is already inherent in the algorithm. Nor by chance, where *chance* is used in the sense of *accidental* or *random*, for chance generates only complex *unspecified* information. Since fixed laws can transmit only the CSI they are given, and since chance cannot generate any CSI, it follows that no combination of law and chance can generate CSI (Dembski 1999:168). Dembski concludes that natural causes are thus incapable of generating CSI (1999:170). Hence any CSI present in a system must be due to intelligent input.

Dembski has developed tools to measure the CSI in a given system. By means of such tools he hopes to promote a scientific research programme to discern and investigate the effects of intelligent causes, thereby challenging naturalistic biology. For example, he asserts that the specified complexity of a living cell is so great that it must be attributed to design (1999:146).

Paul Davies (*Are We Alone?* 1995:28–31) estimates that, over ten billion years, the odds of random permutations of molecules assembling just one molecule of DNA in the observable universe is much less than 1 out of $10^{30,000}$ (*i.e.*, 10 followed by 30,000 zeros)! This is about the same as tossing a fair coin and getting heads 100,000 times in a row.

And these huge odds are just for a single DNA molecule. The chance formation of even the simplest cell, which is much more complex, is enormously less likely. Even Sir Francis Crick, a committed materialist, conceded:

An honest man, armed with all the knowledge available to us now, could only state that in some sense, the origin of life appears at the moment to be almost a miracle, so many are the conditions which would have had to be satisfied to get it going (Crick, 1981:88).

Since Crick wrote these words, the origin of life remains naturalistically inexplicable.

Moreover, many biological organs are *irreducibly* complex, in the sense that they cannot function properly if any part is missing. An irreducibly complex system cannot be produced gradually, by small steps, since the smaller, as yet incomplete systems are non-functional. Function is attained only when all the components of the system (*e.g.*, an eye) are in place simultaneously. This poses a problem for natural selection, which supposedly works through the gradual accumulation of small changes. A gradual process cannot account for irreducibly complex systems, which must be produced all at once.

DOES LIFE HAVE A PURPOSE?

We move on to a further, closely related, mystery pertaining to life. The most remarkable property of living things is their *purposeful* behaviour. Even the simplest forms of life seem to be guided by some definite, pre-ordained plan. This purposeful behaviour is hard to deny. Even the materialist biologist Jacques Monod, observes:

> One of the fundamental characteristics common to all living things without exception [is] that of being *objects endowed with a purpose or project*, which at the same time they show in their structure and execute through their performances . . . Rather than reject this idea (as certain biologists have tried to do) it must be recognized as essential to the very definition of living beings. We shall maintain that the latter are distinct from all other structures or systems present in the universe by this characteristic property, which we shall call *teleonomy* (Monod 1972:20).

This major distinction between life and non-life leads to a perplexing puzzle. Materialists, such as Monod, believe that living organisms are no more than complex machines, consisting of atoms and operating in full accordance with the usual laws of physics. The difference between life and non-life is attributed solely to the higher level of complexity in living things. But how can purposeless laws acting upon purposeless atoms ever give rise to a purposeful organism? That is the central mystery of life. Jacques Monod concedes that the biggest challenge for materialist atheists like himself is to explain how purposeful biological activity arose from random molecular events in a purposeless universe.

Richard Dawkins (1991:13) asserts, 'Biology is the study of complex matters that appear to have been designed purposefully.' The key word here is *appear*. Dawkins tries to escape the dilemma by asserting that any appearance of purpose in biological systems is just an illusion. Monod seems to acknowledge that it is more than that. He writes:

> Objectivity nevertheless obliges us to recognize the teleonomic character of living organisms, to admit that in their structure and performance they decide on and pursue a purpose. Here, therefore, at least in appearance, lies a profound epistemological contradiction (Monod 1972:31).

The contradiction referred to by Monod is that materialism has no place for purpose.

Materialists often try to resolve this profound enigma by appealing to the notion of *emergence*. The idea is that, as systems become more complicated, new properties emerge at each level of organization. A typical example often given is that of hydrogen and oxygen atoms joining up to form a water molecule. A water molecule has properties quite different from those of its constituent atoms taken separately. Regrettably, however, no examples are ever given of a living system emerging from a non-living one. This is simply *assumed* to happen.

A case in point is the reasoning of Paul Davies. Davies (1988:142) holds that 'There exists a propensity in nature for matter and energy to undergo spontaneous transitions into new states of higher organizational complexity.' To account for this, he believes that 'There must be new general principles – organizing principles over and above the known law of physics – which have yet to be discovered.' Thus Davies appeals to some mysterious, as yet unknown, law. This is just another way of saying he has no answer.

In short, the purposeful nature of living organisms remains a deep mystery for naturalism. It is either dismissed as an illusion or attributed to emergence from unknown laws or for no reason at all. Such inexplicable emergence amounts to sheer magic. It seems quite impossible that any purposeless process could ever produce a purposeful being.

Turning Matter into Mind

The sense of mystery deepens when we move from simple life to those advanced forms endowed with conscious mind. Our consciousness consists of our thoughts, sensations, feelings of pain and love, urges, beliefs, and so on. Nothing is more obvious to us than our mental world. This was the one indubitable rock – *I think, therefore I am* – upon which Descartes sought to build his philosophy.

The prime mystery is how to fit conscious mind into the naturalist worldview, which posits that only material things are real. Mind seems to be quite different from matter. Matter occupies space, is perceptible to the senses, and is governed by the laws of physics and chemistry. Mind, on the other hand, experiences, thinks and chooses; it is governed by rational and moral norms. Our *thoughts about atoms* are very different in nature from the actual *atoms* themselves.

How can the huge gap between matter and mind be bridged? How can the interaction of atoms produce feelings of pain, beliefs, desires, and so on? How can non-conscious material entities evolve so as to produce consciousness?

These are tough questions for naturalism. There seem to be only two naturalist options. One is to postulate that there exists no gap between conscious and non-conscious matter. This idea is known as *pan-psychism*. It attributes some form of consciousness to all entities, even atoms. This view, which is currently not very popular, is incorporated in *process theology*, which its supporters consider to be a naturalist form of theism. Process theology will be discussed in a later chapter.

The only other naturalist possibility, held by the vast majority of naturalists, is to postulate that mind somehow evolved from matter. This requires mind to be no more than a complex property of matter. Accordingly, most naturalists are *materialists*. They believe that the universe consists ultimately only of matter. Materialism is a type of *reductionism*, in that it aims to reduce everything in the universe to one type of substance. Many materialists adhere also to *physics-ism*, the belief that all of reality can eventually be explained in terms of the properties of the most basic physical particles and their interactions. This creed is currently popular among scientists.

There are at least four features of mind that need explaining:

1. the existence of consciousness

2. the unity of the conscious self

3. the reality of our beliefs

4. our ability to make and to activate mental choices

Let us look more closely at each of these.

Mysteries of Mind

Consider first the mere existence of consciousness. Consciousness is not a publicly observable phenomenon, since we cannot see another person's conscious states. Each person can experience only his own feelings and pains. How is it that brain cells, which can be objectively described in terms of physical properties, can give rise to our private, subjective, experiences of seeing red and feeling pain?

Neuroscience seeks to explain our conscious experiences in terms of the neural processes of the brain. However, it does not solve the problem to say that my conscious feeling of fear, for example, is caused by certain neural activities. The problem is precisely *how* electro-chemical neural activity can give rise to my subjective conscious experience. As Colin McGinn asks: 'How can subjective consciousness result from the operations of little grey cells all bunched together into a few pounds of bland-tasting meat?' (1999a).

Clearly, our subjective feelings cannot be reduced to the physical neural processes investigated by neuroscience. Something more is needed. The problem of what turns electrical impulses into personal experiences is often called 'the hard problem' of consciousness.

A second, related, problem is why some brain processes are conscious whereas others are unconscious. What makes the difference? Psychologist Susan Blackmore (2002) asks:

> Is there a special place in the brain where unconscious things are made conscious? Are some brain cells endowed with an extra magic something that makes what goes on in them subjective? This doesn't make sense. Yet most theories of consciousness assume that there must be such a difference, and then get stuck trying to explain or investigate it.

In short, the great problem of consciousness is how purely physical processes can give rise to our subjective experiences and why this happens only in very specific circumstances.

What Are Thoughts About?

A further remarkable feature of mind is its *intentionality*. Intentionality is the capacity of the mind to be *about* things, to have meaning beyond itself. My thoughts and feelings refer to things beyond myself. I may think about Mexico or about supper; I may be afraid of snakes, and so on. Intentionality is the ability of the mind to *represent* the external world. It has to do with abstraction and symbolism. As such, it is crucial for language and mathematics.

But what is the nature of such mental representation? How is representation possible in a purely physical system? How can a brain generate mental states that represent the external world? How can neurons become symbols that refer to other things? And if brain cells have intentionality, why don't cells from other organs have the same property?

These are daunting questions. As yet, naturalism has given no satisfactory answer. Naturalists have taken three different approaches to the problems of consciousness: (1) mind-brain identity (2) emergence and (3) denial of consciousness. Let us briefly consider each of these.

IS MIND MORE THAN BRAIN?

One proposed solution is that psychological states are in fact *identical* to states of matter. This is the position of philosopher Richard Taylor (1974:34). Although Taylor concedes that psychological states are not identical with any *known* bodily states, he believes that there may be as yet *unfamiliar* bodily states that will do the job.

The difficulty with this proposal is that it ascribes to matter novel properties rather different from those it has in all other contexts. It does nothing to explain the subjectivity and intentionality of our experiences. Even if each mental event could be shown to be connected to a corresponding neural event, this still does not establish that they are the same event and that this event is purely physical.

Nor does it explain how these unusual alleged properties of matter can arise from the more usual ones. It is not as if mental and physical properties differ only in *degree*, so that one might continuously merge into the other. Rather, they differ in *kind*. Mental states have properties that are totally distinct from those of physical states. Our subjective beliefs, sensations and fears are logically distinct from objective observations of our brains. The former are controlled by logical and moral norms; the latter by the laws of bio-chemistry. Since they differ in kind, mental and physical events cannot be identical.

EMERGING MIND

Most materialists concede that non-physical, mental properties do exist. They propose that these mental properties emerge naturally from physical ones once a certain degree of complexity has been reached. Details as to how this might in fact be accomplished are, however, never given.

Philosopher John Searle believes that consciousness emerges from the brain just like liquidity emerges from water molecules. He writes, 'Consciousness is a mental, and therefore physical property of the brain in the sense in which liquidity is a property of systems of molecules' (1992:14). Consciousness is thus viewed as a high-level property of a system of brain neurons. In Searle's view, such consciousness is entirely explicable in terms of the interactions of brain neurons.

Yet Searle has not really given an explanation of how consciousness emerges from matter. He merely gives an analogy. Unhappily, this analogy is flawed. The liquidity of water *can* be deduced from its composition. There is nothing more to liquidity than molecular bonding. However, even if we were to know everything about our physical brains, we could not deduce a single mental fact, since there is no necessary link between the physical brain and the non-physical mind.

Thus Searle has failed to account for the emergence of consciousness from matter. Indeed, the very notion of such emergence seems impossible. Particularly hard to account for is the problem of intentionality: our ability to have thoughts that are abstract and point beyond themselves (see Moreland and Rae 2000:164).

Hence, the evolutionary biologist Sewall Wright concluded that the emergence of even the simplest mind from no mind is utterly incomprehensible. According to Wright, 'the emergence of mind from no mind at all is sheer magic' (Wright 1977:82). The magic is doubly miraculous in that, according to naturalistic evolution, it is due – not to a magician – but to a presumed purposeless, random process. Similarly, materialist Colin McGinn finds the mind-body problem to be an insoluble mystery (1991:viii). McGinn says:

> It would take a supernatural magician to extract consciousness from matter, even living matter. Consciousness appears to introduce a sharp break in the natural order – a point at which scientific naturalism runs out of steam . . . it seems to need an injection from outside the physical realm (McGinn 1991:45).

Nevertheless, McGinn's commitment to materialism leads him to reject any theistic resolution to the mind-body problem (1991:47). Thus McGinn is left with an intractable problem. Wright, on the other hand, opts for pan-psychism, the notion that all things, even atoms, have both a material and a psychic aspect. Although this may solve the problem of the *origin* of consciousness, neuro-scientist Sir John Eccles, a Nobel prize winner in physiology, argues that pan-psychism fails to explain how consciousness can *evolve* into a causally effective force (1994:5,10).

DISMISSING THE MIND

Some materialists, conceding that consciousness cannot be derived from matter, conclude that we should simply deny the existence of consciousness. For example, naturalist philosopher Paul Churchland asserts:

> The important point about the standard evolutionary story is that the human species and all its features are the wholly physical outcome of a purely physical process . . . If this is the correct account of our origins, then there is neither need, nor room, to fit any non-physical properties into our theoretical account of ourselves. We are creatures of matter. And we should learn to live with that fact (Churchland 1984:21).

Yet a 'theoretical account' is surely, by definition, non-physical. Hence the very fact that Churchland *does* defend his own theoretical account refutes his claim that there is neither need nor room for non-physical properties.

Since mind cannot be reduced to matter, Churchland advocates that we should simply eliminate the mind by denying its existence. He writes, 'If we do give up hope of reduction, then elimination emerges as the only coherent alternative' (Churchland 1988:507–8). Churchland (1999) dismisses all talk of beliefs, desires, feelings and intentions as mere folk psychology. It is all empty talk with no basis in reality. It is mistaken to suppose that anyone has any desires and beliefs. We should thus eliminate such talk as outmoded error and replace it with descriptions of the nervous system. In short, according to Churchland, common-sense folk psychology dabbles in illusions; the mind is a myth.

Similarly, Susan Blackmore (2002) also suggests that consciousness is just an illusion, like a mirage or a visual illusion. She writes:

For the proposal 'It's all an illusion' even to be worth considering, the problem has to be serious. And it is. We can't even begin to explain consciousness . . . How can the firing of brain cells produce subjective experience? It seems like magic; water into wine.

She concludes:

Admitting that it's all an illusion does not solve the problem of consciousness but changes it completely. Instead of asking how neural impulses turn into conscious experiences, we must ask how the grand illusion gets constructed. This will prove no easy task, but unlike solving the Hard Problem it may at least be possible.

One might well ask how calling consciousness an illusion contributes anything at all towards explaining how our personal experiences – whether real or illusory – can arise from neural processes. Dismissing consciousness as an illusion only gives the illusion of making progress in solving the problem of consciousness.

Obviously, such an extreme position is hard to maintain with any degree of consistency. Does Churchland really believe that all his own beliefs, desires, feelings and thoughts are illusions? If so, does this not reduce his materialist belief to just another illusion? Why, then, does he write books arguing for the truthfulness of his theories? Churchland's defence of his position is self-refuting. Moreover, by denying the reality of our conscious thoughts, Churchland's theory fails the test of experience. Any theory that denies the existence of our most basic experience has thereby produced a *reductio ad absurdum* of itself.

Are You for Real?

We move on to further difficulties faced by materialism. Suppose, for the sake of the argument, that consciousness could emerge from matter, as Searle conjectures. What sort of mind would it be? The mind that Searle ends up with is totally inert. It can influence neither the brain nor the body. Its contents are completely determined by the physical properties of the brain.

Such materialism, if consistently applied, leads inevitably to the 'astonishing hypothesis' of Sir Francis Crick, as we saw earlier:

> The Astonishing Hypothesis is that 'You', your joys and your sorrows, your memories and your ambitions, your sense of personal identity and free will, are in fact no more than the behaviour of a vast assembly of nerve cells and their associated molecules (Crick 1994:3).

Imagine what that entails. It means that when, for example, you marry, then your experience of joy, your professions of love, your vows of faithfulness, and your hopeful plans for future bliss are just so much hot air, beyond your control. You are a mere robot, ordered about by neural commands.

A similar stance is defended by biologist Edward Wilson (1998) and philosopher of biology, Michael Ruse (1995). They contend that all our knowledge, beliefs, appreciation of beauty and perception of right and wrong, as well as our sense of personal identity, purpose and free will, are all mere illusions caused by our genes and brain neurons. In a joint article, Ruse and Wilson (1986:179) assert, 'Human beings function better if they are deceived by their genes into thinking that there is a disinterested objective morality binding upon them, which all should obey.' The mind simply reflects the behaviour of the brain, which is totally determined by the interaction of brain neurons. Everything, Ruse and Wilson allege, can in principle be fully explained by the laws of physics.

This raises a number of problems. The first problem concerns our very identity, the notion of our inner *I*. An undeniable feature of our experiences is that they are unified. There is an agent – our *self* – that unifies our experiences, reflects, makes decisions and endures through time. We certainly do not feel that we are just vast collections of molecules, genes, neurons, or thoughts.

Yet Crick claims that our sense of personal identity is no more than an illusion. There is no real purposeful self that controls the brain. There is no 'ghost in the machine'. Rather, there is just a set of competing neural circuits.

Such a denial of our deepest, most obvious experience must surely be considered the greatest *reductio ad absurdum* of materialism. John Eccles comments, 'Since materialist solutions fail to account for our experienced uniqueness, I am constrained to attribute the uniqueness of the self or soul to a supernatural spiritual creation' (Eccles 1994:180).

MEME MACHINE MINDS

According to Edward Wilson, the biggest problem facing naturalistic evolution is how to explain the phenomenon of civilization. Our human minds are much more highly developed than seems to be strictly needed for mere survival. From whence comes our ability for highly abstract philosophical and mathematical thought, for music and literature, and so on? Wilson asks:

> How did natural selection prepare the mind for civilization before civilization existed? . . . That is the great mystery of evolution: how to account for calculus and Mozart . . . Natural selection does not anticipate future needs (1998:51).

Wilson is unable to solve this mystery.

One ingenious attempt to answer Wilson's question looks beyond mere genes. Richard Dawkins extended evolution into the realm of ideas by inventing the concept of *memes*. A *meme* is an idea or behaviour that is imitated and passed on. Memes include all the words in our vocabulary, the games we play, the theories we believe, the songs we sing, the habits we have, and so on. Memes, like genes, are reproduced by being copied. Memes, too, evolve through copying errors and natural selection.

Susan Blackmore has worked this notion out in detail in her book *The Meme Machine* (1999). She asserts that memes use our behaviour to get themselves copied. As the genes use our *bodies* as vehicles for reproduction, so likewise the memes use our *brains*. Indeed, the only real power memes have is that of reproduction. Blackmore writes:

> Instead of thinking of our ideas as our own creations, and as working for us, we have to think of them as autonomous selfish memes,

working only to get themselves copied. We humans, because of our powers of imitation, have become just the physical "hosts" needed for the memes to get around (1999:8).

In short, we are mere meme machines. Blackmore believes many aspects of human behaviour can be explained in terms of competition between memes to get into our brains. This, she alleges, explains such diverse things as the evolution of the enormous human brain, the origin of language, our tendency to talk and think too much, human altruism, and the evolution of the Internet.

Whereas Wilson believes that *genes* determine human culture, Blackmore asserts that *memes* control the genes. Memes, not genes, drive civilization. Blackmore considers religions to be prime examples of powerful, and usually false, memes. The memes took a great step forward when they invented writing, and then printing, and then other forms of communication, from railways and ships to fax machines.

According to Blackmore, memes even create the illusion of our inner self. We are no more than a conglomeration of memes living in a brain. We are not really in charge of our lives at all – the memes are. Our 'self' was created by and for the memes. Blackmore argues that we have no free will. Creativity and foresight owe more to memetic evolution than to individual brilliance. We are meme machines through and through, and we need to learn to live with it.

Richard Dawkins, the inventor of memes, was at one time still hopeful for human freedom. He ended his book *The Selfish Gene* with the optimistic opinion:

We have the power to defy the selfish genes of our birth and, if necessary, the selfish memes of our indoctrination . . . We are built as gene machines and cultured as meme machines, but we have the power to turn against our creators. We, alone on earth, can rebel against the tyranny of the selfish replicators (1976:215).

In his later works Dawkins, perhaps realizing the deeper consequences of Darwinism, is less explicit in defending human freedom. Blackmore, however, does not hesitate to draw out the full implications of meme theory. Her book *The Meme Machine* concludes:

> Memetics thus brings us to a new version of how we might live our lives. We [can] carry on our lives as most people do, under the illusion that there is a persistent conscious self inside who is in charge, who is responsible for my actions and who makes me me. Or we can live as human beings, body, brain, and memes, living out our lives as a complex interplay of replicators and environment, in the knowledge that this is all there is. Thus we are no longer victims of the selfish selfplex. In this sense we can be truly free – not because we can rebel against the tyranny of the selfish replicators but because we know that there is no one to rebel (1999:246).

Not all naturalists are enthused about the notion that we are just meme machines. Philosopher Daniel Dennett, in his book *Darwin's Dangerous Idea*, responds,

> I don't know about you, but I am not initially attracted by the idea of my brain as a sort of a dungheap in which the larvae of other people's ideas renew themselves, before sending out copies of themselves in an informational diaspora. It does seem to rob the mind of its importance as both author and critic. Who's in charge, according to this vision – we or our memes? (1995:346).

Yet Dennett offers no solid argument for human freedom. Indeed, in his earlier work, *Consciousness Explained* (1991), he takes the position, similar to that of Churchland (see p.100), that the mind does not really exist.

As Phillip Johnson astutely notes:

> The potentially rebellious self is not the only casualty of memetic theory. By the same logic Darwinism itself is merely another one of those memes. Memes propagate not because they are true but because brains have some tendency to copy them, in the way they copy commercial jingles or jokes (Johnson 2000:110).

One might add that if Blackmore's meme theory is true, then the theory itself is just another meme. Why, then, should we accept it as true?

Can You Believe Your Beliefs?

What about Sir Francis Crick's claim that all our beliefs are illusions caused by brain neurons? Can such a claim be rationally justified? Consider some of the implications.

First, as pointed out by C. S. Lewis in his refutation of naturalism, if all our beliefs are illusions caused by genes, then so is the belief that our beliefs are illusions caused by genes (1947:15). How, then, does a reductionist explain and justify his beliefs?

Second, Keith Ward (1996:171) argues that the statement that all our beliefs are illusions is self-refuting. It asserts two contradictory things: (1) that we believe certain propositions to be true; and (2) that these propositions are false, because our beliefs are illusions. The law of non-contradiction forces us to give up one of these statements. Which one? If we give up (2) and keep (1), then we believe we are not deluded. On the other hand, if we give up (1) and keep (2), we believe ourselves to see beyond any illusion. In either case, we believe we are not deluded. So the belief that all our beliefs are illusions is self-refuting.

Third, it seems clear that only *conscious* beings can *believe* things. Thus, when reductionism reduces the conscious mind to mere neuron interactions, it destroys the possibility of belief, and, if knowledge is justified true belief, of knowledge itself. Therefore, if reductionism were true we could never know it to be the case!

THOUGHTS ABOUT THOUGHTS

Our beliefs are often the outcome of deliberation, which involves a train of thought. What determines the *flow* of our thoughts? One thought, it seems, often leads to another. We aim to connect our thoughts by logic and purposeful goals.

That, at least, is the common sense view. Yet, according to reductionists such as Crick, this is false. If our thoughts are entirely caused by brain neurons then any apparent rational connection between our thoughts is as illusory as our beliefs. The transition from one thought to the next must then be caused solely by the transition from one brain state to the next. And our brain states are, according to Crick, completely determined by physical laws. It follows that the flow of our thoughts must thus likewise be fully physically determined.

An argument, to be valid, must logically relate the conclusion to the premise. As such, each step in our train of reasoning should be connected by *logical*, rather than *physical* causes and effects. However, if our thoughts are determined purely by physical processes, they are determined by the laws of *physics*, not *logic*. Hence, why should they be true? On such grounds, philosopher Karl Popper pointed out:

> Physical determinism is a theory which, if it is true, is unarguable since it must explain all our reactions, including what appear to us as beliefs based on arguments, as due to purely physical conditions. Purely physical conditions including our physical environment make us say or accept whatever we say or accept (Popper 1972:224).

Similarly, neuroscientist John Eccles comments:

> If physical determinism is true, then that is the end of all discussion or argument; everything is finished. There is no philosophy. All human persons are caught up in this inexorable web of circumstances and cannot break out of it. Everything that we think we are doing is an illusion and that is that . . . the laws of physics and all our understanding of physics is the result of the same inexorable web of circumstances. It is not a matter any more of our struggling for truth to understand what this natural world is and how it came to be . . . All of this is illusion. If we want to have that purely deterministic physical world, then we should remain silent (Popper and Eccles 1977:546).

Physical determinism gives no ground for believing our reasoning to be valid. Hence physical determinism leads to scepticism.

Clearly, we do have some measure of control over our thoughts. We make choices based on our inner beliefs and desires. It is equally obvious that such choices depend, not just on physical factors, but also on non-physical ones, such as our sense of truth, justice, and purpose. Further, it is clear that such non-physical causes cannot be reduced to the physical effects of neurons, if only for the reason that the former are concerned with abstractions, norms and principles – with 'oughts' – whereas the latter obey the laws of physics. As David Hume stressed, we cannot deduce 'ought' from 'is'.

Indeed, reductionists themselves, when publishing arguments aimed at rationally persuading others to change their minds, surely presume that their minds are causally effective (how else could they write out their thoughts?) and that thoughts are caused by other thoughts, rather than solely by brain neurons. It is therefore self-refuting to defend any view of reality that denies the existence of mind or its active role in formulating its own beliefs.

Crick calls his hypothesis 'astonishing' because it is so contrary to our common sense experiences. Perhaps it is even more astonishing that Crick himself seems unaware of the self-refuting nature of his hypothesis, even though he himself remarks on the almost limitless human capacity for self-deception (Crick 1994:262).

Turning Thought Into Action

A further remarkable feature of mind is its ability to influence matter. Having made up my mind to open a book, my mind directs my hands to do so. My body is, at least partly, open to my mind's control. How is the materialist to explain this influence of mind on matter?

Many materialists deny such mental causation. If they acknowledge mind at all, it is an inert mind that is a purely passive product of brain activity, much like the shadow of a moving train. Such a mind (called an *epiphenomenon*) is totally controlled by matter and has no ability to influence matter. A leading materialist philosopher, Jaegwon Kim, has concluded that any form of materialism entails that the mind has no power to cause any physical event. Nevertheless, he acknowledges that the notion that our reasons and beliefs have no influence on our bodily actions is a *reductio ad absurdum* of materialism (Kim 1993:104–6). Indeed, nothing is more self-evident and essential to our daily life than the fact that we *do* constantly transform our mental choices into physical action.

Eccles (1994:10) contends that all materialist theories of mind, as well as pan-psychism, are in conflict with biological evolution. According to biological evolution, mental states could have evolved and developed only if they were causally effective in bringing about changes in the neuron happenings in the brain, with consequent changes in human behaviour. This can occur only if the neural machinery of the brain is open to mental influences. Thus, any theory of mind that asserts the causal ineffectiveness of consciousness fails to account for the biological evolution of consciousness.

The philosopher John Locke (1632–1704), in his *Essay Concerning Human Understanding*, addressed the question, 'Which came first, mind or matter?' He asserted that mind had to come first, since 'It is impossible to conceive that ever bare incogitative matter should produce a thinking intelligent Being.' Three centuries later it is still just as inconceivable.

The failure of a causally effective mind to emerge from matter is a fatal deficiency of materialism. Reductionist biologist Richard Dawkins' boast that Darwin's evolution 'made it possible to be an intellectually fulfilled atheist' (1991:6) becomes rather hollow when the truncated world of naturalistic evolution denies us our very intellect.

Conclusions

In summary, naturalism has great difficulty accounting for the origin of life and mind. With regard to life, we saw that even the simplest forms of life are incredibly complex. Such high degrees of complexity could not have arisen by mere accident. The high information content of DNA, as well as the need to interpret and apply the information, point to intelligent design. Naturalism cannot account for the generation of complex information from chaos. Nor can it explain the generation of purposeful life from purposeless matter.

With regard to mind, naturalism fails to explain (1) how consciousness can arise from matter, (2) the unity of my conscious self, (3) how my thoughts are logically connected, and (4) how I can actualize a mental choice. Consistent materialism leads inevitably to the self-refuting notions that my beliefs are illusions and that my mind has no effective influence on my brain.

7

From Mind to Math

Natural selection is not just a scientifically respectable alternative to divine creation. It is the *only* alternative that can explain the evolution of a complex organ like the eye. The reason that the choice is so stark – God or natural selection – is that structures that can do what the eye does are extremely low probability arrangements of matter . . . The language instinct, like the eye, is an example of what Darwin called 'that perfection of structure and co-adaptation which justly excites our admiration', and as such it bears the unmistakable stamp of nature's designer, natural selection.

STEPHEN PINKER (*The Language Instinct* 1994:371, 373)

* * * * *

And the LORD came down to see the city and the tower, which the children of men builded. And the LORD said, Behold, the people is one, and they have one language; and this they begin to do: and now nothing will be restrained from them, which they have imagined to do. Go to, let us go down and confound their language, that they may not understand one another's speech. So the LORD scattered them abroad from thence upon the face of all the earth.

GENESIS 11:5–8

L anguage is a marvellous thing. It is closely connected with thought, logic and knowledge. Advanced language ability is a prime factor that distinguishes man from animals.

How did man's amazing language ability come about? According to naturalist psychologist Stephen Pinker, the admirably complex structure of language is best explained by the gradual, step-by-step process of natural selection. Whether naturalism can indeed construct a plausible explanation for man's linguistic skill is one of the topics we shall address in this chapter.

In the previous chapter we saw that naturalism has difficulty explaining the origin of life, as well as its evolution to higher forms. Naturalism leaves unresolved also the problem of mind and our ability to have thoughts. Now we move on to consider how well naturalism can account for the *quality* of the thoughts we think. How can we know that our beliefs are true? Why should our thoughts be rational? Are there absolute standards for logic, morality or beauty? If so, how can we gain access to them? How can we justify any knowledge that we think we have? Such questions form the substance of this chapter.

Let's Be Reasonable

We shall address first the question of reason, or rationality. What does it mean for us to be reasonable? Rationality surely requires that our thoughts be purposeful and logically coherent. It includes also an ability to evaluate arguments and beliefs, as well as the capacity to make meaningful choices and decisions.

Closely related to rationality is knowledge. For knowledge to be more than mere opinion or belief, it must be rationally justified and shown to be true. Thus knowledge is often defined to be true, justified belief. Rationality and knowledge entail: (1) a purposeful self; (2) a reliable mind; (3) objective truth; (4) absolute values and logical laws. Let us examine these in more detail.

Who Knows?

For knowledge to exist there must be a *knower*. There must be a united *self* that provides coherence and direction to the intricate web of our perceptions, memories, beliefs and judgments. There must be a purposeful self that makes decisions and activates plans. In the previous chapter we saw that naturalism fails to account for such an essential self. On the contrary, naturalism, with its denial of the reality of beliefs, mental causation and even our inner self, undermines the very possibility of a knower.

Can You Trust Your Mind?

Consider next our ability for *rational* thought. Our thoughts are usually not chaotic or incoherent. Rather, they are generally purposeful and have a logical flow. We presume that they reflect at least some measure of truth. We believe that our thinking process is generally reliable. We may make logical mistakes in our thinking but deeper reflection usually uncovers such mistakes. Can naturalistic evolution give a plausible account of the logical coherence of our thinking?

Survival or Truth?

Darwinism presumes that everything, including our thinking ability, evolved through blind, random mutations coupled with natural selection. Our minds were allegedly honed to promote survival and to maximize fitness. If so, why would we expect our minds to furnish us with true metaphysical beliefs?

Charles Darwin himself worried about this:

> The horrid doubt always arises whether the convictions of man's mind, which has been developed from the mind of the lower animals, are of any value or at all trustworthy. Would anyone trust in the convictions of a monkey's mind, if there are any convictions in such a mind? (Darwin 1881:68).

Post-modern philosopher Richard Rorty similarly states:

> The idea that one species of organism is, unlike all others, oriented not just toward its own increased prosperity but towards Truth, is as un-Darwinian as the idea that every human being has a built-in moral compass – a conscience that swings free of both social history and individual luck (Rorty 1995:32–36).

Evolutionary success is measured by the number of offspring one engenders. It would thus seem that physical prowess and the ability to charm members of the opposite sex are more pertinent to evolution than any ability for theoretical thought. Success in the evolutionary struggle does not in itself guarantee the truth of one's beliefs.

Even naturalists must grant this to be the case. Otherwise, given the large majority of people who believe in a supernatural being, naturalists would have to acknowledge supernaturalism to be true.

On this basis the Christian philosopher Alvin Plantinga (1993) concludes that it is irrational to believe in naturalistic evolution. According to Plantinga, naturalistic evolution gives us no reason to believe that our reasoning tells us the truth about the world. It just tells us what we need to believe in order to survive. But this, though effective, could well be false. Thus, we have reason to doubt the truthfulness of our beliefs, including our belief in naturalistic evolution. So, if naturalistic evolution were true, then we have no good reason to believe it. Therefore, naturalistic evolution is self-defeating and it would be irrational to accept it. Plantinga concludes:

> Naturalistic epistemology conjoined with naturalistic metaphysics leads *via* evolution to scepticism or to violation of the canons of rationality; enjoined with theism it does not. The naturalistic epistemologist should therefore prefer theism to metaphysical naturalism (1993:237).

Naturalist philosopher of biology Michael Ruse, in responding to this argument, simply denies that truth should mean correspondence between one's ideas and reality. Ruse contends that we cannot get beyond the common-sense world to that of metaphysical reality. Rather, Ruse views truth as simply *coherence* among all one's beliefs (1998:297). It is enough for Ruse that our reasoning works in *practice*. But in that case he can hardly argue that his evolutionary views are true in any objective sense.

PHYSICS OR PURPOSE?

We noted earlier that evolutionary biologist Richard Dawkins believes any appearance of purpose in biological systems to be merely an illusion. In that case, what are we to make of purposive human reason? Is that, too, an illusion? If so, no rational argument has any real purpose. Hence, why should we believe it? If all purposes are illusory we have no rational grounds for doing anything. On the other hand, if purpose is not an illusion, how did it arise? How can genuine purpose ever arise from completely purposeless causes and effects? How can meaning ever arise out of meaninglessness? Such questions Dawkins is unable to answer.

Philosopher Richard Taylor (1974:114) gives the following argument against a naturalistic account of human origins. Imagine that, while travelling by train, you see stones on a hillside spelling out the words, 'Welcome to Wales'. This observation may cause you to believe that you have just entered Wales. But this presupposes that the stones have been purposely arranged to accurately convey that information. If you subsequently came to believe that the stones had ended up in this formation purely by accident, through natural laws, then it would be unreasonable to continue to believe that the stones transmitted a meaningful message. In similar fashion, Taylor argues, it is irrational to believe that your brain is the result of purely natural forces and, at the same time, to base this belief on the actual reasoning of your brain. Taylor writes:

> It would be irrational for one to say *both* that his sensory and cognitive faculties had a natural, non-purposeful origin and *also* that they reveal some truth with respect to something other than themselves . . . If, on the other hand, we do assume that they are guides to some truths having nothing to do with themselves, then it is difficult to see how we can, consistently with that supposition, believe them to have arisen by accident, or by the ordinary workings of purposeless forces, even over ages of time (Taylor 1974:118).

Philosopher of religion David Ray Griffin (2002:372) notes that, according to materialism, all causation is *efficient* causation, meaning that each event is completely caused by previous events. Rational thought, however, is guided by goals and *norms*, such as the rules of logic. As such, rational activity reflects *final causation* – causation in terms of a norm or goal – which is quite different from efficient causation. Materialism equates the mind with the brain, whose activities are presumed to be completely determined by the physical activities of its parts (*e.g.*, brain neurons). These, in turn, are held to be fully explicable in terms of purely physical causes. Hence materialism has no room for final causation.

This raises the question: if everything can be explained in terms of physics, where do logical norms enter into our thinking?

Note that it *is* possible for a *physical* mechanism to do *logical operations*. Think of computers, for example. Here there is an exact correlation between the flow of physical states of the computer and the corresponding flow of logical operations. In this case, however, the correspondence is specifically designed by an intelligent agent.

The origin of the brain, on the other hand, is attributed to an allegedly purposeless process. Hence, there are no grounds for believing in a perfect correspondence between the brain's physical flow and the mind's logical thinking. Further, in the case of the computer, the output is meaningless unless it is *interpreted* by an intelligent observer. In a purely material brain, where is there room for an intelligent interpreter?

Justifying Truth

Central to knowledge and rationality are the notions of truth and logic. How can naturalism account for these?

WHERE IN THE WORLD IS TRUTH?

Truth, as we noted in Chapter 1, is concerned with reality. A statement or belief is true if, and only if, it corresponds with what is actually the case. This common sense view of truth is known as the *correspondence* theory of truth.

Knowing something about reality involves the capacity to *represent* some aspect of reality as a thought in our mind. Our beliefs are tentative representations of reality. Our beliefs are judged to be either true or false depending on how well they represent reality.

Truth and falsity are objective properties of our *representations*, not of the external world itself. Physical objects do not, in themselves, represent anything. They do not refer to anything beyond themselves. They can, of course, be *interpreted* by us as representing something other than themselves, but the actual representation is then our mental interpretation. Christian philosopher Dallas Willard argues that no *physical* property or combination of properties can constitute a *representation* of anything (2000:39). Hence truth cannot be reduced to a physical property. It follows that truth cannot be explained by materialism.

It does not help matters to adopt a pragmatic or coherence definition of truth, as Ruse did in response to Plantinga's argument. For truth so defined still applies only to our *beliefs*. As such, truth can never be reduced to a property of material objects or their interactions. So, even within these looser definitions, truth has no place in the materialist world.

A QUESTION OF LOGIC

Closely related to truth is *logic*. Logical propositions are either true or false. Logical laws and relations connect the truth-values of different propositions. Since truth is not a physical property, it follows that neither is logic.

Moreover, logical laws are quite different from laws of physical or psychological fact. Logical laws are neither hypothetical nor inductive, but rather, necessary and universal. They remain valid, regardless of the state of the physical world. Hence they cannot be proven from any physical laws or state of affairs.

Logical laws, like truth, are abstractions. As such, they belong to the realm of ideas, not matter. Christian philosopher J. P. Moreland (2000:67) contends that consistent materialistic naturalism must reject abstract objects of any kind (including sets, numbers, propositions, and properties), if we take these in the traditional sense of being non-physical.

MATH IS IDEAL

These considerations raise particular problems for a materialist view of mathematics. Most mathematicians believe that numbers, equations, perfect circles, and so on, exist in some ideal, abstract sense. Such non-physical objects must be rejected by consistent materialists. But if ideal entities do not exist, this means that any propositions concerning them cannot be true in the sense of corresponding to anything. As Griffin points out (2002:369), one is then forced to either reduce mathematics to a mere game with meaningless symbols or to think of mathematical objects as part of the physical world, which is clearly not the case. Consequently, few mathematicians are materialists. Most materialists just ignore this problem.

One further difficulty for naturalists is that the abstract entities of mathematics are essential for physics, which, as we saw in a previous chapter, relies very strongly on mathematics. Physics, in turn, is essential to materialism. On that ground, philosopher Willard Quine (1981:14–15), who is otherwise a materialist, grants the existence of the abstract objects of mathematics. However, Quine fails to explain how ideal mathematical objects can exist in his otherwise materialist universe.

ARE THERE ABSOLUTES?

Thus far we have stressed that truth, logic and mathematics require the existence of ideal, abstract norms. Rationality concerns the rightness or wrongness of our reasoning. Rationality assumes the existence of objective, rational 'oughts' that prescribe how we are to reason. Given certain arguments and evidence, a rational person *ought* to accept the conclusions they entail. This implies the existence of objective laws of logic and rules of evidence. Philosopher Hilary Putnam, who at one time denied the existence of any ideal truths, later had to concede that the law of non-contradiction, at least, is an absolutely unrevisable ideal truth (Putnam 1983:98–114).

What is the status of such ideal truths? They surely exist in our human minds whenever we think of them. Yet they are not mere human inventions, limited to individual minds. The law of non-contradiction, for example, does not depend on our thinking of it. On the contrary, this law constrains and guides our thinking. Logical and mathematical truths have a universality that transcends human minds.

Michael Ruse denies the existence of any objective criteria for rationality. According to Ruse (1998:206), human rationality is determined solely by genetic traits developed via the evolutionary struggle for survival. But such a claim undermines any claim of Ruse that his thinking is rational. As Hilary Putnam notes, 'If rationality were measured by survival value, then the proto-beliefs of the cockroach . . . would have a far higher claim to rationality than the sum total of human knowledge' (1983:232).

Rationality is closely linked with morality. Both are concerned with 'oughts'. Rationality has to do with how we ought to reason; morality has to do with how we ought to act. Are all moral norms merely convenient social conventions, with no absolute authority? Most people would dispute that. For example, few people would want to defend the rightness of stealing from your neighbours or murdering your parents. Most people believe that all people ought to be fair and ought not to be selfish. Most people believe that promises should be kept and agreements honoured. Most people abhor Hitler's mass murders. This suggests the existence of at least some absolute moral laws that transcend individual minds and cultures.

This poses a difficulty for naturalists. Naturalist philosopher John L. Mackie denied the truth-value of moral claims because he thought that objective moral values must then exist in some ideal world. How, he asked, could such non-physical norms affect our mind so that we could come to know them? Mackie was convinced that one would have to appeal to some occult faculty of intuition. This he rejected. Mackie's naturalism committed him to the belief that the world consists solely of the physical and psychological phenomena that are the objects of natural science. His facts were limited to the way things are and what we think or do. They did not include how we *ought* to think or act. Consequently, Mackie concluded that postulating objective moral values is incoherent (1979:38–41), at least within a naturalist worldview. Hence naturalists have no solid basis upon which to condemn Hitler's acts; moral differences can then be attributed only to different social conventions.

In a later work, Mackie judged that even *subjective* moral properties are difficult to fit into a naturalist world. How can 'is' ever give rise to 'ought'? Mackie contended:

> Moral properties constitute so odd a cluster of properties and relations that they are most unlikely to have arisen in the ordinary course of events without an all-powerful god to create them (Mackie 1982:115).

Unhappily, this conclusion led Mackie not to God but, rather, to the rejection of moral properties.

Philosopher Charles Larmore notes that *moral* oughts are similar in nature to *rational* oughts. Both are ideal and abstract. The notion of moral truth is no more dubious than the idea of there being a truth or falsity to any claim that something ought to be believed (Larmore 1996:99). Hence Mackie's argumentation can just as well be applied to rational norms. Mackie must then conclude that objective rational norms, too, are inconsistent with naturalism. This destroys the very idea of rationality. Any worldview that denies the existence of rational norms inevitably ends up with the self-contradictions of irrationalism.

Larmore asserts that, whereas *natural* facts are found by observation and experiment, *normative* facts involve *reasons*, which are found by reflection. He writes:

> The inadequacy of naturalism is in the end its inability to account for normative truth in general. Thus, the minute we suppose it is

true that we ought to believe something, we have broken with the naturalistic perspective. Acknowledging that there are indeed reasons for belief and action is enough to dispel the mystery . . . By leaving no room for there being reasons for belief, naturalism contradicts itself. Or it does if it presents itself as the truth regarding what we ought to believe about the world (Larmore 1996:115–116).

The great Greek philosopher Plato (427–347 BC) believed that universal truths and ideals existed in a separate ideal world, of which the physical world was but a thin shadow. Larmore concludes that Plato was right. The world is more than the material world. In addition to physical and psychological facts, reality must include also abstract norms.

WHERE ARE THE STANDARDS?

Granted that universal norms do exist, *where* do they exist? Norms are ideas, which exist only in minds. Human thoughts exist in human minds. Since universals exist even in the absence of human minds, in whose mind do they exist?

Augustine (345–430 AD) solved this dilemma by placing universals in the mind of God. He argued that the existence of universal, eternal truths, such as those of logic and arithmetic, implied the existence of an infinite, eternal mind, which can only be that of God.

Naturalism, on the other hand, does not acknowledge such an eternal mind. Hence, even if it were to allow for universals, it has nowhere to place them. Thus naturalist mathematician Reuben Hersch rejects mathematical Platonism (the notion that objective mathematical truths exist) primarily because of the difficulties he has with the ideal Platonic world this entails. Hersch writes:

Recent troubles in the philosophy of mathematics are ultimately a consequence of the banishment of religion from science . . . Platonism . . . was tenable with belief in a Divine Mind . . . The trouble with today's Platonism is that it gives up God, but wants to keep mathematics a thought in the mind of God . . . Once mysticism is left behind . . . Platonism is hard to maintain (1997:42,122,135).

The same sentiment is expressed by mathematician Yehuda Rav, who asserts,

> Whereas the quarrel about universals and ontology had its meaning and significance within the context of medieval Christianity, it is an intellectual scandal that some philosophers of mathematics can still discuss whether whole numbers exist or not . . . There are no preordained, predetermined mathematical 'truths' that just lie out or up there. Evolutionary thinking teaches us otherwise (Rav 1993:81,100).

As a result, Hersch and Rav demote mathematics to a mere human invention, with no pretensions to any objective truth. This is contrary to the realist working philosophy of most mathematicians. Also, it fails to explain the amazing applicability and universality of mathematics.

In summary, naturalism – at least in its materialist form – has place for neither abstract entities nor universal norms. It cannot provide the metaphysical structure needed for rationality and knowledge. Therefore it cannot make any legitimate knowledge claims.

How Do You Know?

Rationality and knowledge, we have argued, demand the existence of abstract ideals that cannot be reduced to material properties. Hence naturalism, to be viable, must move beyond materialism. It must concede the existence of abstractions and universal norms. This raises a further question. Given the existence of non-material entities, how do we acquire knowledge about them?

Naturalists are generally *empiricists*. They believe that all our knowledge comes to us through our senses, through seeing, hearing, touching, and so on. If that is the case, then statements can be known to be true or false only by testing them empirically. Empiricism thus has great difficulty accounting for our knowledge of non-material entities, such as philosophical abstractions and moral norms. This has led some naturalists to prescribe drastic limits on reasonable speech.

Is Non-Science Nonsense?

Take, for example, the interesting tale of *logical positivism*. Logical positivism was an influential anti-metaphysical, naturalist movement prominent in the first half of the twentieth century. Members of this philosophical school were much impressed by empiricism and the success of science. They asserted that, if a sentence was not scientifically verifiable or a matter of logical truth, then it was nonsense.

One of their chief proponents was the British philosopher A. J. Ayer. In 1936 Ayer proposed the *verification principle*, which asserted that statements were meaningful and genuine only if they could be empirically verified. All meaningful statements had to be potentially falsifiable by direct observation. This standard was to filter out genuinely factual statements about the world. Applying this criterion, Ayer concluded that all statements of theology, metaphysics, and ethics were factually meaningless.

It soon became evident, however, that the verification principle itself could not be empirically verified. Hence, according to its own standard, it too was meaningless. Even Ayer (1959:35) himself eventually had to grant the validity of this fatal objection.

Ayer was forced to concede that language, even scientific language, could not be reduced to purely empirical terms. Scientific language must do more than merely *refer* to the physical world. It must accommodate also the world of ideas and concepts. Science needs these if it is to *explain* our observations in terms of theoretical entities and principles.

Philosopher Hilary Putnam (1983:189) argues that the self-refutation encountered by logical positivism applies to any attempt to define rationality in terms of merely *relative, cultural* norms. Any such limited definition of rationality, when applied to itself, will fail its own test for rationality. Why? Because the claim that our rational standards are themselves rational, involves an appeal to a universal standard of rationality. It is what Putnam calls a *transcendental* argument. Arguing about the nature of rationality is an activity that inevitably presupposes a notion of rationality wider than that of purely cultural norms. In short, the notion of rationality itself presumes the existence of universal norms.

MAKING SENSE OF SENSE

Empiricism limits our knowledge to that gained through our senses. If followed through consistently, empiricism leads us unavoidably to Hume's scepticism. As Hume showed, strict empiricism deconstructs our knowledge into a meaningless stream of experiences. Empiricism cannot step out of this flow of data to learn about the external world beyond our experiences, to find any necessary connection between cause and effect, or even to gain knowledge of our inner self.

Further, the empiricist is unable to solve the perplexing problem of how to derive a rational (or moral) 'ought' from a physical or psychological 'is'. Observations alone cannot do the job. All we can ever observe is 'what is', not 'what ought to be'. Nor does logical reasoning offer any help. Even if it were available to the empiricist, logic just establishes the conclusions that follow from given premises. Logic does not tell us whether the premises are true. Moreover, for the strict empiricist, the laws of logic themselves have first to be empirically established and justified.

Clearly, rational norms require more than sense experiences and deductive reasoning. Since rational norms are essential to justify knowledge claims, naturalist philosopher Jaegwon Kim (1994) concludes that an adequate naturalist theory of knowledge is impossible. That being the case, naturalism can offer no rational grounds for embracing naturalism. Hence it is self-refuting to argue that one *ought* to believe in naturalism.

The same holds for moral norms. Dutch naturalist Willem Drees admits that naturalism cannot explain morality. He writes:

> The view that all moral judgments are forced upon us by our past . . . seems to me to be insufficient for morality; it still identifies the moral justification with an explanation of how we came to have the preferences which we do turn out to have; there is no room for a contrast between 'what is' and 'what ought to be'. However, upon a

naturalist view developed here, there seem to be no other sources for substantial moral judgments . . . There is no room for the justification of ethical decisions in relation to entities in some Platonic realm, as if we come to hold moral principles by intuiting an absolute moral order (Drees 1996: 218).

Empiricism denies Drees access to absolute moral norms, even if they were to exist. Therefore, like Mackie, Drees is unable to establish any moral (or rational) 'oughts'. He thus has no means of distinguishing right from wrong. How, then, is he able to defend the rationality or morality of any of his writings or actions?

THE IDEAL CONNECTION

If there does exist an ideal world of universal norms and mathematical objects, how do we gain entry to it? How is moral or mathematical knowledge acquired?

Paul Benacerraf, a philosopher of mathematics, contends that holding true beliefs does not necessarily constitute genuine knowledge. They could just be lucky guesses. True beliefs may be considered to be genuine knowledge only if their truth is *causally* responsible for our belief (1983:412). For example, my true belief that the moon is not made of green cheese does not constitute knowledge if it is based on my underlying belief that the moon is made of candy. Rather, my knowledge should be based on pertinent observations of the moon.

Applying this view of knowledge to mathematics raises a difficulty. Mathematical objects are *ideal*, rather than *physical*, entities. Ideal entities are inert. They have no power to do anything. How, then, can they act upon us so as to cause beliefs? In the theistic worldview this poses no problem, for mathematical objects can be causally effective in the world, and in our minds, by virtue of being in the mind of God. God can always cause the required connections to be made. Those who profess not to believe in God are, however, faced with a daunting problem. Griffin comments:

The implication of Benacerraf's insight . . . is that atheism renders unintelligible the idea that we can have knowledge of a Platonic realm of numbers. Several philosophers of mathematics, including Hersch himself, use Benacerraf's insight as the basis for rejecting a Platonic realm. As Quine points out, however, such a realm is presupposed by physics. Benacerraf's insight, plus Quine's observation, implies that atheism makes an adequate philosophy of mathematics impossible (Griffin 2002:373).

Benacerraf's insight, when applied to morality, similarly undercuts any naturalist claims to moral knowledge.

THE GIFT OF THE GAB

Knowledge and thought are intimately connected with language. Concepts and propositions are formulated by means of words arranged in sentences. Words are abstract symbols representing things beyond themselves. Earlier (p. 117) we noted that physical properties do not represent things in this way. Hence language cannot be derived from mere experiences of physical things. Moreover, for language to be meaningful, its representations must somehow be connected to the concrete world of sense experiences. How can this huge gap be bridged? It seems to call for a high order of intelligence coupled with the necessary linguistic tools.

One amazing feature of language is its high degree of sophistication. It is estimated that there are currently about 6000 languages worldwide. Yet, although some societies are technologically backward, their languages are not. There are no primitive languages. If we trace language back through history it does not become less complex. Ancient Greek, Hebrew or Hittite are no less complex than modern Greek, English or Turkish. Well-developed languages are as old as mankind. All exhibit the same high order of complexity. All languages seem to follow the same general blueprint, using the same universal grammatical rules.

Psychologist Stephen Pinker, a naturalist, writes,

The universality of language is a discovery that fills linguists with awe, and is the first reason to suspect that language is not just any

cultural invention but the product of a special human instinct . . .
There are Stone Age Societies, but there is no such thing as a Stone
Age language (1994:14).

The similarity of languages suggests that all languages stem from
one original language. Regarding the biblical account of language
diversity, at the Tower of Babel (*Gen.* 11), Pinker comments,

> God did not have to do much to confound the language of Noah's
> descendants. In addition to vocabulary – whether the word for
> 'mouse' is *mouse* or *souris* – a few properties of language are simply
> not specified in Universal Grammar and can vary as parameters . . .
> There seems to be a common plan of syntactic, morphological, and
> phonological rules and principles. Once set, a parameter can have
> far-reaching changes on the superficial appearance of the language
> (1994:239).

Pinker argues that God would have had to introduce only a few
minor changes in the original language in order to cause a wide
variety of languages that are, superficially, very different.

Another remarkable feature of language is how readily it is
learned by infants. It seems implausible that babies could learn
as fast as they do if they started off with a completely blank
mind.

How, then, do we acquire language ability? The famous linguist
Noam Chomsky argues that language is essentially innate. He
writes:

> The rate of vocabulary acquisition is so high at certain stages of life,
> and the precision and delicacy of the concepts acquired so remark-
> able, that it seems necessary to conclude that in some manner the
> conceptual system with which lexical items are connected is already
> substantially in place (1980:139).

The whole conceptual system must be in place *before* we can use
it to interpret our experiences. According to Pinker (1994:266),
'All infants come into the world with linguistic skills.' Yet they
don't learn to speak until these skills are actually applied to learning their mother tongue.

How did this astonishing innate language ability arise? Pinker argues that language ability can have arisen only through gradual Darwinian evolution. As we saw (p. 111), he writes:

> Natural selection is not just a scientifically respectable alternative to divine creation. It is the *only* alternative that can explain the evolution of a complex organ like the eye. The reason that the choice is so stark – God or natural selection – is that structures that can do what the eye does are extremely low probability arrangements of matter . . . The language instinct, like the eye, is an example of what Darwin called 'that perfection of structure and co-adaptation which justly excites our admiration', and as such it bears the unmistakable stamp of nature's designer, natural selection (1994:371,373).

His reasoning is that language, like the eye, is much too complex to have arisen as a hugely improbable accident. Rather, it could have arisen only gradually, step by step.

This proposal has a number of weaknesses. First, Pinker gives no plausible scenario as to how language ability came about through any specific gradual process. Language ability, like the eye, would seem to be functional only in its completed form. A half-formed eye does not give half-formed vision. It gives no vision at all. As such, it is useless and unlikely to be passed on via natural selection. Second, if language ability came about gradually, why are there no examples of primitive language ability? There is a huge gap between the gibberish of animals and the highly sophisticated speech of humans.

For such reasons Chomsky is sceptical about the ability of naturalistic evolution to explain language ability. He holds that language is too unusual and too unconnected with anything else in the animal world to have come about through gradual evolutionary changes. Chomsky writes:

> It is perfectly safe to attribute this development to 'natural selection', so long as we realize that there is no substance to this assertion, that it amounts to nothing more than a belief that there is some naturalistic explanation for these phenomena . . . In studying the evolution of mind, we cannot guess to what extent there are

physically possible alternatives to, say, transformational generative grammar, or an organism meeting certain other physical conditions characteristic of humans. Conceivably, there are none – or very few – in which case talk about evolution of the language capacity is beside the point (1972:97–98).

Chomsky suggests that language came about quite suddenly, perhaps as the accidental by-product of an increase in brain size or complexity. However, Chomsky offers no specific proposal as to how this might have happened.

Neither Chomsky nor Pinker explains how naturalistic evolution bridges the yawning chasm between physical properties and abstract representations of those properties. The problem of the origin of language ability thus remains a naturalist mystery.

It is no easier to account for mathematical ability. Chomsky argues that the human ability to manipulate numbers is like language ability in many respects. Concerning our capacity to deal with the number system, Chomsky writes

> It seems reasonable to suppose that this faculty is an intrinsic component of the human mind. The capacity to deal with the number system or with abstract properties of space is surely unlearned in its essentials. Furthermore, it is not specifically 'selected' through evolution, one must assume – even the existence of the number system could not have been known or the capacity exercised until human evolution had essentially reached its current stage (1980:38–39).

It is thus difficult to see how mathematical ability, like linguistic ability, could have arisen gradually. To function at all it, too, must appear as an essentially complete apparatus.

BEAUTY AND THE NATURALIST BEAST

Naturalism has difficulty accounting, not only for rationality and morality, but also for aesthetics. Aesthetics has to do with beauty and our appreciation of it. Our awareness of beauty is not something that would seem to contribute much to our ability to survive. How, then, did this sense develop? Further, our awareness of beauty suggests that there is objective beauty in the physical world. This consists of such things as colourful flowers, majestic mountains, gorgeous sunsets and cheerful birdsongs. Where did all this beauty come from? Where are the aesthetic norms by which we discern beauty? Aesthetic values – like moral and rational values – cannot be derived from merely material properties.

Beauty has a practical aspect, since perceiving it plays an important role in mathematics and physics. Paul Davies writes:

> It is widely believed among scientists that beauty is a reliable guide to truth, and many advances in theoretical physics have been made by the theorist demanding mathematical elegance of a new theory (1992:175).

Could our capacity for beauty be accounted for by natural selection? Davies is sceptical. He argues:

> If beauty is entirely biologically programmed, selected for its survival value alone, it is all the more surprising to see it re-emerge in the esoteric world of fundamental physics, which has no direct connection with biology. On the other hand, if beauty is more than mere biology at work, if our aesthetic appreciation stems from contact with something firmer and more pervasive, then it is surely a fact of major significance that the fundamental laws of the universe seem to reflect this something (1992:175).

If beauty is a standard of truth, then beauty must somehow transcend our human minds and point towards objective aesthetic values.

Our experience of beauty is profound. It seems to put us in contact with a deeper reality. Philosopher Anthony O'Hear, in his book *Beyond Evolution*, writes:

> Art can seem revelatory, just as it does seem to answer to objective standards. It can seem to take us to the essence of reality, as if certain sensitivities in us . . . beat in tune with reality. It is as if our . . . appreciation of things external to us . . . [is] reflecting a deep and pre-conscious harmony between us and the world from which we spring (1997:199).

O'Hear sees a close connection between beauty and religion. He continues,

> But how could we think of an aesthetic justification of experience . . . unless our aesthetic experience was sustained by a divine will revealed in the universe, and particularly in our experience of the beautiful? It is precisely at this point that many of us will draw back. Aesthetic experience *seems* to produce the harmony between us and the world that would have to point to a religious resolution were it not to be an illusion. But such a resolution is intellectually unsustainable, so aesthetic experience, however powerful, remains subjective and, in its full articulation, illusory. This is a dilemma that I cannot solve or tackle head on (1997:201).

At first O'Hear is impressed by the objectivity and profundity of beauty. Yet, when he realizes the theistic implications, he dismisses beauty as illusion.

O'Hear's difficulty stems from his inability to devise a naturalistic explanation of aesthetic experience and norms. Although O'Hear believes evolution is successful in explaining the development of living things, he finds that it cannot give a satisfactory account of such distinctive facets of human life as self-consciousness, the quest for knowledge, the moral sense, and the appreciation of beauty. O'Hear concludes, 'It is above all in aesthetic experience that we gain the fullest and most vividly lived sense that though we are creatures of Darwinian origin, our nature transcends our origin in tantalizing ways' (1997:202). Thus O'Hear is left with yet another naturalist mystery.

Conclusions

To sum up, naturalism has great difficulty accounting for rationality and knowledge. It cannot account for a unified self, the knower. The evolutionary process of random mutation and survival of the fittest cannot account for the development of a rational mind able to discern truth. The notion that the operation of our brain is fully explained at the physical level rules out the possibility that our thoughts are guided by rational norms.

Rationality requires logic and truth. It requires the existence of universal, abstract standards. Such abstract ideals have no place in a naturalist world restricted to physical and psychological phenomena. Nor does the naturalist have any room for aesthetic norms, moral principles or mathematical entities. The naturalist world is void of any truth, goodness, beauty or meaning. The naturalist world has no place for humans as *humans*. Humans may enter only at the price of being reduced to a bio-physical machine, stripped of all values, personality and self.

Even if naturalists were able to account for the existence of universal ideals, they would still need a means to gain access to them. This entails abandoning strict empiricism. Rationality requires us to have some non-empirical mode of experience by which we can acquire knowledge of rational norms and objective truth.

Instead of absolute, objective knowledge, naturalism is left with mere relative, subjective opinion. Naturalism, consistently applied, ultimately undermines itself. One can hardly argue that it is rational to accept naturalism, if such acceptance destroys the very possibility of objective rational knowledge.

8

Mysteries of Mathematics

CROSSFIRE

With this new way of providing a foundation for mathematics, which we may appropriately call a proof theory, I pursue a significant goal, for I should like to eliminate once and for all the questions regarding the foundations of mathematics, in the form in which they are now posed, by turning every mathematical proposition into a formula that can be concretely exhibited and strictly derived, thus recasting mathematical definitions and inferences in such a way that they are unshakeable and yet provide an adequate picture of the whole science. I believe that I can attain this goal completely with my proof theory ... Already at this time I should like to assert what the final outcome will be: mathematics is a presuppositionless science. To found it I do not need God, as does Kronecker, or the assumption of a special faculty of our understanding attuned to the principle of mathematical induction, as does Poincaré, or the primal intuition of Brouwer.

DAVID HILBERT
(*The Foundations of Mathematics* 1927: 464, 479)

* * * * *

One of themselves, even a prophet of their own, said, The Cretians are always liars, evil beasts, slow bellies. This witness is true. Wherefore rebuke them sharply, that they may be sound in the faith.

TITUS 1:12–13

If anything is undisputable and certain, it would seem to be mathematics. Who would doubt that 6 + 1 = 7? Yet, what guarantees the truth of mathematics? In earlier days, it was thought that mathematical truths were certain because they were upheld by an all-powerful and all-knowing God. The rise of naturalism, however, brought with it the need to establish a naturalist basis for mathematics. At first it was thought that mathematics could be firmly anchored by applying rigorous logic to self-evident axioms. David Hilbert (1862–1943), the foremost mathematician of the early twentieth century, was confident that he, using solely human reasoning, could put mathematics on a solid foundation, without having to resort to God.

Earlier chapters revealed several mysteries involving mathematics. We asked why the physical world has such a pronounced mathematical structure. Why is *human* mathematics so highly effective in not just *describing*, but also in *discovering* physical phenomena? Why is mathematics so intimately connected to both the physical world and the human mind?

This chapter focuses more specifically on mathematics itself. Do mathematical objects, such as numbers and theorems, really exist? If so, where do they exist? Can naturalism account for the existence of mathematics? How can we prove that mathematics is true? We shall see that Hilbert's quest for mathematical certainty was thwarted. A major obstacle was the *liar paradox*, which appears in the above quote from Paul's letter to Titus.

The Classical View on Math

We shall consider mathematics to be the discipline dealing with logic, numbers and shapes. The basic question concerning mathematics is this: Is mathematics a mere human construction? Or is it an exploration of an already existent realm? Is mathematical activity *invention* or *discovery*?

Historically, most mathematicians have believed that mathematical truths such as '6 + 1 = 7' are universally and eternally true, independent of human minds. They believed that they were *discovering* properties of, for example, prime numbers, rather than merely *inventing* them.

This view of mathematics dates back to the ancient Greek philosophers Pythagoras (*circa* 569–475 BC) and Plato (427–347 BC). Bertrand Russell, although himself an atheist, concluded from his study of the history of Greek philosophy, that 'mathematics is . . . the chief source of the belief in eternal and exact truth, as well as in a super-sensible intelligible world' (1945:37). This is so, Russell asserts, because of the abstract nature of mathematical concepts. For example, geometry deals with exact circles, but no physical object is exactly circular. This suggests that exact reasoning applies primarily to ideal, rather than physical, objects.

Furthermore, mathematical objects do not seem to be limited by time. Such things as the number '7' or an equilateral triangle seem to exist at all times or even beyond time. Mathematics seems to deal with an ideal, eternal world of pure thought. Russell notes, 'Mathematical objects, such as numbers, if real at all, are eternal and not in time. Such eternal objects can be conceived as God's thoughts' (1945:37).

MATH IN AN IDEAL WORLD

According to Plato, the world consists of two parts – *Cosmos* and *Chaos*. The Cosmos is the more fundamental world, consisting of eternal *forms* or ideas. These eternal forms include mathematical truths, beauty, justice, and so on. This ideal world is itself ordered by higher ordering principles. The highest principle is that of the *Good* or the *One*, the transcendental Spirit. The Good is the ultimate cause of all knowledge and existence. The physical world, on the other hand, was initially unformed matter, called *Chaos*. A transcendental Spirit, called the *Demiurge*, transformed it into our ordered, physical world by following the pattern of the Cosmos. The physical world is thus an imperfect, concrete, temporal copy of the perfect, ideal, eternal Cosmos.

Man, according to Plato, consists of an immortal soul connected to a physical, temporal body. As to our knowledge, the empirical knowledge of our senses gives rise only to knowledge of the *physical* world. Knowledge of the eternal forms is attained only through reason. This non-empirical knowledge is known as *a priori* knowledge. We acquire knowledge of the ideal realm via our soul's memories of its former life there, before it was united with its earthly body.

The notion that mathematics exists objectively in some ideal world is often called *platonism*. In order to avoid association with other features of Plato's philosophy, I shall just refer to this notion as *mathematical realism*. The *realism* here refers to the idea that mathematical truths really do exist in some objective form.

MATH IN THE MIND OF GOD

The existence of eternal, abstract, mathematical thoughts seems to require the existence of something actual in which they exist. This raises the questions of where and how such mathematical entities exist.

The early theistic philosophers Philo (*circa* 20 BC–AD 50) and Augustine (AD 354–430) placed the ideal world of eternal truths in the mind of God. Augustine argued that the existence of eternal necessary truths implied the existence of an eternal, necessary, infinite mind in which all such truths exist.

Indeed, Augustine used this as an argument for the existence of God. He asserted that we all know time-independent truths about logic (*e.g.*, A = A) and arithmetic (*e.g.*, 2 + 2 = 4). Where can such truths come from? Not from the physical world, for changing, material things cannot cause fixed, eternal truths. Nor can they come from finite human minds, since our thinking does not generate eternal truths, but rather, is judged by them. Thus truth must derive from something non-material that is superior to the human mind. Mathematical truths must depend on a universal and unchanging source that embraces all truth in its unity. Such a truth must exist and is by definition God (see Geisler and Corduan: 154).

Thus arose the classical Christian view that mathematics exists in the mind of God. Mathematics was held to be true because of its supposed divine origin. Moreover, since God created the universe according to a rational plan that uses mathematics, and since man's creation in the image of God included rationality, it was thought that man should be able to discern the mathematical structure of creation. As we saw in Chapter 3, such theological considerations were key factors motivating the scientific revolution.

Removing God from Math

Ironically, the very success of mathematical models in physics led to the demise of the classical Christian view. The clockwork universe of Newtonian physics worked so well that it seemed to do so all by itself. It had no apparent need of divine adjustment. Also, the uniformity of nature implied by the mathematical mechanisms contradicted the supernatural events related in the Bible. Over-confidence in scientific models led to a questioning of the possibility of miracles. This undermined biblical authority. Such developments eventually induced many scientists to banish God from their worldview. By the end of the nineteenth century naturalism had become the dominant worldview among scientists.

As we noted in the previous chapter, once theism was dropped, it became difficult to explain, (1) where objective truths might exist, and (2) how we might have access to such truths. Mathematical realism, which was plausible, it seemed, only within a theistic worldview, thus came to be questioned. Nowadays most philosophers of mathematics reject mathematical realism, primarily because of its perceived ill fit with naturalism. Consequently, mathematics has widely come to be considered as no more than a human construction. Nevertheless, most mathematicians remain mathematical realists, at least in their practical work.

However, a godless worldview left mathematics without a solid foundation. If mathematics were not God-given, why should it be true? This raised the question of how the truthfulness of mathematics could be proven.

Putting Math on Its Feet

The preferred approach for proving the truth of mathematics was the *axiomatic* method. This consisted of basing mathematics on a set of undoubtedly true, self-evident principles, called *axioms*. From the axioms everything else was to be derived using deductive logic.

The axiomatic method had been used with great success by the Greek mathematician Euclid. In about 300 BC he was able to derive all the truths about normal (*i.e.*, *Euclidean*) geometry from only 10 axioms, divided into 5 *common notions* (very general axioms) and 5 *postulates* (see Table 1).

Table 1. The Axioms for Euclidean Geometry

Common Notions

1. Things equal to the same thing are equal to each other.
2. If equals are added to equals, the wholes are equal.
3. If equals are subtracted from equals, the remainders are equal.
4. Things that coincide with one another are equal to each other.
5. The whole is greater than the part.

Postulates

1. A straight line can be drawn joining any two points.
2. A finite straight line can be extended indefinitely.
3. A circle can be drawn with any centre and radius.
4. All right angles are equal to each other.
5. Through a point not on a line, there is exactly one line parallel to the line.

From these simple axioms, which seemed quite self-evident, Euclid proved 465 propositions. These can all be found in his book, *Elements*, which was the most successful textbook of all time; at the end of the nineteenth century it was still used in many European schools.

The axiomatic method became the model for the rest of mathematics. Other disciplines, such as physics and even philosophy, tried to follow suit. Towards the end of the nineteenth century the search was on for a set of self-evident axioms upon which all of mathematics could be based. Various systems were proposed.

Unhappily, it was soon found that, in many cases, axioms that all seemed self-evident when considered individually nevertheless led to contradictions when combined into a system. Any such contradictory system must be false, as we saw in Chapter 2.

A system of axioms that will never yield a contradiction is said to be *consistent*. A system is said to be *complete* if *all* true theorems (and no false ones) can be derived from the axioms. The goal, then, was to find a set of axioms that could be proven to be consistent and complete for all of mathematics. This quest was what David Hilbert, quoted at the beginning of this chapter, was working on. It came to be known as *Hilbert's programme*.

Initially, this ambitious programme met with some success. It was proven that simple ('first-order') logic was both consistent and complete. The same was proven true for Euclidean geometry and *Presburger* arithmetic (a simplified arithmetic that uses addition and subtraction but not multiplication or division). Full victory was in sight. Or so it seemed.

The next step was to prove the consistency and completeness of number theory. Number theory consists of all theorems involving just the positive integers $\{0, 1, 2, \ldots\}$ plus the operations of addition and multiplication. It is based on the laws of logic plus a set of axioms pertaining to the integers, as listed in Table 2.

Table 2. Axioms of Number Theory

For any integers A and B
1. $S(A)$ is never 0
2. $A + 0 = A$
3. $A + S(B) = S(A + B)$
4. $A \times 0 = 0$
5. $A \times S(B) = A \times B + A$

In Table 2, S(A) stands for 'the successor of A', which is the next integer after A. For example, S(0) = 1, S(4) = 5, and so on. Axiom 1 states that 0 is the lowest integer. Axioms 2 and 3 define addition; axioms 4 and 5 define multiplication. It was hoped that from these basic axioms all true theorems of number theory could be derived.

In 1930, when David Hilbert retired, he thought his program was on the verge of being completed. His last speech ended with the famous boast, 'Wir müssen wissen, wir werden wissen' – 'We must know, we shall know.'

Math in Crisis

Unfortunately, this early optimism was soon shattered by some surprising mathematical discoveries. The very next year, in 1931, the Austrian logician Kurt Gödel proved two profound theorems:

1. Every system S large enough to contain number theory is incomplete.

2. If system S, large enough to contain number theory, is consistent, then it is impossible to prove that S is consistent by methods within S.

Theorem 1 says that any system of axioms large enough for number theory can never completely cover the branch of mathematics it addresses. There will always be propositions that can be neither proven nor disproven by the system. This means that no finite set of axioms can serve as a basis for *all* of mathematics. Mathematics will always be larger than our human attempts to capture it with a system of axioms.

This theorem is based on the *liar paradox*. This is a famous paradox that can be found even in the Bible. Paul writes: 'One of themselves . . . said, "The Cretians are always liars"' (*Titus* 1:12). This statement, if true, must be false, since it is made by one of the Cretians, who allegedly always lie. On the other hand, if it is false, then it must be true, for it confirms that the Cretian lied. It is like the statement, 'This statement is false.' If the statement is true, then it must be false, for that is what it claims to be. But if it is false, then it must be true, for it says that it is false. So, what is it – true, false, both, or neither?

The paradox arises from the reference of a statement to itself. Self-reference can often lead to incoherence and confusion. It should be noted, however, that self-reference does not always lead to paradox. There is no paradox, for example, in the self-referring sentence, 'This sentence is true.' Self-reference has been used effectively in art. M. C. Escher produced a print in which a man in a print gallery is observing a picture of a town that includes the print gallery and the man himself (see www.mcescher.com).

Gödel found a way to transform any statement *about* number theory into a mathematical theorem *in* number theory. He could transform any proof in number theory into a corresponding proof about number theory. Using this transformation, Gödel proved that number theory contains a theorem equivalent to the statement, about number theory, which asserts, 'This statement is unprovable.'

If that self-referring statement is true, then the statement *is* unprovable. This means that the corresponding theorem in number theory is also unprovable. This means that number theory is incomplete, since at least one true theorem cannot be proven from the axioms of number theory. On the other hand, if the statement is false, then the corresponding theorem in number theory is also false. In that case number theory contains a false statement, which renders it logically inconsistent. Since the self-referring statement must be either true or false, it follows that number theory – full arithmetic – is either incomplete or inconsistent.

Of these two options, inconsistency is by far the worse. In Chapter 2 we showed that any theorem, no matter how silly, can be proven in a system containing an inconsistency. That means that, if number theory were inconsistent, we could prove such things as '1 + 2 = 4'. Clearly, inconsistency would entail the death of arithmetic.

We would thus gladly pay the smaller price of incompleteness. Incompleteness implies that no finite set of axioms can ever encompass the whole of mathematics. Given any finite set of axioms, we can find meaningful mathematical questions that the axioms leave unanswered. Using mathematics we can prove that there is mathematical truth beyond our ability to prove. This, then, is the thrust of Gödel's first theorem.

This brings us to a further question. Granted that number theory is incomplete, could we prove it to be consistent? Alas, no. Gödel's second theorem says that, even if we have a system S that captures most of mathematics, we can never use S to prove that S is consistent. To do that, we have to go beyond S and use a larger system, say S'. Suppose that we could use S' to prove that S is consistent. How reliable is that proof? To ensure that the consistency proof is valid we must first prove the consistency of system S'. To do that, Theorem 2 tells us we have to go to a larger system S''. And so on, *ad infinitum*. In short, we can never prove the consistency of any system containing full arithmetic. It follows that we cannot prove the consistency of arithmetic, even though we use it all the time!

Gödel's theorems have had a devastating effect on the philosophy of mathematics. The logician Christopher Leary writes:

> Mathematics, which had reigned for centuries as the embodiment of certainty, had lost that role. Thus we find ourselves in a situation where we cannot prove that mathematics is consistent. Although I believe in my heart that mathematics is consistent, I know in my brain that I will not be able to prove that fact, unless I am wrong. For if I am wrong, mathematics is inconsistent. And if mathematics is inconsistent, then it can prove anything, including the statement which says that mathematics is consistent (2000:3).

The soundness of mathematics now had to be accepted largely on faith. John Barrow comments:

It has been suggested that if we were to define a religion to be a system of thought which contains unprovable statements, so it contains an element of faith, then Gödel has taught us that not only is mathematics a religion but it is the only religion able to prove itself to be one (Barrow 1992:19).

The loss of certainty in mathematics has had profound effects far beyond mathematics. For millennia, mathematics had been upheld as the model of certain knowledge. It was thought that, if anything could be known with certainty, it would surely be the truths of mathematics. Hence, the demise of mathematical certainty brought with it the demise of human certainty in any discipline. Bertrand Russell, who in his earlier years had done very important work on the foundations of mathematics, concluded later in his life:

> I wanted certainty in the kind of way in which people want religious faith. I thought that certainty is more likely to be found in mathematics than elsewhere. But I discovered that many mathematical demonstrations, which my teachers expected me to accept, were full of fallacies, and that, if certainty were indeed discoverable in mathematics, it would be in a new field of mathematics, with more solid foundations than those that had hitherto been thought secure. But as the work proceeded, I was continually reminded of the fable about the elephant and the tortoise. Having constructed an elephant upon which the mathematical world could rest, I found the elephant tottering, and proceeded to construct a tortoise to keep the elephant from falling. But the tortoise was no more secure than the elephant, and after some twenty years of very arduous toil, I came to the conclusion that there was nothing more that I could do in the way of making mathematical knowledge indubitable (Russell 1956:54–55).

> The splendid certainty which I had always hoped to find in mathematics was lost in a bewildering maze (Russell 1975:157).

Thus, amazingly, the ancient *liar paradox*, transformed into Gödel's theorems, played a major role in thwarting the modern human quest for truth and certainty.

Man-made Math

The rejection of theism, with the consequent concerns for the *soundness* of mathematics, had implications also for the actual *content* of mathematics. Classical mathematics was based on the concept of an *ideal mathematician*. It assumed the existence of a God who was all-knowing, all-powerful and infinite. The operations and proofs allowed in classical mathematics were those that could in principle be performed by such a God.

Some naturalist mathematicians, considering mathematics to be no more than the free creation of the *human* mind, felt that the methods of mathematics should be adjusted accordingly. Only those mathematical concepts and proofs were to be considered valid that could be (mentally) constructed in a finite number of explicit steps. The 'there exists' of classical mathematics was to be replaced by 'we can construct'. Accordingly, this came to be known as *constructive* mathematics. As the constructivist mathematician Errett Bishop notes:

> Classical mathematics concerns itself with operations that can be carried out by God . . . You may think that I am making a joke . . . by bringing God into the discussion. This is not true. I am doing my best to develop a secure philosophical foundation . . . for current mathematical practice. The most solid foundation available at present seems to me to involve the consideration of a being with non-finite powers – call him God or whatever you will – in addition to the powers possessed by finite beings (Bishop 1985:9).

Bishop himself rejected classical mathematics and urged a constructive approach to mathematics. He writes:

> Mathematics belongs to man, not to God. We are not interested in properties of the positive integers that have no descriptive meaning for finite man. When a man proves a positive integer to exist, he should show how to find it. If God has mathematics of his own that needs to be done, let him do it himself (Bishop 1967:2).

Constructive mathematics entailed a new approach to both logic and proofs. Consider, first, the implications for logic. Classical mathematics is based on what is called *two-valued* logic. Any well-posed mathematical proposition is either true or false; there is no third option.

Take, for example, the famous *Goldbach conjecture* concerning primes. A prime is a whole number that is divisible only by itself and 1 (*e.g.*, 2, 3, 5, 7, 11 are the first five primes). In 1742 the Prussian mathematician Christian Goldbach (1690–1764) suggested that any even whole number can be written as the sum of two primes (*e.g.*, 10 = 3 + 7; 20 = 13 + 7). This certainly seems to be true. No one has ever found a number for which this does not hold. But no one has as yet been able to prove it, even though a few years ago an American publisher offered a $1,000,000 prize for the first correct proof.

Classically, Goldbach's conjecture is either true or false, even though we do not yet know which it is. This follows from the logical *law of excluded middle*, which asserts that any proposition is either true or false. Any other possibility is excluded.

Constructivists, however, object to the law of excluded middle. They insist that there *is* a third possibility: a proposition is neither true nor false until we can construct an actual, finite proof.

This radical view of logic places severe restrictions on what constructivists accept as valid proofs. Classical mathematics, in addition to proving theorems directly, by deriving them from the axioms, often uses an indirect method of proof called *proof by contradiction*. It is based on the law of excluded middle. In a proof by contradiction we show that, if we assume the theorem to be false, we end up with a contradiction. The contradiction proves that our assumption was false. Hence, by the law of excluded middle, since the theorem cannot be false, it must be true.

To illustrate, consider the theorem, 'There exists an infinite number of primes.' A direct proof would aim to generate a list of primes and show that it is infinitely long. An indirect proof, due to Euclid, starts off by assuming that the number of primes is *not* infinite. Then there must be a largest prime, say, P. We can then form the number Q by multiplying all the primes together and adding 1 (*i.e.*, $Q = 2$ x 3 x 5 x . . . x P + 1). Now, note that Q is larger than P and is not divisible by any of the primes listed. It follows that Q is either prime or is a multiple of primes larger than P. For example, if we take P to be 7, then $Q = 2$ x 3 x 5 x 7 + 1 = 211, which is divisible only by 1 and 211. But this contradicts our definition of P as the largest prime. Hence, there can be no largest prime. This means that our initial hypothesis (*i.e.*, that the number of primes is not infinite) is false. Thus, by the law of excluded middle, the opposite must be true. Therefore, we conclude that the number of primes is infinite.

Constructivists object that this indirect proof is invalid, because it relies on the law of excluded middle. Moreover, the proof purports to demonstrate that an infinite number of primes exists. Yet it does not tell us how to draw up the actual list of primes, as should be done by a valid constructive proof.

Constructivism entails the rejection of many results of classical mathematics. So many, in fact, that it fails to support the sophisticated mathematics needed in modern physics. For example, philosopher of mathematics Geoffrey Hellman (1993, 1997) contends that it is impossible to reformulate quantum theory without resorting to the law of excluded middle. Advanced mathematical concepts, well beyond the range of constructive mathematics, are required to prove important theoretical results in physics. These include such esoteric mathematical tools as 'infinite Hilbert spaces' in quantum mechanics, the 'Hawking-Penrose singularity theorems' in general relativity, and 'renormalization' in quantum electrodynamics. If one is to believe in the truth of these theories in modern physics, then one must accept the truth also of the advanced classical mathematics that these theories presume. This involves, at the very least, the acceptance of the reality of several levels of infinite sets (*e.g.*, natural numbers and real numbers).

Another weakness of constructivism is that it does not do justice to the fact that mathematicians, when finding a new result, often experience a great sense of *discovery*. New theorems are seen as discoveries rather than inventions. For mathematicians, mathematics is more than a mere human construction. For such reasons most mathematicians are not constructivists.

Further, if mathematics is a human invention, one might ask: How did mathematics exist before humans existed? Do naturalists believe that '2 + 2 = 4' did not hold, so that two pairs of dinosaurs did not add up to four? Or that the Pythagorean Theorem did not apply? This seems absurd.

For theists, mathematics exists independent of human minds. God surely knows whether any proposition is true or false. His mind contains all truths, including truths about mathematics. Hence a mathematical entity need not be explicitly constructed in order to exist. As we shall elaborate in Chapter 14, theism validates two-valued logic, as well as both direct and indirect (*i.e.*, by contradiction) proofs.

Evolution-made Math

If mathematics is just a human invention, as naturalists supposed, how did it ever get started? How did man come to construct, from scratch, the magnificent tower of modern mathematics? We would hardly expect the primitive caveman, so prominent in evolutionary lore, to be proficient in mathematics.

Various evolutionary mechanisms have been proposed. Mathematician and psychologist Stanislas Dehaene (1997) suggests that human brains come equipped at birth with an innate, wired-in ability for mathematics. He postulates that, through evolution, the smallest integers (1, 2, 3 . . .) became hard-wired into the human nervous system, along with a crude ability to add and subtract. A similar position is defended by linguistics professor George Lakoff and philosopher Rafael Nunez (2000). They seek to explain mathematics as a system of metaphors that ultimately derive from neural processes.

To answer the question of where mathematical intuition comes from, philosopher of science Penelope Maddy (1993) sketches another, somewhat similar scenario. She conjectures that our nervous system contains higher-order assemblies that correspond to thoughts of particular sets. Among these is an even higher-order group corresponding to the general notion of a set. These are held to be responsible for various beliefs about sets (*e.g.*, the belief that sets have number properties). Thus our beliefs about sets come not, in some incomprehensible way, from Platonic ideal forms, but, rather, from certain *physical* events, such as the development of pathways in neural systems. In similar fashion, we allegedly acquire intuitions about lines, curves and other mathematical structures.

Such evolutionary explanations seek to derive all our mathematical *thoughts* from purely *physical* connections between neurons. One weakness of the proposed explanations for simple arithmetic is that they are entirely hypothetical. No actual mathematical mechanisms have as yet been found in the brain.

Even if the evolutionary mechanism of random mutation and natural selection could account for an innate ability for simple arithmetic, it is hard to see where more advanced mathematics comes from. An ability for simple arithmetic might be useful for survival. However, our capacity for advanced mathematics seems to be well in advance of mere survival skills. Paul Davies comments:

> One of the oddities of human intelligence is that its level of advancement seems like a case of overkill. While a modicum of intelligence does have a good survival value, it is far from clear how such qualities as the ability to do advanced mathematics . . . ever evolved by natural selection. These higher intellectual functions are a world away from survival 'in the jungle' . . . Most biologists believe the . . . human brain has changed little over tens of thousands of years, which suggests that higher mental functions have lain largely dormant until recently. Yet if these functions were not explicitly manifested at the time they were selected, why were they selected? How can natural selection operate on a hidden ability? Attempts to explain this by supposing that, say, mathematical ability simply piggy-backs on a more obvious useful trait are unconvincing in my view (Davies 1995:85–86).

The evolutionary approach fails to explain also the amazing mathematical intuition of leading mathematicians.

Further, if our mathematical ideas are just the result of the physics of neural connections, why should they be true? Such accounts of mathematics cannot distinguish true results from false ones. Nor can they yield any explanation for *correctness*, a basic issue in mathematics. Indeed, if all knowledge is based on neural connections, so is the idea that all knowledge is based on neural connections. Hence, if true, we have no basis for believing it to be true.

Are Numbers Real?

In spite of what most philosophers of mathematics might believe, most mathematicians remain realists. In the last century realism has been explicitly defended by a number of outstanding mathematicians, including Georg Cantor, Kurt Gödel, G. H. Hardy, and Roger Penrose.

A prime reason for this is the strong sense of discovery that mathematicians experience in their work. Consider, for example, the strange bug depicted in Figure 8.1. If we continuously magnify any portion of this bug, we get ever-finer details, opening up a whole new world to be explored.

Where does this remarkable world come from? Actually, it is just a piece of abstract mathematics, known as the Mandelbrot Set. This immensely complicated structure is in fact generated by a very simple procedure. Each point on the picture is specified by two numbers: x (the horizontal position) and y (the vertical position). To determine whether a point is black or white we apply the following rule.

1. For each point (x, y), let v = x and w = y.
2. Replace v and w with v = v x v − w x w + x, and w =
   2 x v x w + y.
3. Repeat step 2 ten times.
4. If the final point (v, w) is still close to the initial point (x, y), then colour point (x, y) black. Else colour it white.

Figure 8.1: The Mandelbrot Set. Each figure is a close-up of the preceding one. Note that the last figure is very similar to the first. (From H. O. Peitgen and D. Saupe, *The Science of Fractal Images*, New York: Springer Verlag, 1980, p. 202; used with permission.)

For example, for point $(0, 1)$ we generate the sequence $(0,1)$, $(-1, 1)$, $(0, -1)$, $(-1, 1)$, $(0, -1)$, and so on. This sequence remains close to $(0, 1)$, so we colour point $(0, 1)$ black. For the point $(1, 0)$ the sequence is $(1, 0)$, $(2, 0)$, $(5, 0)$, $(26, 0)$, and so on. Since this sequence moves far from the initial point $(1, 0)$, we colour point $(1, 0)$ white. A computer can easily be programmed to do these simple, though tedious, calculations for all the points. We end up with Figure 8.2.

The remarkable thing about the Mandelbrot Set is that its intricate structure was not contrived or invented by any mathematician. At every level of magnification novel, unexpected details emerge. No computer picture can fully capture the structure of the Mandelbrot Set. It seems to have a reality of its own, beyond the imagination of human minds. This led Roger Penrose to exclaim, 'The Mandelbrot set is not an invention of the human mind: it was a discovery. Like Mount Everest, the Mandelbrot set is just *there*' (1990:124).

Likewise, the mathematician G. H. Hardy believed that 'mathematical reality lies outside us . . . our function is to discover or observe it . . . the theorems which we prove, and which we describe grandiloquently as our "creations", are simply our notes of our observations' (1967: 123–4).

Realism has a number of distinct advantages over the rival view that mathematics is merely a human invention. Consider the following factors:

(1) Realism Is Very Effective and Fruitful.

The notion that there is a mathematical universe waiting to be explored provides a powerful incentive for research, much more so than a mere dabbling in arbitrary inventions of the mind. Thus, even if one really did not have a realist view of mathematics, it might be beneficial to pretend to believe in it.

(2) Realism Explains the Universality of Mathematics.

The notion of an objective mathematical world explains why mathematicians widely separated in space, time, and culture come up with the same mathematical theorems and ideas.

(3) GÖDEL'S INCOMPLETENESS THEOREM SUPPORTS REALISM.

Gödel proved that not all mathematical truths can be derived from a finite set of axioms. This implies that mathematical truth extends beyond our construction of mathematical systems. We cannot limit mathematical truth to the logical consequences of our axioms. Also, since this holds for *any* mathematical system, the number of mathematical truths must be actually infinite – more than any finite mind could construct. The vast infinities of objects that mathematics requires can be readily supplied by realism. Roger Penrose comments on the implications of Gödel's theorems, 'There is something absolute and "God-given" about mathematical truth ... Real mathematical truth goes beyond mere man-made constructions' (1990:146). The fact that Gödel's theorems came as an unexpected and unwelcome shock to mathematicians indicates that they themselves were objective discoveries rather than merely human inventions.

(4) REALISM IS INDISPENSABLE FOR SCIENCE.

Modern physics is so heavily dependent upon mathematics that its theories could hardly be even stated without mathematics. Since science deals with real objects, it would seem that mathematics must also deal with real objects. This applies even more so for those embracing a realist view of scientific theories. How can scientific theories be true unless the underlying mathematics is also true?

(5) REALISM EXPLAINS THE APPLICABILITY OF MATHEMATICS TO THE PHYSICAL WORLD.

If mathematics is merely a human invention, why is it that relatively simple mathematical theories yield such accurate representations of the physical world? Sophisticated theories, such as relativity or quantum mechanics, can be aptly summarized in just a few small mathematical equations and their logical implications. The amazing success of physics is largely due to its basic mathematical nature. This suggests that the physical world reflects the same mathematical structure that mathematicians explore. We already noted (p. 54) that Eugene Wigner, a Nobel prizewinner in physics, commented, in a famous article entitled *The Unreasonable Effectiveness of Mathematics*, on the amazing applicability of complex analysis to quantum mechanics. He said:

> It is difficult to avoid the impression that a miracle confronts us here, quite comparable to the . . . miracles of the existence of laws of nature and of the human mind's capacity to divine them (Wigner 1960:8).

> The miracle of the appropriateness of the language of mathematics for the formulation of the laws of physics is a wonderful gift which we neither understand nor deserve (Wigner 1960:14).

There is thus ample evidence indicating that mathematics is much more than a mere human invention. Mathematics seems to have an objective reality of its own.

How do we have access to the world of mathematics? It seems that mathematical intuition is almost like a sixth sense, by which we perceive the mathematical realm or, at least, the mathematical aspect of the physical world. Through mathematical intuition we 'see' the mathematical realm as our eyes see the physical world. In some mathematicians this sense is developed to an extraordinary degree, enabling them to glimpse truths that are not evident to others. This may help to explain why some geniuses have an uncanny ability to make conjectures that are not proven true until much later.

Conclusions

In summary, the classical Christian view of mathematics was that of mathematical realism. It held that mathematical objects existed independently of human minds, in the eternal mind of God. It considered mathematics in terms of what an all-knowing, all-powerful and infinite God could know and do.

With the rejection of theism, mathematics came to be viewed as a purely human invention. The attempt to put mathematics on a solid axiomatic basis was defeated by Gödel's theorems. These theorems proved that mathematics could never be captured by a finite set of axioms and that the consistency of mathematics could never by proven by mathematics. Henceforth, the truth of mathematics had to be accepted on faith.

The rejection of theism led also to the replacement of classical mathematics with constructive mathematics. Constructive mathematics entails the rejection of many results of classical mathematics. As a result, it cannot support the advanced mathematics needed for modern physics.

Evolutionary views of mathematics cannot account for the existence of advanced mathematics, its amazing applicability, its universality, and so on. They fail also in doing justice to mathematics as a form of objective knowledge.

Finally, mathematical realism was found to have numerous advantages over the notion that mathematics is a mere human invention.

9

Beyond Naturalism

CROSSFIRE

Atheistic existentialism, which I represent . . . states that if God does not exist, there is at least one being in whom existence precedes essence . . . This means that, first of all, man exists, turns up, appears on the scene, and, only afterwards defines himself. If man, as the existentialist conceives, is indefinable, it is because at first he is nothing. Only afterward will he be something, and he himself will have made what he will be. Thus, there is no human nature, since there is no God to conceive it. Not only is man what he conceives himself to be, but he is only what he wills himself to be after this thrust toward existence. Man is nothing else but what he makes of himself.

JEAN-PAUL SARTRE (*Existentialism and Human Emotions* 1957:15)

* * * * *

My son, forget not my law; but let thine heart keep my commandments: For length of days, and long life, and peace, shall they add to thee. Let not mercy and truth forsake thee: bind them about thy neck; write them upon the table of thine heart: So shalt thou find favour and good understanding in the sight of God and man. Trust in the LORD with all thine heart; and lean not unto thine own understanding. In all thy ways acknowledge him, and he shall direct thy paths. Be not wise in thine own eyes: fear the LORD, and depart from evil.

PROVERBS 3:1–8

The French atheist philosopher Jean-Paul Sartre (1905–80) rejected naturalism, with its denial of a purposeful self. Sartre was a major promoter of *existentialism*, which holds that each person is the sole judge of his own actions in an absurd, godless universe. Man is to create his own nature and destiny. Indeed, Sartre contended that 'man is the being whose project is to be God' (1957:63). What defines and drives man is his deep desire to be God.

Thus far we have concentrated on the plight of naturalism. Naturalism, we saw, leaves many mysteries unresolved. It has particular difficulty accounting for absolute rational and moral norms. The shortcomings of naturalism have led to various forms of post-modernity. These include Sartre's existentialism and other types of relativism. Like naturalism, post-modernity is motivated by man's urge to become God. Like naturalism, post-modernity, as we shall soon see, is burdened with lethal shortcomings.

Naturalism's Failures

First, we shall briefly summarize the conclusions of the previous chapters. We found that naturalism has great difficulty solving the following mysteries:

why the universe exists and continues to exist.
why the universe is orderly and uniform.
why the universe is mathematically comprehensible to humans.
why the universe has a (particular) mathematical structure.
how a mathematical possibility can be physically actualized.
how purposeful life arose from purposeless non-life.
how random interactions give rise to increasingly complex
    information.
how mind can arise from matter.

how our conscious self unifies our many experiences.
how non-physical factors (*e.g.*, logic and morals) influence the
    mind.
what transforms mental choice into physical action.
why our minds are capable of purposeful, rational thought.
how non-physical absolutes in truth and morals can exist.
how we acquire knowledge of non-physical absolutes.
why advanced mathematics is true and applicable to the
    physical world.

These numerous explanatory gaps are all the more glaring given the grandiose claims of naturalists. Consider, for example, Edward Wilson's Pulitzer-Prize-winning book *Consilience: The Unity of Knowledge* (1998). Wilson, who believes in universal truth, asserts that all truth can be acquired by the reductionist methods of natural science. All knowledge, he believes, can ultimately be reduced to the laws of physics.

How does Wilson account for the failure of naturalism to explain the gaps? He is confident that, since scientific reductionism has answered many questions about the natural world, it will eventually be able to answer *all* questions. This is typical of naturalists. Naturalist explanations are deferred to as yet unknown (natural) laws, to be discovered by future research. But these are mere promissory notes of wishful thinking.

It is not even the case that materialistic science is steadily reducing the mystery even about material reality. For example, the discovery of quantum mechanics *deepens*, rather than explains, the mysteries of how matter behaves and how it connects with mind and mathematics. Similarly, the discovery of DNA, with its intimate connection to information, which is generally a product of intelligence, deepens the mystery of life.

The Magic of Emergence

Naturalists often bridge gaps by an appeal to *emergence*. At certain levels of complexity new properties allegedly emerge, introducing new laws. Emergence, we saw, is held to account for the jumps from non-life to life, to consciousness, to rational thought, and so on. Such appeals are, however, never backed up by any plausible mechanisms. Surely the onus is on naturalists to show how these gaps can be bridged at least in principle, if not in practice.

The difficulty is that these gaps are anything but trivial. It is not a question of merely filling in a few minor details in an otherwise complete naturalist portrait of reality. Rather, these are huge leaps across quite different categories, from non-life to life, from matter to mind, and so on. These *are*, in fact, the fundamental things that need explaining. Naturalism may be able to describe fairly well how matter interacts with other matter but it fails miserably in explaining the deeper mysteries of the universe.

As we saw in Chapter 6, some naturalists have come to acknowledge that assertions of emergence amount to no more than appeals to magic. Yet, if genuine natural emergence is ruled out, what other options do naturalists have? One possibility is to simply concede that the jumps are *inexplicable*. For example, physicist Kenneth Denbigh doubts that genuinely new things can simply emerge from previously existing things. He believes that the emergence of a new level of reality is always indeterminate. It has no cause at all (Denbigh 1975:145). But to say that emergence happens for no reason at all is to give up on rational enquiry, which seeks to explain why things are the way they are. To render the gaps naturally inexplicable is to admit naturalist defeat.

Naturalist philosopher Colin McGinn believes that the deepest philosophical problems – such as free will, the self, and how the brain can give rise to conscious mind – are humanly insoluble. Our minds have inherent limitations, imposed by the biology of our brains. McGinn states that 'it is the purest dogmatism to believe that the human mind, at this particular stage of evolutionary history, has reached the pinnacle of cognitive capacity' (1999b:45). He believes that the problem of consciousness, for example, is so fundamental that we cannot even conceive of any process that could account for it. Nevertheless, he is confident that there *is* a naturalist explanation, even though humans are incapable of conceiving it. He insists that this mystery requires no theistic miracle. Yet, were our human minds indeed as limited as McGinn supposes, his claim that there exists a naturalist explanation is itself pure naturalist dogmatism. McGinn's agnostic solution, too, amounts to an admission of naturalist defeat.

The Dangers of Self-Refutation

Another strategy for naturalists is to deny the real existence of any but material phenomena. Then there are no gaps to cross. Thus, for example, we saw that Sir Francis Crick dismissed all our beliefs, even of our free will and inner self, as just so many *illusions* caused by brain neurons. A fully material world has no place for such immaterial things as consciousness, mental causation, rationality, universal norms, mathematical entities and objective truth. Small wonder, then, that some naturalists have denied the reality of all of these.

Yet, as we noted in Chapter 2, such basic things as a purposeful self, an effective mind, a real external world, absolute rational standards, logic, and objective truth are essential for scientific activity and, indeed, for any intelligent discourse. They are part of what philosopher of religion David Ray Griffin calls our *hard-core* common sense (2000:99). Hard-core common sense beliefs are universal beliefs that must inevitably be pre-supposed in practice.

Any viable worldview must be consistent with what must necessarily be presumed. *Performative contradictions* arise when whatever is being claimed is at odds with the presuppositions or implications of the act of claiming it. Any worldview that denies hard-core common sense beliefs is self-refuting. How can one rationally argue for the truth of naturalism if such naturalism entails the non-existence of rational thought and objective truth? As Griffin astutely notes, 'No worldview can be adequate for "science" that has no room for the activities of scientists!'

(2000:167). Naturalism can be argued for only by means of *non*-naturalistic concepts and philosophical arguments. Since naturalists generally esteem themselves to be highly rational, it is most remarkable that many naturalists seem to be blind to the self-refuting nature of their worldview.

The most tragic consequence of naturalism is its destruction of the central self, the thinking ego. For Descartes this was the one firm certainty that could not be doubted. The naturalist self, on the contrary, is reduced to a pathetic puppet, little more than a ghostly illusion, jerking and dancing to neuronic tunes. *That* is the inevitable conclusion deduced from materialistic evolution.

The Post-Modern Backlash

Naturalism, by positing that the ultimate reality is an objective, material world, inevitably ends up undermining the reality of a purposeful, subjective self. The loss of the self, in turn, entails also the loss of reliable, objective knowledge. The end result is the demise of naturalism as a coherent worldview.

In recent years scholars are increasingly seeing through the vain pretences of naturalism, with its boastful dogmatism and empty promises. Unfortunately, the pendulum has swung too far in the opposite direction. There has been a backlash, not just against naturalism, but also against the basic notions of objective knowledge and truth that underlie modern thought. Many post-modern scholars have reacted by opting for the contrary extreme, adopting various forms of *relativism*. Radical relativists claim that there is no objective knowledge and that all worldviews are entirely subjective. In a sense, post-modernity is merely the logical consequence of naturalism's destruction of objective knowledge.

THE LOSS OF TRUTH

Many post-modern thinkers have abandoned the notion of objective truth. They view truth as a mere social construct, something that varies with culture and history. For example, post-modern philosopher Richard Rorty asserts, 'There is no such thing as "the best explanation" of anything; there is just the explanation that best suits the purpose of some given explainer' (Rorty 1991:60). Rorty contends that we have no objective facts or knowledge, only linguistic constructs. Some relativists go so far as to insist there is no objective structure to anything, not even to logic.

If there is no objective truth, or if we have no access to such truth even if it did exist, then we cannot check whether our beliefs correspond to what actually is the case. In that case we cannot apply a *correspondence* theory of truth. Hence, post-modernists often posit a *coherence* theory of truth. The coherence theory denies that there are any foundational truths upon which to found objective knowledge. Instead, it considers our beliefs to be an intricate inter-connected web, constrained only by the condition that it must cohere consistently. The coherence theory of truth stresses *internal* consistency, rather than consistency with some, allegedly inaccessible, outside reality. Some post-moderns go one step further and drop even this requirement for consistency. Instead, they adopt the *pragmatic* theory of truth, which affirms that we should just believe whatever works best for us. Even logic can then be considered as merely a tool – to be used or ignored as needed.

Playing with Words

Such radical notions of truth have far-reaching implications for language. Many post-modernists question the objectivity of language. The French post-modernist Jacques Derrida writes, 'There is nothing outside the text; all is textual play with no connection with original truth' (Derrida 1976:158). Derrida holds that words refer only to other words, not to an objective reality beyond the words. Words cannot convey objective truths. Further, Derrida contends that there is no fixed meaning in any sentence. We may thus interpret any text freely, without being constricted by considerations of its intended meaning. The meaning of words is then controlled by the interpreter. A text therefore has many meanings, none of which is privileged.

Another French post-modernist philosopher, Jean-François Lyotard, asserts that, since there is no inherent meaning in language, all speech is merely speaking-about-speech (1992:2). Likewise, literary critic Barbara Smith urges that *doing*, rather than *meaning*, should be at the centre of linguistic theory (1997:52). The meaning of a word or sentence depends entirely on its use.

Writers such as Rorty, Derrida and Lyotard argue that our thinking should transcend the rationalist attempt to describe an objective world. They urge us to look at the work of poets and other artists, whose intuitive, aesthetic view of the world conveys a better, deeper, approach to knowledge. The immediate intuition is claimed to provide a surer basis to knowledge than rational reflection. Rational thought is allegedly unable to handle the complexities and nuances of modern – or post-modern – society. The immediate and fragmentary are elevated at the expense of the objective and universal. Poetry, aphorisms and intentional ambiguity are preferred to clear, objective speech. Feeling is held to be superior to reason.

Such thinking is not so much *post*-modern as *pre*-modern, a return to the era of pagan myth and magic, before the alleged corrupting influence of Western philosophy.

POWER MAKES TRUTH

Post-modernists reject the notion of an objective worldview, which they call a *meta-narrative*. A meta-narrative is an account of reality that claims to transcend one's personal, subjective circumstances. Post-modernists deny that meta-narratives can exist. They claim that modern meta-narratives are merely social constructions, lacking any objectivity. They are contrived to serve a particular purpose. That purpose is power and control. By defining what is rational and real, the dominant meta-narrative marginalizes and oppresses minorities. Unity of truth is bought at the price of violence, by repressing whatever does not fit into the system.

In this vein another well-known French post-modernist, Michel Foucault, claims that every assertion is an act of power. Foucault holds that there is no genuine discourse, no rhetoric capable of conveying 'the truth', of showing us 'the thing itself'. On the contrary, all communication is concerned primarily with power. All discourse is violent, in the sense that it represses dissenting voices. Foucault writes, 'Power produces; it produces reality; it produces domains of objects and rituals of truth' (Foucault 1977:196).

By exposing the constructive and oppressive nature of meta-narratives, post-modernists hope to open up room for minority views. Justice may then be done to the hitherto oppressed. According to post-modernists, no meta-narrative is large enough to include all groups. Hence meta-narratives should be abandoned. Instead, each group should be allowed to construct its own local, limited narrative. None of these should be privileged. Grand systems of truth are to make way for a multitude of local stories.

POST-MODERN POST-MORTEM

Post-modernity makes a number of commendable points. It rightly questions the modernist assumption that human reason can answer all questions and solve all problems. It rightly challenges the modernist quest for absolute, perfect, and complete knowledge. It rightly points out the subjective nature of scientific theorizing. It rightly notes that not all knowledge can be conveyed in purely rational, objective form. It rightly insists on making room for subjective intuition and feeling.

Yet post-modernity, in its denial of *all* objective truth and language, goes much too far in the other direction. Consider, for example, the post-modern claim that no true meta-narrative can exist. This assertion, insofar as it makes a claim about reality, is itself a meta-narrative. Even the more modest claim that meta-narratives are unknowable, because a person's perspective can never be overcome to obtain objective knowledge, is self-defeating. It amounts to the *objective* claim that objective knowledge is impossible. As the English writer G. K. Chesterton commented, 'We do not know enough about the unknown to know that it is unknowable' (cited in Marlin 1987:336).

To avoid such difficulties of self-refutation one must modify one's relativism to allow for at least some objective knowledge. For example, one can hardly deny the common-sense world of rocks and chairs.

Consider next the post-modern notion that language cannot communicate truth. If no text has any objective meaning, how can post-modernists make use of language to convey that purported truth to us? Why do they write thick volumes that tell us language cannot convey truth? Their writing, in expectation of being understood, contradicts the very thesis they are defending. It is self-refuting to use language to convey the presumably objective notion that language cannot convey objective meaning.

Further, if language cannot represent the external world, as some post-modernists maintain, how is it that they can use language to convey *that* aspect of the external world (*i.e.*, that language cannot represent it)? If language cannot be used to represent the external world, then it is self-contradictory to use language to represent this alleged fact about the external world.

Political scientist Joseph Wagner (1991) argues that all language presupposes objectivity, which, in turn, presupposes truth. Our ability to identify and to express subjective thoughts requires a capacity for objectivity. This, in turn, depends upon an ability to observe distinctions based on rules. The meaning of words depends on their *consistent, objective* usage. Else we could not speak coherently.

Indeed, we could not challenge truth claims if we did not possess a capacity for objectivity and truth. Philosopher Jürgen Habermas comments that the relativist's own words depend on the essential nature of *assertion*. We cannot assert that something is the case without relying on the rules of logic, including the true/false distinction. For example, the sceptic asserts a certain thing, rather than its opposite. According to Habermas, the sceptic, in making a specific argument against objectivity, must inevitably presume certain rational rules that contradict the content of his objection

(1991:82). Therefore, to challenge truth or objectivity is by its nature self-refuting. Again we have a performative contradiction.

Although language may be a human convention that determines what we say *about* the world, it does not determine the *contents* of the world. As Shakespeare noted, 'That which we call a rose by any other name would smell as sweet.' Logical consistency and objectivity form universal standards that restrict meaning in any language.

Of course, this critique presupposes a regard for consistency and coherence. As we already noted, some post-moderns view these as no more than convenient weapons, to be used or discarded as desired. Thorough-going relativists may well shrug off the charge of inconsistency by objecting that, since they are repudiating logic, why should they be concerned with consistency? The difficulty is that, once they leave the shelter of their studies, even relativists must behave rationally. How else could they survive in their daily lives? They can hardly disregard the objective meaning of traffic signs or labels on medicine bottles. The fact that they cannot live out their worldview demonstrates its practical, as well as rational, absurdity.

The concern of post-moderns for oppressed minorities is praiseworthy. Yet, if all human judgments are subjective, on what basis are oppression and violence deemed bad? Are such judgments themselves then not merely post-modern constructions? Moreover, in practice, a proliferation of local stories can still lead to violence when opposing groups clash. Richard Middleton and Brian Walsh comment:

> Given the clash of ideologies and aggressive violence which so characterizes post-modern plurality, why should we trust the outcome, unless we are rooted in a meta-narrative that demands this? The post-modernist is thus caught in a performative contradiction, arguing against the necessity of meta-narratives precisely by (surreptitious) appeal to a meta-narrative (1995: 77).

The very concept of post-modernity presupposes a master-narrative, an all-embracing perspective that envisions a transition from one stage of society to a new one. Humans seem to have a need for meta-narratives. Local stories usually end up becoming universal ones.

Naturalism placed ultimate reality in objective matter, at the cost of the subjective inner self. Post-modernity, on the other hand, places ultimate reality in the subjective self, at the cost of objective truth and values. Man no longer knows where he is, why he is, or who he is. The post-modern self is thus reduced to a meaningless absurdity, lost in a trackless void.

THE GHOST OF NATURALISM

The shift from modernity to post-modernity was helped, if not caused, by dramatic changes in science.

The main scientific model for the modern era was Newtonian physics. In Newtonian physics the universe was viewed as a huge clock, composed of material parts acting according to fixed laws in a fully deterministic manner. Man was viewed as an independent, objective observer.

This view was challenged in the early part of the twentieth century, with the advent of relativity and quantum mechanics. Relativity stressed that what we observe depends on the position and motion of the observer. Quantum mechanics introduced uncertainty and indeterminacy – at least from a human perspective. The hitherto independent observer now became an integral part of the closely inter-related quantum world. In mathematics, Gödel's theorems further underscored the inherent limitations of human knowledge. All of these scientific developments helped to undermine the modernist quest for complete, objective knowledge of reality. They helped set the stage for post-modernity.

Most post-modernists, in spite of their alleged rejection of meta-narratives, are still naturalists. They still view the universe as a closed system, with no room for the supernatural. In particular, the bulk of academia and media still uphold the grand evolutionary story as truth. Perhaps this is not surprising. If the supernatural is denied, how else is one to account for the origin of all that we see? Moreover, evolution, which connects everything to a common origin and substance, fits in well with the post-modern emphasis on community and inter-connectedness.

Thus post-modernity inherits modernity's problem of explaining how bare, purposeless matter can give rise to a creative mind. Post-moderns, with their stress on pragmatic results and power, rather than on truth, rarely give this problem the attention it deserves.

What Does a Worldview Need?

Viable worldviews, we have argued, must account for science and common sense. They must explain such essentials as the existence of other minds, the existence of a common language by which we can communicate meaningful ideas to those minds, dependable means of communication, effective minds, reliable thought processes, and objective logical and rational standards.

These imply the existence of three distinct worlds: the physical world in which we live, the mental world of our conscious perceptions, and the ideal world of universal truths. These are essentially the three worlds of Roger Penrose (1994), discussed in Chapter 1. Any coherent, rationally defendable worldview must at least acknowledge the existence of these three distinct worlds.

Which of these is ultimate? Which came first? Penrose, we noted, believed that the abstract world was primary, the other two being mere shadows of it. He was led to this conclusion by the fact that the material world has a definite mathematical structure. World 1, our physical world, is just one of an infinity of possible worlds contained in the ideal realm of World 3; it is the physical actualization of one particular member of World 3. Hence Penrose viewed World 3 as more basic than World 1.

What provides the coherence between these three worlds? Note that the actualization of one particular contingent world from an infinity of abstract possibilities requires an active power that makes a specific choice. Since the abstract universals are themselves inert, Keith Ward suggests that this requires a rational Creator (1996:38).

One problem with the ideal realm is how it could exist. Penrose does not elaborate on this, beyond asserting that this world is timeless and without physical location. One wonders, however, how ideas can exist other than in a mind. Eternal norms, Augustine argued, entail an eternal mind. If so, reality must have at least four components:

World 1: the material world
World 2: human minds
World 3: abstract universals
World 4: an eternal mind and source of coherence

Since neither abstract universals nor bare matter can generate mind, we are left with only two options. The existence of World 2 requires that either (1) mind has a supernatural origin (*i.e.*, *theism*) or (2) all entities – even atoms – have some degree of consciousness (*i.e.*, *pan-psychism*).

Any workable worldview must include a viable theory of knowledge. Empirical knowledge, we noted, cannot acquire any knowledge of universals. We must thus have some other means of accessing the ideal realm, whether through innate knowledge (perhaps wired into our minds at birth), intuition (perhaps a sixth sense whereby we apprehend universals), or by divine revelation (perhaps in written form).

Creating a Natural God

Can naturalism be sufficiently adapted to fulfil the requirements of a viable worldview? A naturalist alternative to materialism has been promoted by David Ray Griffin, who develops the *process theology* of British mathematician and philosopher Alfred North Whitehead (1861–1947).

Process theology is based on the following presuppositions:

1. All entities, even atoms, have a subjective, experiential aspect, as well as a material aspect. Because of this remarkable feature,

process theology is often referred to as *pan-psychism* (*pan* is Greek for *all*). In the more complex entities the experiential aspect is more developed, eventually appearing as mind and consciousness.

2. Entities at one level can give rise to entities at a higher level. Mind is the experiential aspect of the brain, which is made up of brain cells, each of which has its own experiences.

3. All entities have a non-sensory, intuitive form of perception, called *prehension*. The mind and its brain cells interact by prehending each other's experiences. As our brain cells prehend our mind, so do our minds likewise prehend God. Since the primordial mind of God is the home of all ideal norms, we can prehend these norms.

4. Since all entities can directly experience God, God can influence the world in the same way that the mind influences brain cells (Griffin 2000:103). God does not contravene natural laws; he does not perform any miracles.

5. This notion of God rules out any divine revelation of absolute truth, which would require special intervention (Griffin 2000:10,13).

This complicated philosophy bills itself as a naturalistic theism. It rejects the God of orthodox Christianity. Instead, it views God as having two poles. In his *primordial* nature God is the (unconscious) order of all unity in the world. He upholds all universals. In his *consequent* nature God is conscious, dependent on the world, and the source of novelty. God never coerces, he never breaks the natural order. Rather, he always works through persuasion. God does not, and indeed cannot, control the free choices of creatures.

The world is the body of God, but God also has a mind. This is not pan-theism, which equates the world with God, but pan-*en*theism, which asserts that the world is *in* God. According to process theology, God did not create the world nor give it its structure. Matter has always existed. Matter and metaphysical principles exist independent of God (Griffin 2000:91). Perhaps better put: God, the world, and absolute norms are all mutually dependent. Since God did not create the world and is unable to control its events, he is thus not responsible for the presence of evil in the world.

The God of process theology is thus not omnipotent. His powers are very limited. He can perform no miracles. Also God's knowledge is limited. Process theology holds that God has perfect knowledge of the past and present but not of the future. To leave room for the free actions of man, the future is indeterminate, so that not even God can know it.

DO ATOMS HAVE FEELINGS?

Process theology rightly seeks to remedy various deficiencies of materialism. In particular, it makes room for subjectivity and for non-empirical knowledge. Thereby it avoids the self-contradictions of materialism and provides a better fit with our experiences. Nevertheless, process theology has a number of serious shortcomings.

First, it has no experimental basis. If pan-psychism were true we would expect to see indications of that. Physically indistinguishable systems would be expected occasionally to diverge in their physical behaviour because of their mental aspects. But this is never observed. There is no empirical evidence that non-living systems have any form of experience, subjectivity or purposeful behaviour.

Second, it is not made clear how advanced forms of consciousness can develop from lower ones. Griffin (2000:167) wants to distinguish between mere collections (such as rocks), where the highest experiences are those of the constituent molecules, and compound individuals (such as dogs and humans), where higher-level conscious experience emerges. But Griffin provides no mechanism for this. Nor does he explain why conscious mind is associated only with matter found in the *brain*.

At first sight, by postulating a two-in-one God, process theology seems to solve the problem of the One and the Many. The two poles of God seem to provide unity between the diverse realms of abstract universals and material particulars. However, unlike the Christian trinity, this divine duality is not absolutely sovereign. The God of process theology has no control over the universals and he has only a very limited control over the physical world, even though that physical world is considered to be his body.

Moreover, this God is the Creator of neither the physical world nor universals. Originally, universals, physical particulars and God all exist independently of each other. No explanation is given why these three were originally present or why they should have a positive affinity for each other. The Many is grounded in no deeper unity; there is no genuine unifying principle. Yet, a Many makes no sense unless there is a common property shared by each, so that they can be correlated. The philosopher Norris Clarke (1987:228) argues that, in the last analysis, process theology asserts a priority of the Many over the One. This entails a fatal lack of coherence. For coherence, the One and the Many should be equally ultimate in harmonious co-existence.

A further problem concerns our knowledge of universal norms. According to Griffin, we learn about such norms through our intuitive prehension of God's mind. The difficulty is that not everyone has the same intuition of moral or mathematical norms. Not everyone seems to have the same experiences of God. In case of a dispute, how are we to distinguish genuine norms from mere human imagination? How are we to decide which intuitions truly reflect the divine mind? This requires an objective form of divine revelation, which process theology explicitly denies. Thus process theology has no means by which to test non-empirical knowledge claims.

Finding Firm Ground

Rejecting God has terrifying consequences. Jean-Paul Sartre, the existentialist philosopher quoted at the beginning of this chapter, sadly commented,

> The existentialist . . . thinks it very distressing that God does not exist, because all possibility of finding values in a heaven of ideas disappears along with Him; there can no longer be an *a priori* Good, since there is no infinite and perfect consciousness to think it. Nowhere is it written that the Good exists, that we must be honest, that we must not lie: because the fact is we are on a plane where there are only men. Dostoevsky said, 'If God didn't exist, everything would be possible!' That is the very starting point of existentialism. Indeed, everything is permissible if God does not exist, and as a result man is forlorn, because neither within him nor without does he find anything to cling to (Sartre 1957:22–23).

The removal of God leaves man without any absolute values. Everything is then permissible. Forlorn man is left adrift in a moral fog, with neither compass nor solid ground to anchor on.

Our ideas are true only to the extent that they correspond to reality. They must reflect 'God's view' of things. A God's view of things can, however, be known only to the extent that God reveals it to us in objective form, such as in sacred books. Without such divine help we are reduced to idle speculation.

Has God given us verbal revelation? There are many different religions. Some, such as Buddhism and Confucianism, do not believe in any supernatural being. Others, such as Hinduism and Shinto, do not claim to have any divinely inspired, normative scriptures. The only religions that claim to possess divine scriptures are Christianity, Judaism and Islam, plus various sects that derive from these. All of these are based, to at least some extent, on the Bible. Christianity accepts the entire Bible as the Word of God. Judaism adheres to the Old Testament. The Islamic Koran asserts that the original Christian Bible was God-given (see *Surah* 3:3) but was subsequently corrupted (God allegedly sent Mohammed to correct the errors). Hence all three religions 'of the book' believe that at least significant parts of the Bible are divinely revealed.

In the following chapters we shall examine what the Bible has to say about the worldview issues we have been addressing.

*****

Appendix: How to Refute Scepticism

Scepticism about human ability to acquire knowledge is as old as philosophy. The Greek philosopher Pyrrho (*circa* 360–270 B.C.), who had been in the army of Alexander the Great, taught scepticism regarding the senses, logic, and morals. He affirmed that there were no rational grounds for preferring one belief above another. Hence, one should renounce all claims to knowledge.

A somewhat more recent advocate of scepticism was the British philosopher David Hume (1711–76). Hume believed that all of our knowledge derives from sense impressions. Consequently, he denied the validity of all abstract ideas, including notions of causation, the external world, and even the self.

Scepticism is appealing to the intellectually lazy because, if all knowledge is reduced to the status of mere opinion, the ignorant sloth is as wise as the learned scholar.

TESTING ASSUMPTIONS

How would one refute scepticism? All worldviews, we noted, consist of various presuppositions, accepted on faith, together with their logical consequences. One might start, therefore, by analysing the plausibility of each of the sceptic's premises. Take, for example, Hume's assumption that our minds consist entirely of a succession of perceptions, without any trace of intellectuality. This presupposition alone already leaves no room for any thinking *about* our perceptions or how they are linked. Once one adopts a more comprehensive view of mind, Hume's sceptical conclusions no longer follow.

Often, however, the initial errors are small and not easily discerned. It is only later, after a long train of thought, that they produce significant consequences. As Aristotle noted in *De Caelo*, 'The least initial deviation from the truth is multiplied later a thousand-fold . . . that which was small at the start turns out a giant at the end' (Aristotle 1952:362).

TRYING OUT THE SYSTEM

This suggests a second, more indirect approach. Instead of examining presuppositions individually, we can examine them together, as a unit. One way we can test the plausibility of a set of presuppositions is to examine the reasonableness of the conclusions they entail. In any logically valid argument, the conclusion follows from the premises. One must then either accept the conclusion or reject the premises. To make a rational choice, one must ask: what is more plausible, that the premises are true or that the conclusion is false?

Often, of course, our comparison of plausibility is itself rather subjective, coloured by our worldview. Sometimes, however, the conclusions are so strongly contrary to common sense that the choice should be clear. In that case, we have a *reductio ad absurdum* of the premises.

Consider, for example, George E. Moore's refutation of Hume's scepticism:

> It seems to me that, in fact, there really is no stronger and better argument than the following. I *do* know that this pencil exists; but I could not know this, if Hume's principles were true; *therefore*, Hume's principles, one or both of them, are false. I think this argument really is as strong and good a one as any that could be used: and I think it really is conclusive. In other words, I think that the fact that, if Hume's principles were true, I could not know of the existence of this pencil, is a *reductio ad absurdum* of those principles (Moore 1953:119–120, italics in the original).

Moore argues that, since it is more certain that his pencil exists than that Hume's premises are true, Hume's set of premises must therefore be rejected as false.

Moore's argument is similar to that of Aristotle, in *Physica*, who met the scepticism of his day with the reply:

> That nature exists it would be absurd to try to prove, for it is obvious that there are many things of this kind and to prove what is obvious by what is not is the mark of a man who is unable to distinguish what is self-evident from what is not (Aristotle 1952:268).

In brief, if the falsity of the conclusion is more plausible than the truthfulness of the premises, then it is rational to reject the premises. This is particularly the case if the conclusions deny that which is directly evident to our senses. After all, worldviews are supposed to *explain* our observations. If any theoretical explanation is at odds with our personal experiences, then it is clearly the explanation, rather than our experience, that will have to be revised. The advantage of this method of refutation is that one need not pinpoint exactly where the initial error occurred.

An Impossible Life

Hume's scepticism also fails the test of livability. Consider, for example, Hume's own writings on scepticism. Surely Hume, by writing and publishing arguments for scepticism, expected others to read and comprehend them. This, in turn, assumes the existence of an external world consisting of at least paper with symbols on it, as well as other minds to whom the symbols on the paper are directed. It assumes further that, in reading Hume's book, the senses of other people will reliably transmit to the mind what is actually written down. Hence Hume's written defence of scepticism is self-refuting. Hume's book itself refutes the theory of mind it contains.

Indeed, Hume confessed his own inability to consistently maintain his scepticism:

> The great subverter of Pyrrhonism or the excessive principles of scepticism is action, and employment, and the occupations of the common life. These principles may flourish and triumph in the schools; where it is, indeed, difficult if not impossible to refute them.

But as soon as they leave the shade, and by the presence of the real objects, which actuate our passions and sentiments, are put in opposition to the more powerful principles of our nature, they vanish like smoke, and leave the most determined sceptic in the same condition as other mortals . . . Nature is always too strong for principle. And though a Pyrrhonian may throw himself or others into a momentary amazement and confusion by his profound reasonings; the first and most trivial event in life will put to flight all his doubts and scruples . . . When he awakes from his dream, he will be the first to join in the laugh against himself, and to confess that all his objections are mere amusement' (Hume 1777: 177–179).

Hume's failure to integrate scepticism into his daily life is itself the practical refutation of scepticism. Deeds, not words, are the most telling indicator of a philosopher's deepest convictions.

Hume conceded that 'custom . . . is the great guide of human life' (Hume 1777:47). Only Hume's habits of mind enabled him to accept such things as, for example, the principle of causality, whereby he could successfully navigate life. However, he was unable to give these a rigorous philosophical grounding in terms of his empirical presuppositions. Hume's sceptical worldview failed to adequately account for the reliability of such common-sense knowledge.

The dilemma of relativism is that it asserts a non-relative claim, which inevitably leads to its self-refutation. As Thomas Nagel notes:

The claim 'everything is subjective' must be nonsense, for it would itself have to be either subjective or objective. But it cannot be objective, since in that case it would be false. And it cannot be subjective, because then it cannot rule out any objective claim, including the claim that it is objectively false (1997:15).

Similarly, the sceptical claim, 'there is no objective truth', is itself a truth claim, contradicting itself.

If relativists were consistent with their professed beliefs, then they would have to remain silent. Scepticism renders philosophical discourse null and void. Hume concluded his *Enquiry concerning*

Human Understanding with the following advice on how to choose books:

> *Does it contain any abstract reasoning concerning quantity and number?* No. *Does it contain any experimental reasoning concerning matter of fact and existence?* No. Commit it then to the flames: for it can contain nothing but sophistry and illusion (Hume 1777:184).

Unfortunately for Hume, this severe standard dooms his own works to ashes.

In sum, a worldview may be assessed directly, by examining the plausibility of its presuppositions, or indirectly, by considering the consequences of the set of presuppositions. It is irrational to accept a worldview whose consequences are less plausible than the denial of one or more of that worldview's presuppositions.

Extreme forms of scepticism or relativism cannot be rationally defended. Any viable worldview must allow for (and justify), at least to some extent, objective logic and language, as well as other factors that are presumed in normal intellectual discourse. The relativist may claim that he is not concerned with rationality or consistency. He may prefer to live inconsistently rather than opt for another worldview. However, this amounts to giving up on explaining reality and resigning oneself to superficiality.

10

The Christian Worldview

One had better put on gloves before reading the New Testament. The presence of so much filth makes it very advisable . . . I have searched the New Testament in vain for a single sympathetic touch; nothing is there that is free, kindly, open-hearted or upright. In it humanity does not even make the first step upward – the instinct for cleanliness is lacking . . . Only evil instincts are there, and there is not even the courage of these evil instincts. It is all cowardice; it is all a shutting of the eyes, a self-deception. Every other book becomes clean, once one has read the New Testament.

FRIEDRICH NIETZSCHE
(*The Antichrist* 1920, SECT. 46)

* * * * *

For men shall be lovers of their own selves, covetous, boasters, proud, blasphemers, disobedient to parents, unthankful, unholy, without natural affection, trucebreakers, false accusers, incontinent, fierce, despisers of those that are good . . . But continue thou in the things which thou hast learned . . . that from a child thou hast known the holy scriptures, which are able to make thee wise unto salvation through faith which is in Christ Jesus. All scripture is given by inspiration of God, and is profitable for doctrine, for reproof, for correction, for instruction in righteousness: that the man of God may be perfect, throughly furnished unto all good works.

2 TIMOTHY 3:2–3, 14–17

Friedrich Nietzsche (1844–1900), in spite of being the son of a Lutheran pastor, did not have much good to say about the Bible. That is clear from the above quote. Yet, as we saw, non-biblical worldviews, such as naturalism and relativism, fail to explain the three worlds of matter, mind and mathematics. They leave us with no firm foundation for either truth or morals. As for Nietzsche, his atheism led to the nihilist conclusions that life was meaningless, devoid of absolute morals or values, with no prospect of a hereafter.

Only divine revelation, which Nietzsche vigorously rejected, can provide the solid ground needed for making us wise, wise even unto salvation. Accordingly, in the next few chapters, we shall examine what light the Bible can shed on the issues we have studied. What does the Bible have to say about the basic worldview questions? How well does it explain the mysteries we have encountered?

In this chapter we shall elaborate on the presuppositions of the Christian worldview. Succeeding chapters will deal with various specific applications of the Christian worldview.

Basics of the Christian Worldview

In terms of our basic worldview questions, discussed in Chapter 2, the Christian answers are as follows.

1. God is the Ultimate Reality

Central to the Christian worldview is belief in a sovereign, all-knowing, tri-personal, good and infinite God, who has revealed himself through his written Word, the Bible. This God is the creator of everything. He sets logical and moral absolutes. He gives meaning to all that happens. God has revealed to us various characteristics of himself.

GOD IS SOVEREIGN

God is self-sufficient, dependent on nothing beyond himself, and the ultimate cause of everything else. God can ultimately be defined only in terms of himself. As God said to Moses, in response to the question as to who God was: 'I AM THAT I AM' (*Exod.* 3:14). God is independent in his thought: 'How unsearchable are his judgments, and his ways are past finding out! For who hath known the mind of the Lord?' (*Rom.* 11:33–34). God is independent in his will: 'For who hath resisted his will?' (*Rom.* 9:19) and independent in his power: 'He hath done whatsoever he hath pleased' (*Psa.* 115:3). God is totally self-contained.

GOD IS ALL-POWERFUL

God's sovereignty is manifested in his omnipotence. It is abundantly clear in the Bible that God is all-powerful: 'Whatsoever the LORD pleased that did he in heaven, and in earth' (*Psa.* 135:6); 'with God all things are possible' (*Matt.* 19:26); 'For the Lord God omnipotent reigneth' (*Rev.* 19:6). Nothing happens by chance: 'The lot is cast into the lap; but the whole disposing thereof is of the LORD' (*Prov.* 16:33).

GOD KNOWS EVERYTHING

God's sovereignty is further shown in his omniscience. God knows everything. His knowledge is complete and perfect. 'God . . . knoweth all things' (*1 John* 3:20). His knowledge encompasses all things actual and possible. This includes all events: 'The eyes of the LORD are in every place, beholding the evil and the good' (*Prov.* 15:3). It also covers the contents of our minds and hearts: 'The LORD knoweth the thoughts of man' (*Psa.* 94:11); 'the LORD looketh on the heart' (*1 Sam.* 16:7); 'the LORD searcheth all hearts, and understandeth all the imaginations of the thoughts' (*1 Chron.* 28:9).

God's knowledge encompasses also the future: 'Behold, the former things are come to pass, and new things I do declare: before they spring forth I tell you of them' (*Isa.* 42:9); 'Declaring the end from the beginning, and from ancient times the things that are not yet done, saying, My counsel shall stand, and I will do all my pleasure' (*Isa.* 46:10).

God Is a Spirit

The Bible tells us that 'God is a Spirit' (*John* 4:24). This means, first, that God does not depend on matter ('a spirit hath not flesh and bones', *Luke* 24:39). God has a substantial Being all his own and distinct from the physical world. He is also invisible to the bodily senses ('the invisible God', *Col.* 1:15). The idea of spirit includes also that he is alive ('the living God', *Matt.* 16:16). He is a *person*, a self-conscious and self-determining Being ('I AM THAT I AM', *Exod.* 3:14; *Rom.* 9:11).

God Is Tri-Personal

The biblical God is a tri-personal God. There is one God, but he exists in three distinguishable persons: the Father, the Son, and the Holy Spirit. The persons of the Trinity are sometimes distinguished by their different functions. Thus the creation is often attributed to the Father, redemption to the Son, and sanctification to the Holy Spirit (see *Eph.* 1:3–14). Yet there exists a fundamental unity whereby all three persons participate in the activity of the others. For example, creation is said to be the work also of the Son (*John* 1:3) and the Holy Spirit (*Isa.* 40:13).

God Is Everywhere

The Bible portrays God as being omnipresent. On the one hand, he *transcends* all spatial limitations. On the other hand, he is present in every point in space: 'Though he be not far from every one of us: For in him we live and move and have our being' (*Acts* 17:27–28); or, 'Can any hide himself in secret places that I shall not see him? saith the LORD. Do not I fill heaven and earth? saith the LORD' (*Jer.* 23:24).

Nevertheless, even though God is present everywhere, he does not manifest himself everywhere in the same manner. There are numerous biblical references to God dwelling particularly in a special place: 'I dwell in the high and holy place' (*Isa.* 57:15). Moreover, the place of God's particular manifestation is not fixed in time; motion is often attributed to God: the Spirit of God moves over the face of the deep (*Gen.* 1:2); God walks in the garden in the cool of the day (*Gen.* 3:8); the Lord comes to Abraham (*Gen.* 18), The Lord goes before the Israelites in a pillar of cloud (*Exod.* 13:21); the Lord comes down to Mount Sinai (*Exod.* 19:20), Moses sees God pass by (*Exod.* 33), and so on. In the Incarnation Christ came down, from God's place, to man's place, taking on himself a human nature; in his ascension Christ's risen human body goes from man's place to heaven – to a specific place – where he now sits at the right hand of God (*Rom.* 8:34). God is a personal, living God who transcends the universe he has created.

GOD IS GOOD

The prime ethical characteristic of God's personality is his *goodness*. This is shown in his righteousness, truthfulness, holiness, love, faithfulness, patience, and mercy. He proclaims, 'I am the LORD which exercise lovingkindness, judgment, and righteousness, in the earth: for in these things I delight' (*Jer.* 9:24). Paul writes, 'Or despisest thou the riches of his goodness and forbearance and longsuffering; not knowing that the goodness of God leadeth thee to repentance?' (*Rom.* 2:4).

GOD IS INFINITE

The infinity of God refers to his *unboundedness*: he is free from all limitations. He is in no way limited by the universe or confined to it. God is absolutely *perfect*, with no defects ('Be ye therefore perfect, even as your Father which is in heaven is perfect' *Matt.* 5:48). His greatness knows no bounds ('his greatness is unsearchable', *Psa.* 145:3). God is also perfectly wise, true, good, holy and righteous.

God's infinity is further manifested in his *eternity*, which has no bounds in time ('From everlasting to everlasting thou art God', *Psa.* 90:2), and his *immensity*, which has no spatial limitations.

2. *The Universe Totally Depends on God*

The sovereignty of God is such that he freely created the universe out of nothing and that it completely depends on him for its continued existence. No creature is autonomous; none can act independently of God's sustaining power.

ALL THINGS WERE CREATED BY GOD

We note first that God is the Creator of everything in heaven and earth. 'In the beginning God created the heaven and the earth' (*Gen.* 1:1). Although this creation is derived from God the Father, it came about through Christ in whom 'all things were created in heaven and on earth, visible and invisible ... all things were created by him and for him, and he is before all things and by him all things consist' (*Col.* 1:16–17).

GOD CREATED FREELY

God transcends his creatures. He is 'above all' and 'over all' (*Rom.* 9:5). The infinite, uncreated, self-sufficient Creator must be sharply distinguished from all his creatures. God is distinct from his creation. God may thus not be identified with the universe or any portion of it. Only God is worthy of worship. Consequently, man is to be admonished against serving 'the creature rather than the Creator' (*Rom.* 1:25) and is commanded not to worship any graven image (*Exod.* 20:4).

The creation must be understood not as a *necessary* act, but as a *free* act of God's sovereign will (cf. *Eph.* 1:11, *Rev.* 4:11). He did not need to create the universe (cf. *Acts* 17:25), but freely chose to do so. The universe is thus not necessary, but contingent. This means that the universe could have been different, had God wanted it to be. Out of an infinity of possible worlds, God chose this particular one. God's awesome power is such that he can actualize his choice by the mere command of his Word. God's decision to actuate *this* particular universe indicates that the Creator is a *personal* God.

THE WORLD ALWAYS DEPENDS ON GOD

God is not only the creator, the originator of the universe, but also the cause of its continuous existence: 'Upholding all things by the word of his power' (*Heb.* 1:3). The universe is at all times entirely dependent upon God's sustaining power. Without God's continual upholding Word the universe would instantly cease to exist.

CREATION OUT OF NOTHING

The explicit formulation of *creatio ex nihilo* (Latin for 'creation out of nothing') arose in the early church in reaction to the belief that matter had always existed. This challenge came in two forms: dualism and pantheism. The dualists held that God created the universe by ordering pre-existent material. Thus there were two fundamental entities: the world and God. Pantheism, on the other hand, identified God and the world, thus denying any independent reality to the world.

In opposition to such views, the traditional Christian teaching is that the universe was created out of nothing, that is, without the use of any previous substance. 'In the beginning God created the heaven and the earth' implies that the physical universe had a beginning in time, being created by God. Another text often cited in support of *creatio ex nihilo* is Hebrews 11:3, 'Through faith we understand that the worlds were framed by the word of God, so that things which are seen were not made of things which do appear.' Also: 'For thou hast created all things, and for thy pleasure they are and were created' (*Rev.* 4:11). Nothing would have existed if it were not for God's will.

How, then, did God create the universe? Simply through his Word of power. He simply spoke: 'And God said, Let there be light: and there was light' (*Gen.* 1:3); 'for he spake and it was done; he commanded, and it stood fast' (*Psa.* 33:9). During the creation week God performed a series of specific creation acts, culminating in the creation of Adam and Eve (*Gen.* 1).

Creation *ex nihilo* applies not only to the material universe but also to all laws, principles and even possibilities. It stresses that

God is absolutely sovereign, the ground of all being, all necessity, and all possibility. Nothing that exists is self-sufficient; everything is totally dependent on God.

3. Man Was Created to Be God's Steward

Man is not a complex machine, assembled accidentally for no particular purpose. Rather, God specifically created man for a purposeful task. God formed man to glorify and enjoy him as his earthly steward and friend.

CREATED IN THE IMAGE OF GOD

Man is the crown of creation. He was made in the image of God ('so God created man in his own image', *Gen.* 1:27). As God's image-bearer, man is given dominion over the earth and all creatures on it (*Gen.* 1:28). Man, and all of creation, was originally created unblemished ('God saw everything that he had made, and, behold, it was very good', *Gen.* 1:31).

Man was made by a direct act of God: 'And the LORD God formed man out of the dust of the ground, and breathed into his nostrils the breath of life; and man became a living soul' (*Gen.* 2:7).

The image of God initially consisted of true *knowledge* ('and have put on the new man, renewed in knowledge after the image of him that created him', *Col.* 3:10), *righteousness* and *holiness* ('and that ye put on the new man, which after God is created in righteousness and true holiness', *Eph.* 4:24). Note that these refer, respectively, to man's mind, acts, and heart. The image of God can be extended to other characteristics that we seem to share, to a very limited extent, with God: self-consciousness, personality, creativity, rationality, the unity of the self, and so on. In short, Adam was created with the full ability to serve God in perfect submission.

THE FALL AND ITS FALL-OUT

Yet Adam wilfully rebelled against God. He wanted to be independent, putting himself in the place of God ('Ye shall be as gods, knowing good and evil', *Gen.* 3:5). The rebellion involved Adam's heart (whose pride rejected God's command), his mind (which sought for knowledge beyond that which God had revealed to him), and his action (in the physical eating of the forbidden fruit).

Through Adam's disobedience, sin and death entered the world and spread to all men. All three aspects of the image of God became grossly distorted. Instead of being inherently receptive to God, man wilfully suppresses God and his revelation (*Rom.* 1:18–23). Fallen man serves himself, rather than God. Man did not want to retain God in his knowledge, so God gave him up to a corrupted mind and all manner of unrighteousness and unholiness (*Rom.* 1:24–32). Fallen man is wholly inclined to reject God and do evil (*Rom.* 3:9–19). 'The natural man receiveth not the things of the Spirit of God: for they are foolishness unto him: neither can he know them' (*1 Cor.* 2:14).

God cursed also the ground, so that it would now bring forth thorns and thistles (*Gen.* 3:17–18). Indeed, 'the whole creation groaneth and travaileth in pain together until now' (*Rom.* 8:22).

REDEMPTION THROUGH CHRIST

Through the redeeming work of Christ – his incarnation, death and resurrection – salvation came into this world of sin and death. But even then sinners are saved only through the working of the Holy Spirit, by the grace of God ('For by grace are ye saved through faith; and that not of yourselves: it is the gift of God: not of works, lest any man should boast', *Eph.* 2:8–9). The new regenerated man regains, at least partially, the original image of God (see *Col.* 3:10 and *Eph.* 4:24 as cited above).

God through Christ will reconcile to himself all things, whether on earth or in heaven (*Col.* 1:19–20). All of creation will be set free from its bondage to decay (*Rom.* 8:19–22). At the end of this era Christ will come to judge all men and to determine their eternal destiny (*Rev.* 20:11–15).

The first heaven and earth shall then pass away and there will be a new heaven and a new earth (*Rev.* 21:1). 'For behold, I create new heavens and a new earth; and the former shall not be remembered, nor come into mind' (*Isa.* 65:17). Then the holy city, the new Jerusalem, shall come down from heaven and God shall dwell with his people for evermore (*Rev.* 21:2–3).

4. God Created Man to Know

God's infinite knowledge forms the norm for all truth. Our belief about anything can be considered to be true only to the extent that it corresponds to God's knowledge about the issue. It follows that we can justify our beliefs only to the extent that God reveals his knowledge to us. An essential premise of the Christian worldview is that God has revealed truths to us through his written Word, the Bible.

THE BIBLE IS OUR STANDARD

A Christian theory of knowledge is grounded upon a proper attitude of obedient submission to God, listening to his Word and doing his will. 'The fear of the LORD is the beginning of knowledge' (*Prov.* 1:7). This implies that we accept his Word as inerrant. We do so, not because we can prove it to be such, for that would make human reason the ultimate judge. Rather, because it comes from him who is truth. 'Thy word is truth' (*John* 17:17). An inerrant Bible is our basic presupposition, not our final conclusion.

This entails further that we must strive to listen to God's Word with open ears and mind, applying proper principles of interpretation that are consistent with this high view of Scripture. Since God's Word is truth, we can expect it to be internally consistent. Hence, Scripture must interpret Scripture, the more clear parts clarifying the less clear. Further, we must take God at his Word. Thus, to minimize human distortion of the text, its most direct, natural interpretation is to be preferred, unless internal scriptural evidence indicates otherwise.

The notion that the Bible is God's Word is consistent with what the Bible attests about itself. 'All scripture is given by inspiration of God' (*2 Tim.* 3:16).

OUR FACULTIES WERE CREATED RELIABLE

God created man so that he can acquire knowledge. This entails that God created man so that his senses and rationality functioned reliably. 'The hearing ear, and the seeing eye, the LORD hath made even both of them' (*Prov.* 20:12). The Bible presumes that God has created man in such a way that he can attain reliable knowledge of nature. Alvin Plantinga comments:

> God has . . . created us with cognitive faculties designed to enable us to achieve true beliefs with respect to a wide variety of propositions – propositions about our immediate environment, about our own interior lives, about the thoughts and experiences of other persons, about our universe at large, about right and wrong, about the whole realm of *abstracta* – numbers, properties, propositions – . . . and about himself (Plantinga 1993: 201).

There is a close connection between divine wisdom and the wisdom of righteous men. In Proverbs 8, where wisdom is personified, we read:

> The LORD possessed me in the beginning of his way, before his works of old. I was set up from everlasting . . . When he prepared the heavens, I was there . . . and my delights were with the sons of men . . . whoso findeth me findeth life (*Prov.* 8: 22–35).

The message is clear: the same wisdom used by God is available also to man, if only he seeks it in the right place.

OUR HEART IS IN CONTROL

Our reasoning ability is not confined to the mere application of deductive logic. It includes also the capacity for abstract, speculative thought. Being created in the image of God includes an element of creativity or inventiveness, the ability to think novel thoughts.

However, our reasoning is a tool manipulated by our inner heart, with its will and desires. As such, it can easily be misguided, 'For out of the heart proceed evil thoughts' (*Matt.* 15:19). As we already noted, the Fall profoundly diminished the image of God in man. Man lost his original righteousness and holiness; his knowledge became distorted.

Fallen man still possesses some innate knowledge, not derived from experience but present in the mind from birth. Man still has an innate awareness of God, plus a limited sense of right and wrong ('which shew the work of the law written in their hearts, their conscience also bearing witness', *Rom.* 2:15). These imply also an innate rationality, the ability to think logically.

Fallen man's ability to acquire true knowledge is such that he should still be able to discern God through nature (*Rom.* 1, *Psa.* 19). Man's problem is that he wilfully suppresses this knowledge. He rejects God's Word in any form. He no longer uses his senses and rationality in the service of God, as they were intended, but in service to himself. It is this erroneous presupposition – the autonomy of man – that causes him to misinterpret everything he experiences. Consequently, nothing retains any meaning.

In short, a Christian view of knowledge embraces the Bible as the ultimate source of truth, while granting also a proper place to the senses, rationality and innate knowledge. However, our present knowledge can be only partial: 'For now we see through a glass, darkly; but then face to face: now I know in part; but then I shall know even as also I am known' (*1 Cor.* 13:12). The central question is whether man uses his knowledge, however limited, in service to God or in rebellion against him.

5. God Sets the Standards

Since God is sovereign, he sets the ultimate standards. God, the Absolute, is the only one who can set absolute norms. He alone can endow life with meaning and value. Since God is truth, he sets the norms for logic, truth and rationality. God, the Holy One, the overflowing fountain of all good, determines moral standards. Our morality must thus be based on those standards he has given in his Word. The Ten Commandments form the central core of biblical morality (*Deut.* 4:13, *Matt.* 5:17–20). Christians are to 'love the LORD [their] God, walk in his ways, and keep his commandments' (*Deut.* 30:16). All meaning and beauty finds its source in God. Universal norms and values exist because God upholds them as such.

6. History Unfolds God's Plan

The Christian worldview does not view history as chaotic or meaningless. Since God is a *rational* Sovereign, everything he does is done for a sufficient *reason*, so that his eternal *plan* might be fulfilled (*cf. Eph.* 1). Hence everything, no matter how seemingly trivial, occurs, not by chance, but according to God's purposes. The *principle of sufficient reason* is thus grounded in God's will, wisdom and power.

Everything that happens unfolds according to God's eternal plan. The ultimate explanation of everything and anything is God's will. Not all of God's will has been revealed to us ('The secret things belong to the Lord our God: but those things which are revealed belong unto us and to our children for ever, that we may do all the words of this law', *Deut.* 29:29). Nevertheless, Christian believers take comfort in the fact that, even though they may not know why certain things happen, they do know that they happen in full accord with God's purpose. 'All things work together for good to them that love God, to them that are called according to his purpose' (*Rom.* 8:28).

The universe is purposeful because of its purposeful Creator. The ultimate purpose of God's work of creation is to reveal his glory: 'For I have created him for my glory' (*Isa.* 43:7) and 'the heavens declare the glory of God' (*Psa.* 19:1).

Examining the Christian Worldview

Having outlined the basics of the Christian worldview, a few comments are in order.

A Total Worldview

Since *everything* has been created by God for a specific purpose, the Christian worldview is all-encompassing. Like naturalism, it sets out to explain everything in terms of its basic tenets. Everything finds its true meaning only in God, in relation to his comprehensive plan.

The Bible addresses the full range of our experiences: issues of matter, mind, and heart. It even explains naturalism in terms of man's rebellion against God. We must therefore strive to bring all our thoughts, words and actions into line with biblical norms and insights. Scripture is 'profitable for doctrine, for reproof, for correction, for instruction in righteousness: that the man of God may be perfect, throughly furnished unto all good works' (2 *Tim.* 3:16–17). Ours should be a deeply felt heart commitment, involving our whole being: 'And thou shalt love the LORD thy God with all thine heart, and with all thy soul, and with all thy might' (*Deut.* 6:5). 'And whatsoever ye do in word or deed, do all in the name of the Lord Jesus' (*Col.* 3:17).

Justifying Worldview Tests

Since the Christian worldview is comprehensive, it should, among other things, address also our criteria for testing worldviews. These, as outlined in Chapter 2, were (1) consistency (2) experience and (3) livability.

We note first that the Bible itself tells us that truth claims must be tested. The Apostle John exhorts, 'Beloved, believe not every spirit, but try the spirits whether they are of God: because many false prophets are gone out into the world' (*1 John* 4:1). Paul, likewise, urges, 'Prove all things; hold fast that which is good' (*1 Thess.* 5:21).

How are we to test the spirits? The Bible cites a number of specific tests.

(1) THE TEST OF EXPERIENCE.

First, we consider the criterion of experience. One test for false prophets was the falsity of their predictions:

> And if thou say in thine heart, How shall we know the word which the LORD has not spoken? When a prophet speaketh in the name of

the LORD, if the thing follow not, nor come to pass, that is the thing which the LORD hath not spoken, but the prophet hath spoken it presumptuously' (*Deut.* 18: 21–22).

The Bible proclaims that only God can predict the future unerringly; the falsity of other gods is shown by their failure to make correct predictions (*Isa.* 41:21–26).

More positively, various experiences can testify to the power and faithfulness of God. 'The heavens declare the glory of God; and the firmament showeth his handiwork' (*Psa.* 19:1). When John the Baptist sent his disciples to ask Jesus whether he was the One who was to come, Jesus answered them, 'Go and shew John again those things which ye do hear and see: The blind receive their sight, and the lame walk' (*Matt.* 11:4–5). These experiences should have clearly answered their question. Indeed, many were thereby led to belief: 'many believed in his name, when they saw the miracles he did' (*John* 2:23).

Belief in Jesus' resurrection is grounded in the disciples' actual experiences: 'When therefore he was risen from the dead, his disciples remembered that he had said this unto them; and they believed the scripture, and the word which Jesus had said' (*John* 2:22). Paul backs up his claim of Christ's resurrection by appealing to eye witnesses of the risen Christ (*1 Cor.* 15:5–8); John, too, bases his teachings on what he has personally heard and seen (*1 John* 1:1–5).

(2) THE TEST OF SCRIPTURE

Nevertheless, the test of experience is often inadequate, since our experiences are frequently open to differing interpretations. Suppose, for example, that a prophet made a prediction that was fulfilled. Could we infer that he was therefore a true prophet? No, to make that conclusion would be to commit *the fallacy of affirming the consequent* (see Chapter 2: the appendix on logic). It is still possible that the prophet is a false prophet. A further test must be applied. If the prophet makes true predictions but urges the people to follow other gods, then he is a false prophet. In that case God is just testing his people (see *Deut.* 13:1–3).

The test applied here is the test of Scripture. Christians must reject teachings that contradict the Bible. Thus we read that the Bereans 'searched the scriptures daily, whether those things were so' (*Acts* 17:11). Jesus said, 'Ye do err, not knowing the scriptures' (*Matt.* 22:29). Since the Bible is the Word of God, and since God is truth, whatever contradicts the Bible must be rejected as false.

(3) THE TEST OF CONSISTENCY

A third biblical criterion of truth is that of *consistency*. The above criteria already entail that our beliefs should be consistent with Scripture and experience. There is, however, also the aspect of *internal* consistency. Our beliefs should not contradict each other. Rather, they should form a coherent whole. The Bible implies the need for such consistency whenever it presents logical arguments. For example, when the Pharisees charge that Jesus' casting out of demons is a Satanic act, Jesus responds: 'If Satan cast out Satan, he is divided against himself; how shall then his kingdom stand? And if I by Beelzebub cast out devils, by whom do your children cast them out?' (*Matt.* 12:26–27). In this confrontation Jesus' miracles, which should have proved his divinity, were interpreted in a contrary manner. Jesus notes, however, that the Pharisees' interpretation is incoherent. An inconsistent worldview, like a divided house, will eventually collapse.

(4) THE TEST OF LIVABILITY

A final test is that of lifestyle. Christianity is not just academic talk. It is a very practical worldview that must be fully lived out. The Bible continually stresses that our *works* must be *consistent* with the faith we profess:

> Beware of false prophets, which come to you in sheep's clothing, but inwardly they are ravening wolves. Ye shall know them by their fruits. Do men gather grapes of thorns, or figs of thistles? Even so every good tree bringeth forth good fruit; but a corrupt tree bringeth

forth evil fruit . . . Not every one that saith unto me, Lord, Lord, shall enter the kingdom of heaven; but he that doeth the will of my Father which is in heaven (*Matt.* 7:15–21).

Likewise, James writes, 'But be ye doers of the word and not hearers only, deceiving your own selves' (*James* 1:22). Of course, as sinful humans, we all fall short in fully living the life required by the Christian worldview, even after we have been regenerated by the Holy Spirit.

The Danger of Compromise

Worldviews come as package deals. Compromising Christianity with modern, post-modern or pagan ideals introduces an inconsistency into our lives that will eventually undermine our commitment to God. 'No man can serve two masters' (*Matt.* 6:24). Likewise, no inconsistent worldview can hope to survive. Hence, we should diligently test the spirits of the day, discerning their source and implications:

> And be not conformed to this world: but be ye transformed by the renewing of your mind, that ye may prove what is that good, and acceptable, and perfect, will of God (*Rom.* 12:2).

This is no easy thing. It is difficult to avoid contamination from the society in which we live. It requires us to test and cleanse our every thought, bringing it in line with God's Word and will:

> For the weapons of our warfare are not carnal, but mighty through God to the pulling down of strong holds; casting down imaginations, and every high thing that exalteth itself against the knowledge of God, and bringing into captivity every thought to the obedience of Christ (*2 Cor.* 10:4–5).

Christianity, like its rivals, is all-embracing. Hence, worldview wars are total wars, covering every aspect of reality. The Christian must therefore be constantly alert, relying on God and applying the full armour he supplies:

> Finally, my brethren, be strong in the Lord, and in the power of his might. Put on the whole armour of God, that ye may be able to

stand against the wiles of the devil. For we wrestle not against flesh and blood, but against principalities, against powers, against the rulers of the darkness of this world, against spiritual wickedness in high places (*Eph.* 6:10–12).

Conclusions

In this chapter we have outlined the basics of the Christian worldview. Since these all flow from the Bible, the key Christian presupposition is that the Bible is God's written Word and, as such, the absolute standard of truth. The prime worldview teaching of the Bible is the total sovereignty of God, who is the ultimate reality.

We argued that the Christian worldview justifies the general worldview criteria of consistency, experience and livability. In addition to these, it adds the test of Scripture. The Christian worldview justifies also the principle of sufficient reason (*i.e.*, everything that happens has a place in God's purposeful, all-encompassing plan) and, consequently, the principle of causality (*i.e.*, everything that happens is caused, directly or indirectly, by God).

The Christian worldview seeks to explain everything in terms of its basic tenets. In succeeding chapters we shall examine what it has to say regarding worldview-type questions concerning matter, mind and mathematics.

11

God and the Physical World

Man's knowledge and mastery of the world have advanced to such an extent through science and technology that it is no longer possible for anyone to seriously hold to the New Testament view of the world – in fact there is no one who does . . . It is impossible to use electric light and the wireless and to avail ourselves of modern medical and surgical discoveries and at the same time to believe in the New Testament world of spirits and miracles. We may think we can manage it ourselves, but to expect others to do so is to make the Christian faith unintelligible and unacceptable to the modern world.

RUDOLF BULTMANN (*Kerygma and Myth* 1964:3–5)

* * * * *

Jesus saith unto him, Thomas, because thou hast seen me, thou hast believed: blessed are they that have not seen, and yet have believed. And many other signs truly did Jesus in the presence of his disciples, which are not written in this book: But these are written, that ye might believe that Jesus is the Christ, the Son of God; and that believing ye might have life through his name.

JOHN 20:29–31

Can we still believe the Bible when it speaks of spirits or miracles? The famous New Testament scholar Rudolf Bultmann (1884–1976) thought not. Bultmann believed that the world operated according to purely natural causes and effects. He was convinced that modern science had proven that there was no room for spiritual agents or supernatural causes. Consequently, his worldview was essentially naturalistic. He rejected even the resurrection of Jesus as primitive nonsense.

Spirits and miracles are, however, central to the gospel of Jesus Christ. Paul writes, 'And if Christ be not risen, then is our preaching vain, and your faith is also vain' (*1 Cor.* 15:14). If Christ has not risen then those placing their trust in him are most to be pitied (*1 Cor.* 15:19).

In this chapter we shall examine the implications of the Christian worldview for the physical world. How does God act in this world? Is there room for miracles? Does God create through chance? Does God limit himself in his power or knowledge? As we address these questions we shall revisit various issues that were previously examined from the perspective of naturalism.

God's Creation

We saw in the previous chapter that God is the Creator of everything that exists in heaven and earth (*Gen.* 1). God created everything through his Word of power. This creation was a free act of the transcendent God. The universe exists in its specific, detailed form because God fashioned it in accordance with his all-encompassing plan. It was a creation from nothing – nothing except the idea of God's eternal plan.

WHY WE CAN UNDERSTAND THE UNIVERSE

The fact that God created the universe according to a rational plan has implications for the question of why the universe is comprehensible. Man is a major part of God's plan; God created the universe so that it would be a fit place for man. 'He created it not in vain, he formed it to be inhabited' (*Isa.* 45:18). God created man in his image – which includes rationality and creativity – to serve and enjoy him as his steward and friend. Man is 'to replenish the earth and subdue it' (*Gen.* 1:28). To accomplish the task set him by God, man needs to know how the earthly environment functions. It is thus to be expected that man should be able to discern something of the universe's structure, and that it is user-friendly to him. The human comprehensibility of the physical world is thus no longer a mystery. Rather, it is an expected consequence of God's plan.

God's Providence

We are told that God 'rested on the seventh day from all his work, which he had made' (*Gen.* 2:2). God rested, however, only in that he ceased creating new things. God remained active in *preserving* the universe that he had created.

The biblical God should not be confused with the watchmaker God of the deists, who serves only to assemble the universe, which thereafter runs by itself. The biblical God continues to uphold his creation by the 'Word of his power' (*Heb.* 1:3). God's continuous preservation of the world is needed to keep it in existence. No creature can exist by itself. Nothing can exist independent of God. Without God's sustaining power the world would cease to exist. In this sense, God works always (*John* 5:17).

The Reformed theologian Herman Bavinck (1854–1921) distinguished between creation and preservation as follows. In *creation* God called into being things that had no previous existence other than in the ideas and decrees of God. In *preservation*, on the other hand, God, with his same power, upholds his creatures in the existence that he has created for them. Whereas creation *initiates* existence, preservation grants *persistence* to that existence. In short, although in creation God's creatures receive their own unique existence, distinct from God's being, their existence can never persist independent of God (Bavinck 1999:247–8).

God does not merely preserve the universe, he also *governs* it. His governance has to do with that continued activity of God whereby he rules all things to secure the accomplishment of his divine purpose. God 'worketh all things after the counsel of his own will' (*Eph.* 1:11). God is the *primary* cause of all events. He is the necessary and sufficient cause of all events, no matter how seemingly trivial they may appear to us. Even the birds of the air and the lilies of the field receive his detailed care and attention (*Matt.* 6:26–28). Everything occurs for a purpose, in accordance with God's comprehensive plan.

GOD USES SECONDARY CAUSES

Although God is the *primary* cause of everything, he usually works through *secondary* causes. Secondary agents include physical objects, animals, humans, and spiritual beings such as angels.

God generally upholds the universe, from one moment to the next, in accordance with the properties he has assigned to his creatures. The moon, for example, orbits the earth in accordance with its gravitational character; animals follow their specific instincts; humans act according to their individual characters; and so on. Yet none of their actions can occur without God's *concurrence* or co-operation. Thus every normal natural event has two causes: a primary, divine cause and a secondary, natural cause.

God is a God of order (*1 Cor.* 14: 33). He has made a covenant with his creation that summer and winter, day and night will not cease as long as the earth exists (*Gen.* 8:22; 9:11–12; *Jer.* 33: 25). He has set bounds for his creatures (*Job* 38–41). Hence we can expect secondary causes to be *uniform*. This makes it possible for us to plan our lives and to do science. The Christian worldview solves the problem of *induction* by grounding it in the faithfulness of the God of the Bible. No additional special assumption is needed.

MIRACLES HAPPEN

However, the uniformity of nature is not absolute. God does not inflexibly restrict himself to secondary causes. In extraordinary cases God may withhold his concurrence and substitute some other effect.

Miracles should not be seen as violations of the natural order. Miracles are not divine interventions in a world that otherwise runs by itself. As we have just seen, the world must at all times be sustained by God. Hence, miracles are merely less regular manifestations of God's will. Likewise, natural laws are not rigid rules but, rather, the more regular manifestations of God's will.

Some miracles clearly involve natural forces. Consider, for example, the parting of the Red Sea: 'Moses stretched out his hand over the sea; and the LORD caused the sea to go back by a strong east wind all that night and made the sea dry land, and the waters were divided' (*Exod.* 14:21).

This has led some commentators to suggest that this was a purely natural event. They claim that the miracle consisted only of the fact that God knew exactly when it would happen. Some have gone so far as to assert that all biblical miracles have totally natural explanations. For example, the scientist-theologian James Jauncey, a theistic evolutionist, believes, 'The supernatural events in the world are merely natural events being used by God to bring about his purpose' (1971:36). His reasoning is as follows:

> If God had to break His own laws to bring about miracles, then obviously they were not flexible enough for every purpose of God when He originally made them, which is another way of saying His original creation was imperfect. When God created the world, He saw that it was good. This also included the existence of natural law, which must be flexible enough for every purpose God has in mind. So we have to abandon the idea of miracles as broken laws … It means that miracles are exhibitions of God's knowledge rather than mere brute power or show of magic (Jauncey 1971:36).

This erroneous notion overlooks a number of pertinent factors. First, there is the effect of spiritual agents such as angels and demons. Angels can be forces of physical destruction (*2 Sam.* 24:15–17 and *2 Kings* 19:35). Satan has the ability to perform signs and lying wonders (2 *Thess.* 2:9). Thus some natural events clearly have a secondary *spiritual* cause.

Second, the point of many of God's miracles is to demonstrate that he is the only true God, who alone has power even over nature. We think here of the dramatic confrontation between Elijah and the priests of Baal on Mount Carmel:

> Then the fire of the LORD fell, and consumed the burnt sacrifice, and the wood, and the stones, and the dust, and licked up the water that was in the trench. And when the people saw it, they fell on their faces: and they said, The LORD, he is the God (1 *Kings* 18:38–39).

Consider also the calming of the storm by Jesus, after which his disciples exclaim, 'What manner of man is this! for he commandeth even the winds and water, and they obey him' (*Luke* 8:25). Many miracles of Jesus were recorded so that we might believe that Jesus is the Christ (*John* 20:30–31).

We thus conclude that many biblical miracles are not explicable in terms of purely natural causes. Miracles display not only God's comprehensive knowledge but also his awesome power.

Thus the Christian worldview, with its allowance for miracles and spiritual agents, entails that not all natural events have natural explanations. Naturalists will, of course, rule out the possibility of miracles since, by definition, these are supernatural events. This is based on their notion that the laws of nature are unbreakable. However, as we saw in our discussion on induction (see Chapter 4), this naturalistic assertion is unprovable by either experience or logic. It is mere assumption.

Does God Play with Dice?

A number of recent writers believe that God creates through chance, so that not even God knows the future outcome of all events. They use the word 'chance' in the sense of genuine randomness, rather than mere coincidence or human ignorance. They consider chance events to be an inherent part of creation, necessary for creatures to have creative freedom.

For example, the biochemist and Anglican priest Arthur Peacocke asserts that God creates through law and chance. Consequently, he argues, the future of the physical world is open, rather than being fully determined. Not even God knows the future fully (Peacocke 1993:121). The notion that God has limited knowledge of the future is promoted by adherents of *Open Theology*, which has recently become quite popular in North America.

According to Peacocke, God has so made the world that there are certain areas over which he has chosen not to have control. By using chance, God has self-limited his omnipotence and omniscience. God takes risks. Only thus could the world produce beings fit for fellowship with God (Peacocke 1993:157). Chance, Peacocke asserts, manifests itself mainly through quantum uncertainty and human free will (1993:122). Open theologian Greg Boyd (2000:111) likewise claims that quantum mechanics confirms that the future is partly open.

PROVIDENCE AND CHANCE

Can chance be reconciled with the biblical God? Is it conceivable that God could create an entity whose actions are unpredictable even by God himself, its omniscient Creator?

This seems implausible. Consider, for example, a quantum event. In our discussion on quantum mechanics (Chapter 5) we saw that quantum mechanics certainly limits our *human* ability to know the quantum world. However, quantum mechanics does not *demand* chance. That is merely one possible *interpretation* of quantum physics. We found that it is possible to interpret quantum mechanics without appealing to chance. Further, even if it could be shown that quantum events have no sufficient *physical* cause, this still leaves open the possibility of *non-physical* causes.

Suppose a quantum event were fully determined by physical causes. Then, no matter how complicated the chain of causes leading to the event, an omniscient God would know the outcome. Suppose, on the other hand, that a quantum event is not fully determined by physical causes. Then it lacks a sufficient physical cause. But physical causes are only *secondary* causes. Since God is the primary cause of *all* that happens, this still leaves God as the *primary* cause. The absence of a secondary cause would imply only that God is in this case acting directly. Thus here, too, God must foreknow the outcome.

Authors who postulate that God works through chance rarely pause to consider how it is possible for an all-knowing, all-powerful God to create genuine chance events. The statistician D. J. Bartholomew is a notable exception. He writes:

> It is difficult to conceive of how God could be 'responsible' in some sense for pure chance without having designed the mechanism giving rise to it. Speaking personally, I find it impossible to frame any statement about God's action in generating random events which avoids the notion of design on his part and so justifies us in saying that chance events are without any explanation whatsoever. It is more congenial to both faith and reason to suppose that God generates the requisite degree of randomness much as we do, by deterministic means (1984:102).

Yet, if God generates randomness much as we do, by deterministic means, this means that 'chance' events are actually fully deterministic and that it is only God's *knowledge* of the outcome that is uncertain. In this vein Bartholomew adds, 'this does not imply or require foreknowledge of the consequences at the micro-level on God's part' (1984:102). Bartholomew argues that, at bottom, chance is bound up with the notion of *independence* rather than lack of cause:

> To allow the existence of pure chance in any sense is rather like saying that God can choose to act so that his left hand does not know what his right is doing. Or to put it more formally: that there must be independent sources of independent action within the one Godhead. There seems to be nothing logically impossible in such a suggestion but whether or not it can be usefully developed is not clear (1984:102–103).

The notion that 'God's left hand does not know what his right hand is doing' implies a severe limit on God's self-knowledge of the *present* instant. Moreover, it is just a limit on God's *knowledge*. It does not make the universe any less deterministic. Thus it offers no explanation of genuine chance. It just hampers God's ability to make predictions.

Further, Bartholomew's suggestion contradicts the omniscience, unity and simplicity generally attributed to the God of the Bible. Appeals to the multi-personhood of God do not help. The orthodox notion of the Trinity asserts an essential unity to God, particularly as it relates to knowledge: each Person is essentially and equally omniscient (i.e., the Father: *1 John* 3:20; the Son: *Matt.* 11:27; *John* 21:17; and the Holy Spirit: *1 Cor.* 2:11). Hence, the orthodox conception of the biblical God has no room for the notion that he could generate pure chance.

This conclusion is further strengthened when we consider God's concurrence. At each instant, for God to actuate the universe at the next instant, he must have prior knowledge of all the intended actions of all his creatures. Such knowledge is needed to decide whether or not to concur. Indeed, how could God actuate the universe at each instant without first having full knowledge of all its details? However, if God can fully predict the next state of the universe then, again, genuine chance seems to be ruled out. As the Bible says, 'The lot is cast into the lap; but the whole disposing thereof is of the LORD' (*Prov.* 16:33). God determines the outcome of the lot, no matter how random it may seem to us.

DOES GOD LIMIT HIMSELF?

Arthur Peacocke tries to make room for chance by suggesting that God has self-limited his power and knowledge (1993:212). He suggests that God has so made the world that there are certain areas over which he has chosen not to have control. There are certain systems whose future states are in principle unknowable, even to God (Peacocke 1993:212). In a similar vein, the Christian philosopher William Alston goes so far as to assert, 'To deny that God can voluntarily limit Godself in this way would itself be to deny God's omnipotence' (Alston 1996:191).

However, God's omnipotence means that he can do all things that are *logically possible* and consistent with his character. For a *rational*, omniscient, omnipotent God to construct a purely *random*, indeterministic mechanism seems logically *impossible*. It entails that God causes an effect (*e.g.*, a quantum event) that has no cause.

Furthermore, it is an essential characteristic of God that he is *sovereign*. He is the *only* independent being, upon which everything else depends for its existence. It is contrary to God's essential nature that he would make creatures that are independent of him. God would then no longer be *God*. Omnipotence and omniscience are *necessary* properties of God. God cannot give these up without ceasing to be God. Hence God, as *God*, must necessarily retain his full omnipotence and omniscience at all times.

According to Peacocke, God's omniscience has to be construed as God knowing at any time whatever it is *logically possible* for him to know (1997:145). This, Peacocke asserts, does not include uncertain future quantum events, since these do not yet exist (1997:146). Nevertheless, even this limited definition of omniscience still implies that God has complete knowledge of the past and present. This rules out Bartholomew's suggestion that, at any instant, God's left hand does not know what his right hand is doing. One is then still left with the problem of constructing a viable mechanism for generating pure chance.

The physicist W. G. Pollard (1958:22) and, more recently, the philosopher Nancey Murphy (1995:339) advocate that the apparently random events at the quantum level are all specific, intentional acts of God. However, God limits his action at this level. First, God respects the integrity of the entities with which he co-operates. For example, God doesn't change the electron's mass arbitrarily. Second, God restricts his action to produce a world that, for all we can tell, is orderly and law-like. God, then, is the hidden cause of quantum events. Murphy asserts, rightly, that this position is theologically preferable to indeterminism. It has the further advantage of consistency with the principle of sufficient reason (Murphy 1995:342). Of course, if God is directly responsible for quantum events this entails that these events are therefore predictable by God.

In short, the Christian view of God's providence affirms that the universe is fully determined from God's perspective. Whether quantum events, say, are strictly determined in terms of purely secondary, physical causes remains an open question. Such secondary causes, if they do exist, may well be too deep for finite humans to fully comprehend, let alone to utilize for prediction. However, even if secondary causes were to be incomplete, this still leaves God as the primary cause.

KNOWING AN UNCERTAIN FUTURE

One could approach the question of chance also in terms of God's foreknowledge. If God has complete and certain knowledge of the future, does this in itself not rule out the possibility of chance events and the uncertain future they entail? Some Christians dispute this. Various attempts have been made to preserve God's foreknowledge of future events in a world containing chance.

Consider, for example, the theologian John Jefferson Davis. Davis argues that the Bible depicts God as having a complete knowledge of future events (*Isa.* 41–46), extending even to human thoughts (*Psa.* 139:1–6) and quantum events. Hence Davis (1997:135) rejects Peacocke's limited view of divine omniscience. Yet, at the same time, Davis concurs with Peacocke that quantum events *are* truly indeterministic, governed by genuine chance.

How does Davis square these two seemingly contradictory notions? How can God foreknow an as yet uncertain future event? To resolve this dilemma, Davis appeals to the notion of *middle knowledge*. This concept dates back to the Jesuit theologian Luis Molina (1553–1600). Molina held that God has three types of knowledge: (1) *natural* knowledge of all necessary truths, including all possible worlds, logic and mathematics (2) *free* knowledge of the actual world he created and (3) *middle* knowledge of what any creature would freely do in any given hypothetical situation.

Davis extends the notion of divine middle knowledge to quantum events. He postulates that God knows whether or not a given radium atom, placed in a given physical situation, would randomly decay at a given time. According to Davis, 'God "sees" that a given nucleus is about to disintegrate, and is free either to concur – and so to make certain – or not to concur in the propensities and tendencies of the creature in question' (Davis 1997:144).

In response, Arthur Peacocke (1997: 147) asks how God could possible know exactly when a particular nucleus will disintegrate if there are no underlying laws that determine this. Peacocke argues that, if quantum events are genuinely random, God's middle knowledge can be only of the *probability* of a quantum event occurring.

Indeed, one wonders how God could know with *certainty* the future outcome of an as yet *uncertain* quantum event. By definition, it is impossible to know the outcome of an indeterministic event before it occurs. To say, with Davis, that God knows how a particle will behave in a given *hypothetical* situation implies that, given specific circumstances, the particle will *always* behave in exactly the same way. In that case the outcome is *not* indeterministic at all. Rather, it is fully determined by the circumstances. In short, divine middle knowledge presumes determinism.

Note, by the way, that a mere foreknowledge of the future does not enable God to *control* the future. God then merely sees what is about to happen. If God is to have some measure of control, then God must have detailed knowledge of how creatures will react in particular hypothetical circumstances. Such middle knowledge allows God to predict possible future states of the universe. He can then effectively plan and direct the unfolding of history. As the Creator of all that exists, God surely has fully comprehensive middle knowledge. He knows exactly how any of his creatures will act in any conceivable situation.

BUTTERFLIES AND STORMS

Chaotic systems, as we saw in Chapter 5, offer a mechanism whereby small effects can be greatly amplified. Thus, a chaotic system could transform a tiny quantum event into a major physical catastrophe. Recall, for example, the butterfly effect in weather prediction.

It follows that if, as open theists affirm, God cannot predict quantum events, then neither can he predict the future behaviour of chaotic systems. This puts severe limitations on God's knowledge of the future. For example, the God of open theology cannot predict, say, a future storm, nor those killed by it. Hence, it is not the case, as argued by proponents of open theology, that a God who does not know the outcome of quantum events can still know the future approximately. Chaotic events entail that, for such a limited God, the future cannot be known even roughly. He can overcome the difficulties caused by the chaotic amplification of quantum effects only by continuous direct intervention. To ensure that his future goals are met, the God of Open Theology must constantly perform miracles to keep his plan on track.

Conclusions

In summary, the Christian worldview stresses the sovereignty of God. The universe is structured because God made the universe according to a rational plan. It is comprehensible to man because God made man in his image to be his steward.

God has created everything in the world and he continues to sustain it in its continued existence. God is the primary cause of all events. Everything happens in accordance with God's eternal plan. God's faithfulness is reflected in the fact that he usually works through orderly, secondary causes. However, these are not absolute; God has at times acted directly in miraculous ways.

God's sovereignty and omniscience rule out the existence of genuine chance. Genuine chance in the world would imply that some events happen without being fully caused. It is inconsistent to think that a rational, omniscient, omnipotent God could create a genuinely random device, of which he would not be able to predict the outcome. If God were to limit his powers so that his creatures would be independent agents then God would no longer be God. God's omnipotence and omniscience are essential to his divine nature.

Free Will and Responsibility

CROSSFIRE

Given our best scientific theories, factors beyond our control ultimately produce all of our actions . . . we are therefore not morally responsible for them.

DERK PEREBOOM (*Living without Free Will*, 2001: front flap).

* * * * *

A good man out of the good treasure of the heart bringeth forth good things: and an evil man out of the evil treasure bringeth forth evil things. But I say to you, That every idle word that men shall speak, they shall give account thereof in the day of judgment. For by thy words thou shalt be justified, and by thy words thou shalt be condemned.

MATTHEW 12:35–37

The philosopher Derk Pereboom believes that all our acts and choices are ultimately produced by factors beyond our control. He embraces the naturalist position that our minds are run by our brains, which in turn are completely controlled by biochemical laws. As a result, he concludes that we have no free will. Hence we cannot be held morally responsible.

Free will is perhaps the most perplexing philosophical mystery. It gives rise to many deep questions. Do we have such a thing as free will? Do we really have a choice when we make a choice? Or are our choices completely pre-determined by our character and circumstances? If our choices are pre-determined, should we be held morally accountable? Is free will possible in a determinist world, where all our choices can be completely explained in terms of prior causes? Or does free will require an element of chance? Can God fully predict all our human choices? How can we reconcile human free will with divine sovereignty?

Many philosophers believe that human free will is impossible in a deterministic world, where all events and choices are fully predictable (at least by God). This has led to either a denial of the existence of free will or to a denial that the world is deterministic.

The statistician D. J. Bartholomew asserts in his book *God of Chance* (1984) that the universe must contain chance in order to have room for genuine human freedom and moral responsibility. Consequently, Bartholomew believes that many worldly events were not specifically planned by God. God can therefore not be held responsible for the undeserved suffering that his creatures may experience.

Again, I remind the reader that the word 'chance' refers here not to mere coincidence or human ignorance. Rather, a chance event is one that happens without a sufficient cause. A chance event, in this sense, is one that is inherently unpredictable. The quantum events of the atomic world, for example, are often said to involve chance. The existence of chance has major implications regarding God's interaction with the universe and his knowledge of the future.

In the previous chapter we discussed the possibility of chance in the quantum realm. There we noted that quantum events can be explained without resort to chance. Moreover, we concluded that chance is inconsistent with God's sovereignty, as manifested in his creation, providence, and full foreknowledge of future events.

Nevertheless, in spite of these considerations, many Christians believe that human free will is one aspect of creation that must be genuinely chance-like. It is widely thought that determinism rules out human freedom and responsibility. Thus, for example, the Oxford theologian Keith Ward (1999:12) argues that the universe, if it is to generate freely creative beings, must be indeterministic (*i.e.*, the future must be open or indefinite, not determined). Similarly, Nancey Murphy (1995:355) asserts that indeterminism is needed for human moral responsibility, since determinism makes God responsible for evil. Arthur Peacocke believes that human free will rules out the possibility that God fully knows the future (1993:122).

The question of how human free will relates to divine sovereignty is a basic issue that has been much debated throughout history. There are two main positions. The first says that humans are to some degree autonomous (*i.e.*, self-governing and independent of God). It says that we are free agents who make our own choices, in isolation from God's plan. The second says that our character and circumstances make our choices completely predictable by God, our Creator; our choices form part of God's overall plan.

What Is Human Free Will?

Before comparing these two positions, let us first define what we mean by human *free will*. By free will we mean the *freedom* of the *will* to choose and act of itself, without coercion. Such freedom we experience when we deliberate about a decision (how to vote in an election), make a choice (I decide which candidate I prefer), and actualize that choice into a physical action (I direct my hand to put a mark beside the chosen name).

Human free will surely requires a genuine ability for us to make a mental choice. It involves also the power to convert this mental choice into a physical action. My mental choice may depend on various abstract, non-physical factors such as, for example, the moral qualities of the candidates running for office. Hence, human free will certainly implies physical indeterminism, in the sense that a physical event (raising my hand) might have a non-physical (*i.e.*, mental) cause. In the same physical situation different non-physical factors (my character, beliefs and moral standards) might well cause me to choose and act differently.

Free will entails that we make our choices freely, without coercion. We should be free to choose what we want, in accordance with our own character, history, and moral standards. Such freedom is essential for moral responsibility. To be morally responsible we must make our own decisions. They may not be forced on us contrary to our will. Responsibility for our actions implies that we have a measure of control. Only then can we be held accountable for our free decisions and subsequent actions.

Two Views on Free Will

Most Christians will concur that we have a will, that we make genuine choices, and that we are morally responsible. But now we come to the central point of contention. Are our decisions fully predictable? In the same comprehensive situation, with the same external conditions plus the same internal (*i.e.*, mental) characteristics and circumstances, would the same person always make exactly the same decision?

There are two responses to this question, representing two different notions of free will. Those who answer 'yes' believe in a freedom of *spontaneity*. We choose and act as we please. As long as our acts are expressions of what we want to do they are to be regarded as free, even if what we want is in some way determined. This notion of freedom is compatible with determinism. Hence it is commonly called *compatibilism* or 'soft' determinism (as opposed to the 'hard' determinism of Crick's materialism).

The compatibilist argues that our choices are always based on reasons, even though we may not always be fully aware of them. Our choices are made in accordance with our character and experiences. Hence God, who knows us perfectly, can surely predict our free choices. Our choices are free because they were willingly made by us, rather than coerced against our will.

On the other hand, those who answer 'no' believe in a freedom of *indifference*. We have the freedom to choose either of two different actions with equal ease and out of no necessity. We have the freedom to act contrary to our nature. Our decisions are not fully determined by our character and history. This is called *libertarianism*. Since the word *libertarian* is sometimes used also in connection with certain political and social theories, I stress that I use this word here only in connection with free will, as defined.

Freedom within Uncertainty

We shall consider first libertarianism. Libertarians contend that our will is genuinely free only if our choosing is not pre-determined by external and internal conditions. They assert that our motives and beliefs may incline us toward a particular choice, but they should not guarantee it.

THE NEED FOR CHANCE

Libertarianism assumes that our choices are not entirely caused by such things as character and circumstances. This implies that our choices are, at least to some extent, indeterministic. Only thus, with an element of pure chance, might the same agent choose differently in identical situations. Hence Bartholomew asserts, 'The reality of chance is not merely compatible with the doctrine of creation but is required by it . . . only in a world with real uncertainty can people grow into free responsible children of their heavenly Father' (1984:145).

Not all libertarians believe that our choices require an element of randomness. The evangelical theologian Norman Geisler (1999), for example, contends that human decisions are neither determined nor uncaused but, rather, self-caused. Now, the issue is not whether a human self makes its own decisions, after due deliberation and without external coercion. That much is granted by compatibilists. The issue is whether the circumstances and constitution of the self fully determine its decisions. Will the same self, under the same conditions, always make the same decision? Libertarians answer 'no'. But then we must ask: what is the decisive factor in making a choice, if not the internal constitution of the self and its external circumstances? What other cause can there be? The inevitable implication of libertarianism is that the self's decisions are, at least to some extent, uncaused.

The libertarian lack of a sufficient cause implies that our decisions involve an essential element of genuine chance. Such a position faces much the same difficulties as quantum chance. For one, the notion that our choices are to some extent uncaused contradicts the basic principle of sufficient reason (*i.e.*, that nothing happens without a sufficient reason). Hence David Hume (1777:105), arguing against libertarian free will, writes, 'Liberty, when opposed to necessity, not to constraint, is the same thing with chance; which is universally allowed to have no existence.'

A MISSING PROOF

Libertarianism faces a further weakness. How can we ever prove that our decisions are not fully determined by causes? Theologian R. K. McGregor Wright (1996:52) notes that belief in libertarianism seems to require omniscience. There may well be subtle causes we are not aware of. As the French scientist and philosopher Blaise Pascal remarked, 'The heart has its reasons of which the mind knows nothing.' The assertion that pure chance is necessary for free will is no more than a metaphysical assumption.

Human free will is often linked to quantum events. For example, neuroscientist Sir John Eccles (1994:146) believes that quantum uncertainty leaves room for humans to act in the physical world. Yet, as we have seen, quantum mechanics does not require nature to be inherently chance-like. Determinist interpretations of quantum mechanics are possible. Moreover, no relation between quantum effects and mental choices has ever been found. For example, there is no evidence that the human mind can influence where a photon will hit a photographic plate or when a radium atom will decay.

FREEDOM SHACKLED

Libertarianism, to the extent that it requires an element of chance, seems to entail that I make choices based on no good reason but, rather, capriciously, somewhat like flipping coins. Yet, as physicist Henry Stapp (1993:92) notes, any play of chance would falsify the idea that I, from the ground of my essential nature, make a true choice.

Indeed, uncaused, random events, occurring without sufficient reason, are beyond our control. They do not enhance our human free will at all. Philosopher Richard Taylor (1974:51) remarks, 'The conception that now emerges is not that of a free man, but of an erratic and jerking phantom, without any rhyme or reason at all.'

How can I make any practical plans, if I do not have control over my choices? Imagine that I set out to fly an aircraft from London to Vancouver. Keeping the aircraft safely aloft and on course will keep me very busy. It will require many quick decisions. How can I hope to arrive at my planned destination, if all my actions involve an element of chance? In that case I cannot predict how I shall act. I may do things that will astonish, not only my passengers, but even myself.

Further, if my free acts are outside my full control, how can I be held responsible? Responsibility is closely tied to causation. I cannot be held responsible for something I did not cause or intend to cause. As theologian Terrance Tiessen (2000:247) points out, moral responsibility requires our acts to be intentional. Hence random actions are not free in the sense required for account-ability. Wright (1996:47) asserts that chance events cannot be the stuff of character. To be of good character means that our moral actions are reliably predictable. We cannot be held responsible for actions of the will unless these are tied directly to our character. In short, chance *undermines*, rather than bolsters, moral responsibility.

LIMITING GOD

There is another difficulty with libertarian free will. How are we to reconcile it with divine sovereignty? Libertarianism holds that humans are, at least to some degree, uncaused causers, an attribute normally limited to God. This puts a severe restraint on God's powers. Bartholomew acknowledges, regarding the existence of genuine chance:

> But such a view . . . places limitations on the manner in which God can interact with creation. It implies, for example, that the vast majority of events are not directly planned by God to achieve some immediate and specific end (Bartholomew 1984:145).

In our discussion of quantum events we already noted the difficulty of fitting in chance with the notions of God as Creator and Upholder of the universe. The same problems arise in connection with libertarian free will.

The biblical view of providence attributes *all* events to God's purposeful plan. This includes human choices. We are 'predestinated according to the purpose of him who worketh all things after the counsel of his own will' (*Eph.* 1:11). We are told, 'Both Herod, and Pontius Pilate, with the Gentiles, and the people of Israel, were gathered together, for to do whatsoever thy hand and thy counsel determined before to be done' (*Acts* 4:27–28). Or, as Joseph said to his brothers, 'Ye thought evil against me; but God meant it unto good, to bring it to pass . . . to save much people alive' (*Gen.* 50:20). Joseph's brothers wilfully followed their sinful inclinations. Yet even their sinful choices formed part of God's comprehensive plan.

Creatures, unlike God, can neither create from nothing nor sustain themselves in being. They, and their powers, continue to exist only through God's providential power. It follows that all the actions of creatures must likewise depend on God's sustaining power. Hence creatures cannot act independently of God. Ron Highfield, responding to a defence of libertarianism by open theists (recall that Open Theology posits that the future is open, so that even God does not yet know it), comments,

> Acknowledging that God must act for the agent and its powers to continue in existence and yet contending that God need not – indeed,

for the sake of our freedom, must not – act in our action so that it may have being . . . lands open theism in a self-contradiction (Highfield 2002: 296).

Libertarian freedom requires that an action of an agent, to be free, must originate and be carried out independently of God. This contradicts God's sovereignty, which is essential to his nature.

Even if our decisions were to lack sufficient *secondary* causes, this still leaves the direct, *primary* causation of God. However, attributing our choices directly to God makes God responsible for our sinful decisions. This defeats Murphy's argument that libertarianism is necessary to make humans – not God – responsible for their sins.

Moreover, as we noted in our discussion of quantum events (Chapter 11), it is inconceivable that an all-powerful, all-knowing God could make a creature so sophisticated that God would not be able to predict its every action.

GOD'S KNOWLEDGE OF OUR CHOICES

Libertarianism poses problems also for God's omniscience, particularly regarding future events. The biblical God foreknows the future fully, in all its details. If our future decisions are inherently uncertain, how can God foreknow them? If God knows our decisions beforehand, does this not imply that they are fully predictable?

One might conjecture that, if God were timeless, he would not literally *fore*know anything. Yet, as William Craig (1987:65) points out, the statement, 'God knows timelessly that some event occurs in my future', is still true prior to the event. One is thus still faced with the problem of how God can have certain knowledge of an as yet uncertain future.

On what basis can God know what libertarian decisions I shall make next year? Some libertarians appeal to Molina's concept of middle knowledge, which we discussed in the previous chapter. This referred to God's knowledge of how men would act in hypothetical situations. There are a few biblical incidents that suggest that God has such knowledge. For example, God told David that the men of Keilah would betray David *if* he were to stay in Keilah (*1 Sam.* 23:12). Thus forewarned, David left Keilah and the hypothetical event never took place. Also, we are told that the people of Tyre and Sidon would have repented *if* the mighty works of Jesus done in Bethsaida and Chorazin had been done there (*Matt.* 11:21). However, such divine middle knowledge implies that identical agents in identical situations make identical choices. How else could God know how we would act in a *hypothetical* situation? It follows that God's middle knowledge does not help libertarianism.

How, then, according to libertarianism, does God know our future decisions? It might be thought that such a question is impious. How can we presume to ask how God knows? Yet, we may expect God to act coherently. One might conjecture that perhaps God's view of the future is like consulting a crystal ball or previewing a film. But what makes the crystal ball or film? What forms the future, if not God? The notion that God simply foreknows the future, without predetermining it, entails that there exists an independent force that forms the future. Such an independent force, we just saw, contradicts God's sovereignty. The sovereign God of the Bible has complete knowledge of the future because he has decreed all that comes to pass.

On such grounds the Reformer Martin Luther (1483–1546) refuted the famous humanist Desiderius Erasmus (1466–1536), who defended libertarian free will. Luther, in his book *The Bondage of the Will*, writes:

> For if we believe it to be true, that God fore-knows and fore-ordains all things; that He can be neither deceived nor hindered in His Prescience and Predestination; and that nothing can take place but according to His Will, (which reason herself is compelled to confess;) then, even according to the testimony of reason herself, there can be no 'Free will' – in man, in angel, or in any creature! (1525: Section 167).

Luther's affirmation of the sovereignty of God led him to embrace a compatibilist view of free will.

WHERE DOES IT LEAD?

Libertarianism has various negative theological implications. One consequence is that it diminishes the gospel message. Indeed, Martin Luther believed that the essential issue at stake in the Reformation was precisely the denial of human (libertarian) free will. At the end of *The Bondage of the Will* Luther praises Erasmus, whom he is rebutting, for raising the matter:

> You alone, in pre-eminent distinction from all others, have entered upon the thing itself; that is, the grand turning point of the cause; and have not wearied me with those irrelevant points about popery, purgatory, indulgences, and other like *baubles,* rather than *causes,* with which all have hitherto tried to hunt me down, though in vain! You, and you alone, saw what was the grand hinge upon which the whole turned, and therefore you attacked the vital part at once (1525: Section 168).

To Luther, the denial of libertarian free will was the foundation of the biblical doctrine of grace. He held that the principle, *sola fide* (by faith alone), must be based on the broader principle, *sola gratia* (by grace alone). A faith based on man's will is similar to a salvation based on works. It is then up to man to save himself. Rather, faith is itself a gift of grace: 'For by grace are ye saved through faith; and that not of yourselves: it is the gift of God' (*Eph.* 2:8). Hence Luther stressed that our salvation is due entirely to God's merciful intervention in our hearts.

Another casualty of libertarianism is God's knowledge of the future. Open theists correctly note that libertarianism is inconsistent with divine foreknowledge. Their prior commitment to libertarianism thus leads them to deny that God has full knowledge of the future.

Libertarianism also affects divine sovereignty. Human autonomy and genuine chance imply that some areas of the universe are not fully under God's control. They are independent of God. This entails a reduced God, who no longer upholds all things by the mere Word of his power. Wright (1996:59) contends that libertarianism leads eventually to process theology, discussed in Chapter 9.

The Bible is very insistent on God's comprehensive sovereignty and foreknowledge. Any denial of these thus requires also a rejection of the corresponding biblical texts. However, once we pick and choose which portions of the Bible to uphold, we have undermined any genuine biblical authority. This contradicts the Christian worldview, which requires us to judge all our thoughts in the light of Scripture, rather than vice versa.

To sum up, libertarianism faces serious problems. It is based on an unprovable assumption. Its reliance on chance contradicts the principle of sufficient reason. It introduces a fatal lack of control that destroys our freedom and responsibility. Theologically, it undermines God's grace, sovereignty and omniscience.

Why, then, is libertarianism so widely held? Mainly because it is thought that the prime alternative, compatibilism, is even worse off. Let us then examine the case for compatibilism.

Freedom within Reason

Compatibilism, unlike libertarianism, holds that our choices are fully caused. We make decisions for reasons, in accordance with our character and circumstances. In the same circumstances the same person will always make the same decisions.

Our choices are therefore quite predictable to someone who knows us well. How often, for example, does my wife comment to me, 'I knew you would say that'? Consider, then, the predictive ability of God, our Creator, who knows us completely. The author of Hebrews writes:

> For the word of God is quick, and powerful, and sharper than any two-edged sword, piercing even to the dividing asunder of soul and spirit, and of the joints and marrow, and is a discerner of the thoughts and intents of the heart. Neither is there any creature that is not manifest in his sight: but all things are naked and opened unto the eyes of him with whom we have to do (*Heb.* 4:12–13).

And David elaborates:

> O LORD, thou hast searched me, and known me. Thou knowest my downsitting and mine uprising, thou understandest my thought afar

off. Thou compassest my path and my lying down, and art acquainted with all my ways. For there is not a word in my tongue, but, lo, O LORD, thou knowest it altogether. Thou hast beset me behind and before, and laid thine hand upon me. Such knowledge is too wonderful for me (*Psa.* 139:1–6).

God, who knows us perfectly, even our inmost thoughts and intents, surely knows exactly what future decisions we shall make.

There are three common objections to compatibilism: (1) it reduces us to puppets, (2) it is equivalent to fatalism, and (3) it removes moral responsibility. Let's examine each of these claims.

MORE THAN PHYSICS

Compatibilism should not be confused with *physical determinism*. Physical determinism is the notion that all our thoughts, choices and actions are ultimately completely explicable in terms of purely *physical* laws and concepts. This is the materialism of Sir Francis Crick. In this case our thoughts and choices are just illusions and we are indeed reduced to mere puppets.

Compatibilism, on the other hand, is a much wider form of determinism. It gives proper recognition to the important role of our mind, beliefs and choices. There is a real self, who deliberates and makes decisions. Yet the self makes its decisions for reasons, determined by its character and wants.

Previously (in Chapter 6) we noted that physical determinism implies we are physically determined to believe whatever we believe, regardless of its truth. Hence the rational defence of physical determinism is self-refuting. That critique does not apply to compatibilism. Although what we believe is still determined, the determining process now includes our beliefs, our ideas of rationality and also our assessment of the truthfulness of the belief in question. What we believe therefore *does* depend on the truth of any particular belief. If our thinking apparatus were foolproof, then our thinking, though determined, would nevertheless be determined to produce only true beliefs.

FORMING YOUR FATE

Compatibilism implies that God, with his complete knowledge of all his creatures and their decisions, can fully predict all future states of the world. It follows that God knows the future completely. Moreover, God fully knows also how that future would change if he were to alter some current detail. God can thus completely plan how the future will enfold.

Does divine foreknowledge leave room for human freedom? A common objection is that, if God knows that tomorrow I shall mow my lawn, it is therefore true that I shall mow my lawn. Hence I do not have the power to refrain from mowing my lawn. Thus I am not free.

Such reasoning confuses *determinism* with *fatalism*. Determinism means that all events are rendered unavoidable by their causes, *which include our choices and actions*. Fatalism, on the other hand, holds that all events happen unavoidably, *regardless of our choices and actions*; there is nothing we can do to escape our fate.

Fatalism is a fallacy. It fails to take into account that my will is an active cause that helps to determine my future. Clearly, our choices do make a difference. Else there would be no point in getting out of bed in the morning or driving your car with your eyes open. The fact that our decisions are predictable does not detract from their effect on the future. Although we cannot *change* the future we can surely help *determine* what the future will be.

It is sometimes said, even by Christians, 'You won't go before your time.' This saying is fine, as long as its intent is to stop us from undue worry about things beyond our control. It is certainly comforting to know that everything is ultimately in God's hands. However, this gives us no excuse for irresponsible behaviour, such as, for example, driving an unsafe car at high speed. The time of our death is often closely related to our prior actions. Thus, while our time is surely foreknown by God, it may well have been set largely by our own foolish decisions.

Further, God's knowledge of our future decisions does not, in itself, influence our decisions. How could it, seeing that we have no access to such divine knowledge? Hence divine foreknowledge in itself does not constrain our freedom. Were our decisions to be different, God's foreknowledge of our decisions would be correspondingly different.

Such considerations apply also to the need for prayer. One might ask, if all things are determined by God's eternal plan, why should we bother to pray? The proper answer to this, as Terrance Tiessen (2000:239) notes, is that God has foreseen our prayers and his responses to them. As the prophet Isaiah proclaims, 'Before they call, I will answer; and while they are yet speaking, I will hear' (*Isa.* 65:24). Our prayers help determine the future. They are part of God's eternal plan.

DO YOU REALLY HAVE A CHOICE?

The most common objection to compatibilism is that it seems to lead to a denial of moral responsibility. Compatibilism implies that all the causes of my choices have previous causes. The series of causes that formed my character goes back to my birth, and even before that. All my character traits, dispositions, wants, and so on can then be traced to prior conditions, such as genetics and environment, beyond my control. Had these conditions been different, I would have been different. How, then, I might ask, can I be held accountable for my choices?

Compatibilists reply that all that is required for moral responsibility is that we wilfully act upon our wants, regardless of how these were formed. We shall elaborate upon this in the next section. First, we shall examine several other views.

The Christian philosopher William Hasker argues that, if compatibilism were true, I could not have acted differently, even had I wanted to. How, he asks, could I have wanted something different from what I want? Since my wants are determined, my freedom to choose is illusory. According to Hasker, real freedom requires that I should be free to change my wants. Hasker concludes that compatibilism is incompatible with moral responsibility (1983:36). This, in turn, Hasker takes to be a strong argument for libertarianism, which he deems to be the only alternative.

Suppose, however, that I were free to change my wants. On what basis would I choose my new wants? On the basis of my present character, with all its wants? That would lead back to compatibilism. Nor does a random change help, for that removes my wants from my control. Thus, Hasker's objection has no substance.

As we saw, libertarianism, to the extent that it requires chance, is even less compatible with moral responsibility. Although Hasker denies that libertarianism requires chance, he offers no explanation of how libertarianism can be indeterminate without some degree of chance. Nor does he explain how libertarianism can establish moral responsibility.

If moral responsibility were indeed undermined by both compatibilism and indeterminism, where would that leave moral responsibility? As we saw earlier, Derk Pereboom, in his book *Living without Free Will* (2001), argues that we have no moral responsibility. He maintains that we can be held morally responsible only if we are the ultimate causal source of our actions. Pereboom contends that, according to our best scientific theories, our world is wholly governed by the laws of physics. Factors beyond our ultimate control cause all our actions. Hence, we are not morally responsible for any of them.

Pereboom concludes that, since we cannot be held morally accountable for our actions, we should therefore change our notions of justice. A murderer, for example, should not be held morally responsible for killing. Therefore Pereboom urges that he should not be given a severe punishment, such as death or imprisonment. Instead, the courts should aim at modifying his criminal behaviour, perhaps through rehabilitation programmes. Obviously, one's views on free will and responsibility can have serious implications for society.

Leaving aside the perplexing question of how moral and rational 'oughts' can function in a world completely determined by physical laws (see Chapter 7), Pereboom's reasoning still seems incoherent. He affirms that, even though we are not morally responsible for our actions, they *can* be judged to be morally good or bad. Further, Pereboom clearly expects courts and judges to respond to moral 'oughts'. Yet, if we are not responsible for our actions, as Pereboom claims, surely this applies equally to judges as well as criminals. How, then, can Pereboom venture to instruct us in how we *ought* to treat criminals? In doing so he presumes that we *are* in fact morally accountable, thus contradicting his central thesis.

WHO IS RESPONSIBLE?

Contrary to the claims of Hasker and Pereboom, compatibilism does not destroy moral responsibility. This becomes clear when we examine what morality entails. Morality has to do with the rightness and wrongness of actions. In practice, we hold someone responsible for a crime, if that crime was directly caused by an intentional action based on a wilful, informed choice, with full knowledge of the wrongness of the act and the consequences of doing it.

If Jack, a sane man, deliberately sets his neighbour's house on fire, knowing full well that it is illegal and that it may cause injury or death, would we not hold Jack morally responsible for his misdeed? The critical factor is that Jack's choice was his *own* choice, rather than one forced upon him. We might not hold him responsible if he acted at gunpoint or under hypnosis.

Moral responsibility does *not* require that there are no reasons for our decisions. The freedom needed for moral responsibility is not a libertarian freedom from *causation* but, rather, a freedom from *coercion* by forces outside ourselves. Such is the freedom underlying moral responsibility.

What, then, of the argument that, since Jack did not cause his own nature, he is therefore not morally responsible for his actions?

It fails. Moral responsibility, as outlined above, involves merely our *present* capabilities. We are morally responsible when we can act upon our *own* wants, in accordance with our *own* will, regardless of how our wants and will may themselves have come to be what they are. We would still hold Jack responsible, even if his vicious character were due largely to an unhappy childhood.

In fact, our nature is such that we intuitively *know* we are responsible for our actions. We take ownership over our decisions. Our own conscience, a deep sense of guilt and shame, convicts us of our misdeeds. Within our innermost self, we know we cannot shift the blame for our actions on to our past or our parents.

Such considerations also refute a widely held defence of homosexual behaviour. It is often argued that homosexuality is caused by one's genetic make-up and, hence, the homosexual is not responsible for his behaviour. Whether homosexual desire is indeed genetically determined has still to be proven. Perhaps it is due more to upbringing and life experiences. Perhaps it is more like an addictive habit. However, no matter how one came to have homosexual desires, the fact remains that the homosexual willingly chooses to act upon these desires, knowing that it is sin. Thus, he *can* be held morally accountable.

We conclude that compatibilism does not erase moral responsibility but establishes it. Moral responsibility exists because we make our choices for *reasons*. Hence we can be influenced by reasoning, criticism or the prospect of reward or punishment. The knowledge that we shall be held accountable for our actions is itself a factor that influences our actions. On such grounds David Hume (1777:104–107) asserted that it is only on the assumption of determinism that there can be moral responsibility.

The Bible and Responsibility

Thus far we have discussed various philosophical factors regarding moral responsibility. Ultimately, however, morality is established by God. He sets the absolute standards for right and wrong. He assesses our degree of responsibility. He rewards and punishes our actions. The Bible is thus the most pertinent authority to consult on moral responsibility.

What does the Bible teach about responsibility? We can summarize its main teachings as follows:

1. We are held accountable for all our deeds and words, even though these are determined by our heart:

> A good man out of the good treasure of the heart bringeth forth good things: and an evil man out of the evil treasure bringeth forth evil things. But I say to you, That every idle word that men shall speak, they shall give account thereof in the day of judgment. For by thy words thou shalt be justified, and by thy words thou shalt be condemned (*Matt.* 12:35–37).

Judas is held responsible, even though his betrayal of Jesus was predetermined: 'And truly the Son of man goeth, as it was determined: but woe unto that man by whom he is betrayed!' (*Luke* 22:22).

Since we are held responsible for all our voluntary decisions, we are responsible also for the extent that these have formed our character through developing bad habits, addictions, and so on.

2. Our hearts are enslaved to sin (*Rom.* 6:20), so that of ourselves we have no ability to change them. 'The natural man receiveth not the things of the Spirit of God: for they are foolishness unto him: neither can he know them, because they are spiritually discerned' (*1 Cor.* 2:14). 'So then they that are in the flesh cannot please God' (*Rom.* 8:8).

The Bible does not support the notion that inability limits responsibility. Man's heart is sinful from birth and is beyond man's ability to change. Yet he is still held accountable. The key fact is that we sin *willingly*. Indeed, 'Men loved darkness rather than light' (*John* 3:19) and, 'Knowing the judgment of God, that they which commit such things are worthy of death, [they] not only do the same, but have pleasure in them that do them' (*Rom.* 1:32).

Adam, the first man, was created good and upright, in the image of God. Though good, he was not yet perfect: he had the potential to fall. He could freely choose between good and evil. He had the capacity to serve God. Unhappily, Adam chose not to serve that glorious purpose. Giving in to the devil, he wilfully subjected himself to sin and death. Thereafter man became enslaved to sin.

Adam was not forced against his will to eat the fruit. Nor did he do it arbitrarily. On the contrary, Adam did it for reasons sufficient to himself. He acted knowingly, willingly, and spontaneously, with no violence being done to his will. God created Adam as he was; God knew that Adam's nature and circumstances would lead to his fall. Yet Adam was held fully responsible for his actions.

Fallen man is free to do what he wills, but his will is not free in the sense that it can determine itself. As Henry Stob (1978:152) notes, man responds to his nature, which is what it is, either by sin or by God's sovereign grace. This leaves human responsibility fully grounded. Nothing more is required for holding a man accountable than his acting with the consent of his will, however much his will may be determined by nature or nurture.

3. Salvation is offered to all who hear the gospel of the Lord Jesus Christ: 'For God so loved the world, that he gave his only begotten Son, that whosoever believeth in him should not perish, but have everlasting life' (*John* 3:16). Yet we are so inclined to evil that, of ourselves, we reject God's merciful offer.

Jesus remarked, 'No one can come to me, except the Father which hath sent me draw him' (*John* 6:44). Only the almighty operation of the Holy Spirit can change our sinful hearts. 'Except a man be born of water and of the Spirit, he cannot enter the kingdom of God' (*John* 3:5). This is a free gift of grace, entirely unmerited by us. 'By grace are ye saved through faith; and that not of yourselves: it is the gift of God: not of works, lest any man should boast' (*Eph.* 2:8–9). And, 'For it is God which worketh in you both to will and to do of his good pleasure' (*Phil.* 2:13).

The Holy Spirit does not work faith in everyone. Not all but many, 'a great multitude which no man can number, of all nations, and kindreds, and people, and tongues' (*Rev.* 7:9) – the elect, are thus saved: 'He hath chosen us in him before the foundation of the world, that we should be holy and without blame before him in love: Having predestinated us unto the adoption of children by Jesus Christ to himself, according to the good pleasure of his will' (*Eph.* 1:4–5). 'And as many as were ordained to eternal life believed' (*Acts* 13:48).

Some Christians argue that such election is based on human-generated faith, which God merely foresees ahead of time. One difficulty with this explanation is that it implies that God does not fully foreordain the future. As we noted before, God's sovereignty entails that all that happens occurs in accordance with God's eternal decree. Hence, if God foresees our faith, this requires that he has also chosen the world to be such that our faith would come about. Out of all possible universes, God chose that one in which the elect consist precisely of those whom he wanted to be saved.

God could have created each human to have such a character and such experiences that the elect – and only the elect – would of their own free will choose to believe in Jesus Christ. In such a plan, salvation would then depend *both* on God's sovereign decree of election and on human choices. It is clear from the Bible, however, that this is *not* how the elect are saved. As we noted above, the special and powerful operation of the Holy Spirit is needed to bring even the elect to faith.

4. One may object that this is unjust. How can God blame us if our actions are the inevitable consequences of the heart and nature he has given us? This question is addressed in Romans 9:

> What shall we say then? Is there unrighteousness with God? God forbid. For he saith to Moses, I will have mercy upon whom I will have mercy, and I will have compassion on whom I will have compassion. So then it is not of him that willeth, nor of him that

runneth, but of God that sheweth mercy . . . Thou wilt say then unto me, Why doth he yet find fault? For who hath resisted his will? Nay but, O man, who art thou that repliest against God? Shall the thing formed say to him that formed it, Why hast thou made me thus? Hath not the potter power over the clay, of the same lump to make one vessel unto honour, and another unto dishonour? What if God, willing to shew his wrath, and to make his power known, endured with much longsuffering the vessels of wrath fitted to destruction: and that he might make known the riches of his glory on the vessels of mercy? (*Rom.* 9:14–23).

We are responsible to God because he is the Creator and we are his creatures. The potter has the authority to make of the clay what he wills. Responsibility entails accounting for our actions to a higher authority. The ultimate authority is God. God is responsible only to himself. Responsibility is what it is because of the power and authority of God. God's will sets the final standards for morality and justice. Who are we to argue with God?

One might ask, if election is not based on human faith or works, on what basis does God choose his elect? To answer this question we can go no further than the words of God to his ancient people: he set his love upon them and chose them simply 'because the LORD loved' them (*Deut.* 7:7–8). God's electing love is free, sovereign, unconditional. It is not drawn forth because of anything good or desirable in the object of that love. That is why the Apostle Paul quotes the Lord's words to Moses, 'I will have mercy upon whom I will have mercy, and I will have compassion on whom I will have compassion.'

The Problem of Evil

The main reason unbelievers give for rejecting Christianity is the problem of pain and suffering. It is often argued that, if God is all-loving he *would want* to stop all pain; if he were all-powerful he *could* stop the pain; yet there is pain in the world; hence, God must be lacking in either love or power.

Process theologians assert that God does not have the power to destroy evil. He just persuades, but never coerces. Since this solution to the problem of evil denies God's sovereignty, it is not a viable Christian option.

Similarly, the (libertarian) free-will defence of Alvin Plantinga and others posits that, since God has left us free, evil is not in his control. However, as we noted s earlier, since libertarian free will calls for indeterminism, this removes the responsibility for evil from man. The responsibility is then shifted either to uncaused chance, which denies God's sovereignty, or to God as the primary and only cause, which makes God directly responsible for our evil decisions. Either option is biblically unacceptable.

What does the Bible tell us about the existence of evil? We note first that, in the Bible, evil is the opposite of good. Evil has a broader meaning than sin. *Physical* evil refers to pain and suffering; *moral* evil refers to sinful thoughts, words and actions.

The world was created good: 'And God saw everything that he had made, and behold, it was very good' (*Gen.* 1:31). Moral evil entered our world through the fall into sin of Adam and Eve. God punished them by introducing pain, sorrow and death; he also cursed the ground (*Gen.* 3:16–19). Much pain and suffering is clearly due to the moral evil of human selfishness and wickedness. Other physical evils may come in the form of droughts, plagues and other natural disasters that are due to the curse on nature.

Eventually, Christ will completely conquer evil, so that pain, sorrow and death will be no more (*Rev.* 21: 4). Meanwhile, God uses physical evil to punish wickedness (*Amos* 3:6), to chastise sinners (*Heb.* 12:5–7), to deepen our faith (*James* 1:2–4) and to prepare us for glory (*2 Cor.* 4:17).

Nothing happens that is not foreordained by God as part of his plan. God is the ultimate cause of all that happens. This includes physical evil. God proclaims, 'I form the light, and create darkness: I make peace, and create evil: I the LORD do all these things' (*Isa.* 45:7). 'Shall there be evil in a city and the LORD has not done it?'

(*Amos* 3:6). 'The LORD has made all things for himself; yea even the wicked for the day of evil' (*Prov.* 16:4).

Nevertheless, God is not responsible for moral evil; he is not the *author* of sin. God himself does not sin. God is wholly good: 'A God of truth and without iniquity, just and right is he' (*Deut.* 32:4). Nor does God himself tempt anyone: 'God cannot be tempted with evil, neither tempteth he any man' (*James* 1:13).

The sin that God has foreordained all comes to pass through secondary causes. 'But every man is tempted, when he is drawn away of his own lust, and enticed' (*James* 1:14). The moral responsibility of sin remains with those who actually *do* the sin. Man is held accountable for his own voluntary choices, however predictable they may be. Man is directly responsible for his sins and their consequences of pain and suffering.

Adam and Eve were enticed by Satan. How did Satan acquire his wickedness? We are told of the devil: 'He was a murderer from the beginning, and abode not in the truth, because there was no truth in him. When he speaketh a lie, he speaketh of his own: for he is a liar, and the father of it' (*John* 8:44).

Calvin notes that the words 'abode not in the truth' imply that Satan was once in the truth (*Institutes* I.xiv.16). He was created a good angel but fell into sin. His initial sin seems to have been pride (see *1 Tim.* 3:6). The descriptions of the kings of Babylon (*Isa.* 14:12–15) and Tyre (*Ezek.* 28:11–19) seem to symbolize Satan, at least to some extent. We infer that Satan wanted to be like God. How did Satan come to be tempted? The above words, 'when he speaketh a lie, he speaketh of his own', suggest that Satan's depraved nature originated wholly from within himself. Satan is held fully responsible for his wilful rebellion, even though God had created Satan as he was, knowing that Satan's nature and circumstances would lead to his fall. God, evidently, had created Satan good but with the potential to fall. The details of Satan's fall have, however, not been revealed to us.

One might ask why God made a world where evil was inevitable. Would it not have been better for him to create a perfect world – like the future heaven – from the start? The elect, to be sure, are amply rewarded for their suffering. But, one might wonder, if God is so merciful, why are all people not among the elect?

This question is all the more pressing in the light of passages such as *1 Tim.* 2:4 that indicate that God desires the salvation of all men. What restrains God's desire to save all men? Libertarians might reply that it is God's higher commitment to human self-determination, with its implications for deepening the relationship between God and man. A compatibilist response is given by the theologian John Piper:

> My answer to the question about what restrains God's will to save all people is this: it is God's supreme commitment to uphold and display the full range of his glory through the sovereign demonstration of all his perfections, including his wrath and mercy, for the enjoyment of his chosen and believing people . . . This everlasting and ever-increasing joy of God's people in all of God's perfections is the shining forth of God's glory, which was his main aim in creation and redemption (Piper 2000:339).

Thus, although God has compassion for all men, his commitment to the glorification of his sovereign grace restrains him to save only those whom he chose to be his elect.

God has a morally sufficient reason for everything he does, including all the suffering and evil that he foreordains. 'We know that all things work together for good to them that love God, to them who are the called according to his purpose' (*Rom.* 8:28). Since God himself is good and righteous we may be assured that God's purposes will be fulfilled in goodness and righteousness. As the Reformed theologian Robert Reymond suggests,

> The ultimate end which God decreed he regarded as great and glorious enough that it justified to himself both the divine plan itself and the ordained incidental evil arising along the foreordained path to his plan's great and glorious end (1998:377).

The ultimate end of all things is the comprehensive glorification of God himself in his righteous judgments against his enemies, and his great mercy and grace to his people through Jesus Christ.

This answer may not satisfy worldly conceptions of responsibility and justice. Critics may say that the problem of pain shows that the Christian worldview is inconsistent. However, to demonstrate inconsistency in any worldview one must use the presuppositions and definitions of that worldview. In this case, then, one must use biblical definitions of love, goodness, responsibility, justice, evil and so on. By such definitions, as we have shown, there is no contradiction. Contradictions occur only when humanistic notions are imposed on the Christian worldview.

The issues that we have discussed are very deep. Remaining questions we must leave unanswered, since they ultimately concern matters of the hidden will of God, into which we may not pry. Here we must refrain from vain speculation and humbly abide by the wise words of the Belgic Confession (1561; revised 1619) in its discussion of God's providence and the existence of evil:

> Nothing happens in this world without His appointment; nevertheless, God neither is the author of, nor can be charged with, the sins which are committed . . . And as to what He does surpassing human understanding, we will not curiously inquire into it further than our capacity will admit of; but with the greatest humility and reverence adore the righteous judgments of God, which are hid from us, contenting ourselves that we are pupils of Christ, to learn only those things which He has revealed to us in His Word, without transgressing those limits (Art. 13).

Conclusions

In conclusion, a libertarian view of free will entails that our decisions are not fully caused. This defeats, rather than supports, the notions of human choice and responsibility. To the extent that it leaves our decisions to the primary causation of God, it makes God directly responsible for our evil decisions.

On the other hand, a compatibilist view of human freedom stresses that we wilfully make our decisions for sufficient reasons, in accordance with our nature, beliefs and desires. Since this is so, God, our Creator and Sustainer, who knows us completely, can fully predict all our decisions and actions. The Bible teaches that we are fully accountable for what we knowingly will and do. Although God foreordains everything that occurs, humans are responsible for the evil that they do.

13

Body and Soul

When you die, you're not going to be surprised, because you're going to be completely dead. Now if I find myself aware after I'm dead, I'm going to be really surprised! But at least I'm going to go to hell, where I won't have all of those grinning preachers from Sunday morning listening . . . Let me summarize my views on what modern evolutionary biology tells us loud and clear . . . There are no gods, no purposes, and no goal-directed forces of any kind. There is no life after death. When I die, I am absolutely certain that I am going to be dead. That's the end of me. There is no ultimate foundation for ethics, no ultimate meaning in life, and no free will for humans, either . . . Christian humanism has a great deal going for it. It's warm and kindly in many ways. That's the good part. The bad part is that you have to suspend your rational mind. That part is really nasty. Atheistic humanism has the advantage of fitting natural minds trying to understand the world . . . Since we know that we are not going to live after we die, there is no reward for suffering in this world. You live and you die.

WILLIAM PROVINE (*Darwinism: Science or Naturalistic Philosophy?* 1994:9)

* * * * *

Verily, verily, I say unto you, He that heareth my word, and believeth on him that sent me, hath everlasting life, and shall not come into condemnation; but is passed from death unto life . . . Marvel not at this: for the hour is coming, in the which all that are in the graves shall hear his voice, and shall come forth; they that have done good, unto the resurrection of life; and they that have done evil, unto the resurrection of damnation.

JOHN 5:24, 28–29

Benjamin Franklin said, 'In this world, nothing can be said to be certain except death and taxes.' Death is unavoidable. We must all come to terms with the fact that, sooner or later, we shall die. The natural question that arises is: What then? What happens after death? Is there life after death? Or not? Few questions are of greater significance. As Blaise Pascal remarks,

> The immortality of the soul is of such vital importance to us and affects us so deeply that we must have lost our wits if we no longer care about it. All our actions and thoughts will follow different paths, according to whether there is hope of eternal blessing (Pascal:120).

One path we examined was that of naturalism. We saw that naturalism has great difficulty with the notion of an immaterial soul or mind. If man evolved solely from matter, how can he ever acquire an immaterial soul? If mind evolved from purposeless matter, then mind must ultimately be explicable solely in terms of neuro-physiological activities. Such a matter-based mind or soul could not survive bodily death. That is the inevitable conclusion drawn by the materialist historian of science, William Provine, in the above quote. For him there is no hope of everlasting life. The path of naturalism leads, quite literally, to a dead end.

The path of Christianity, on the other hand, leads to eternal life. Biblical Christianity views humans as consisting of two distinct substances: a material body united with an immaterial soul. Christianity stresses the importance of our soul and its proper relation to God. The soul is vital to spiritual life. It survives physical death. Ultimately the soul of the Christian is rejoined with his (renewed and transformed) body, when he receives his eternal reward.

In our day, mind-body dualism is widely thought to be scientifically untenable. Even many Christian philosophers and scientists assert that the human soul is just a complex property of the body and, as such, cannot exist apart from it.

In this chapter we shall examine the relation between body, mind and soul. What is the soul? How is it related to the mind? How are both related to the body? What does the Bible have to say on these issues? Is an immaterial soul essential to Christianity? How strong are the objections against mind-body dualism? Questions such as these will be our prime concern.

What is the Soul?

What is the soul? Aristotle, in *De Anima (i.e., On The Soul)*, distinguished between three aspects of the soul: the *zoe* (the property of life, which included plants and animals), the *psuche* (a sensitive awareness, which is shared by animals and humans) and the *pneuma* (the rational mind, which only humans have). Similar distinctions were made by Augustine and Thomas Aquinas (1225–74). Aquinas viewed the soul as a substance present in *any* living organism, whether human, dog, or simple one-cell life. The Thomistic soul is a self that directs the formation of the body and mind as the organism grows. The soul gives purpose and direction to the developing body. This concept of the soul is promoted also by the Christian scholars J. P. Moreland and Scott Rae (2000:201). In this view, the soul is present in the body at the point of conception.

John Calvin defined the soul to be the essence of a person. It was the proper seat of God's image in man. To Calvin, the soul is an immaterial substance, dwelling in the body but separable from it. The soul has various powers, the two most basic ones being the power to understand and the power to will (Calvin, *Institutes* I.xxv.7).

René Descartes reduced the human soul to the mind, identifying the person with a purely conscious substance. He considered the human body to be a machine controlled by an immaterial spirit, much as a captain steers a ship. Because animals did not speak, although they have the physical means to do so, Descartes believed that animals lacked souls. Consequently, he considered animals to be physical automata, without any actual feelings or experiences. Most pet-owners would probably disagree with Descartes. One wonders whether Descartes ever walked with a dog or befriended a horse. That he played with machines is well-known. Descartes was so enthused about mechanical life that he acquired a human-like machine, a female robot he called 'Franchina', who sometimes accompanied him on his travels (Herbert 1993:111).

Body and Soul in the Bible

The broader view of Augustine and Aquinas is more in line with the Bible's conception of soul/spirit than is the more limited notion of Descartes. The pertinent biblical words are *nephesh* (Hebrew) and *psuche* (Greek), which are generally translated in English as *soul;* and *ruach* (Hebrew) and *pneuma* (Greek), which are usually translated as *spirit*. In the Bible, *soul* and *spirit* are often used interchangeably.

The Bible tells us that God, the ultimate person, is a Spirit (*pneuma: John* 4:24), a non-material reality. In the beginning, the Spirit (*ruach*) of God moved upon the face of the waters (*Gen.* 1:2). Similarly, angels and demons (fallen angels) are persons who are spirits (*ruach* or *pneuma*). Angels are said to be 'ministering spirits' (*Heb.* 1:14). There are also the 'spirits of devils' (*Rev.* 16:14). Thus it is evident that persons can exist without physical bodies, as immaterial spirits.

Such spirits can relate with bodies. For example, God and angels can take on physical forms (*Gen.* 18; *Gen.* 19:1). Demons can dwell in human bodies ('the evil spirits went out of them', *Acts* 19:12), as well as in swine (*Matt.* 8:28–32). Further, the fact that Satan and his angels were expelled from heaven – 'Neither was their place found any more in heaven' (*Rev.* 12:8) – implies that spirits occupy a spatial position, albeit in the spiritual realm that transcends our physical universe. Spirits, then, are immaterial persons that occupy space and can be embodied.

With respect to the creation of Adam, the Bible teaches that his spirit was added to flesh and bones to form a living person: 'And the LORD God formed man out of the dust of the ground, and breathed into his nostrils the breath of life (*ruach*); and man became a living soul (*nephesh*)' (*Gen.* 2:7; see also *Ezek.* 37:1–10).

The 'breath of life' (*ruach*) given to Adam is found also in animals: 'And they went in unto Noah into the ark, two and two of all flesh, wherein is the breath of life (*ruach*)' (*Gen.* 7:15). Similarly, *nephesh*, the word for soul, is also translated as 'life' and applies to animals: 'And to every beast of the earth, and to every fowl of the air, and to every thing that creepeth upon the earth, wherein is life (*nephesh*), I have given every green herb for meat' (*Gen.* 1:30). Thus animals, too, are said to have a soul or spirit.

How do human souls differ from those of animals and plants? As Augustine notes, human souls are surely more complex and intelligent. We alone are formed in the image of God. Since we are made in the image of God, the properties most important for understanding our personhood are those we have in common with God. These include such things as the conscious self, rationality, creativity, knowledge, righteousness, and holiness, limited as these may be for humans.

HUMAN SOULS SURVIVE DEATH

What happens to man when he dies? At that point his soul is separated from his body: 'Then shall the dust return to the earth as it was: and the spirit (*ruach*) shall return unto God who gave it' (*Eccles.* 12:7). The body dies and disintegrates; the spirit returns to God.

That the soul or spirit survives physical death is indicated in various other biblical texts. We are told, for example, 'Fear not them which kill the body, but are not able to kill the soul (*psuche*)' (*Matt.* 10:28). Christ, when he died, was still alive in the spirit – 'being put to death in the flesh, but quickened by [or 'in'] the Spirit [or 'spirit'] (*pneuma*): by which he also went and preached unto the spirits in prison' (*1 Pet.* 3:18–19). Jesus' words to the thief on the cross, 'Today shalt thou be with me in paradise' (*Luke* 23:43), imply that the thief was to be with Jesus in the intermediate, spiritual state after their physical deaths. Paul says that to be absent from the body is to be present with Christ (*2 Cor.* 5:1–10; *Phil.* 1:21–24), intimating that the spirit can exist separate from the body. The intermediate state (between death and resurrection) is a state in which believers enjoy a conscious communion with God (*Luke* 16:19–31; *1 Thess.* 5:10; *Rev.* 6:9; 7:9; 20:4).

In line with these texts, the Reformed creeds teach that at death the soul is separated from the body, to be re-united to it at the last judgment:

> For all the dead shall be raised out of the earth, and their souls joined and united with their proper bodies in which they formerly lived (*Belgic Confession, Article 37*).

> QUESTION. What comfort does *the resurrection of the body* afford you?
> ANSWER. That not only my soul, after this life, shall immediately be taken up to Christ, its head [Luke 16:22; 23:43; Philippians 1:21, 23]; but also my body, raised by the power of Christ, shall again be united with my soul, and made like unto the glorious body of Christ [Job 19: 25, 26; 1 John 3:2; Philippians 3:21] (*Heidelberg Catechism, Lord's Day 22; Question & Answer 57*).

> The bodies of men, after death, return to dust, and see corruption: but their souls, which neither die nor sleep, having an immortal substance, immediately return to God who gave them: the souls of the righteous ... are received into the highest heavens . . . And the souls of the wicked are cast into hell . . . Besides these two places, for souls separated from their bodies, the Scripture acknowledgeth none (*Westminster Confession* xxxii:1).

A further difference between human souls and animal souls is that animal souls do not seem to survive physical death. At least, that is the implication of the text: 'All are of the dust and return to dust again. Who knoweth the spirit of man that goeth upward, and the spirit of the beast that goeth downward to the earth?' (*Eccles.* 3:20–21).

Since the spirit survives bodily death, it cannot be identified with the body. Nevertheless, the biblical view of man indicates a strong connection between the body and the immaterial spirit. In our earthly life, the two are integrally united into a living soul. The separation of human body and soul is unnatural. Although separation occurs at death, when the soul continues alone, the soul is ultimately to be re-united with a renewed body.

In short, the Bible teaches that humans have a dual nature, consisting of a physical body and an immaterial soul. For elaboration on the biblical teaching of the duality of body and soul the reader is referred to J. P. Moreland and Scott B. Rae, *Body and Soul* (2000) and John W. Cooper, *Body, Soul and Life Everlasting* (1989).

Body, Mind and Common Sense

The biblical position supports the common-sense view that most people hold: body and mind are separate entities, closely connected yet distinct. This fits in well with our previous conclusion that mental properties are quite distinct from physical properties. The former are subjective, the latter objective; the former are controlled by logical and moral 'oughts', the latter by the laws of physics. Since they differ in *kind*, mental events cannot be reduced to physical events. Our minds cannot be just a complex property of our body. It follows that the mind must derive from some non-material source. In short, reality consists of more than material things. There must be room also for mind.

Clearly, mind and body are intimately related. Physical events can cause mental events (*e.g.*, a blow to my head causes me pain). Conversely, mental events can cause physical events (*e.g.*, I decide to write down a mathematical equation). This is called *interactive* dualism. Our *mind* is that aspect of our person involved in mental events. Our mind is controlled by our inner self, which unifies all our mental experiences. The physical aspect of our person we refer to as our *body*. These two together function as our integrated person. This is the common sense view of mind, body and person.

Do You Need a Soul?

Many Christians, particularly scientists and philosophers, while believing that God is spirit, hold that man is wholly physical. They assert that man's soul has no special substance of its own. Man's soul is no more than a complex property of his body. This is the view promoted by physicist and neuroscientist Donald MacKay (1979), Arthur Peacocke, and others. William Dembski (1990:215) refers to this view as *semi-materialism*, seeing that in many respects it is closely related to materialism.

Aside from the materialist difficulties already discussed in previous chapters, semi-materialism faces additional theological problems. The chief concern is how to account for the survival of the soul after the body dies. If the soul is merely a function of the brain, then the death of the brain seems to entail also the death of the soul. Such a conclusion contradicts the above biblical passages that assert the continued existence of the soul.

Most semi-materialists hold that at death man ceases to exist until he is resurrected with a new, transformed body. However, the extinction of the person at death raises questions about his future resurrection. If, on the day of judgment, God re-creates a person with all my characteristics and memories, can this be said to be me? Or is it just a *copy* of me? In principle, two such identical persons could be resurrected. Which is the real continuation of myself? The only plausible solution is to say that both are copies. It seems that, without the *continued* existence of my soul, my personal, subjective identity is lost. My resurrection at some future time then becomes problematic.

Some semi-materialists, such as William Hasker, concede that, in order to safeguard eternal life, it is essential that the 'core person' survives bodily death and continues in existence (Hasker 1983:80). How could that be done? Hasker notes that a physical device may generate a magnetic field distinct from the device. Likewise, he suggests, the complex functioning of the human brain may produce a 'soul-field' distinct from the brain (Hasker 1983:73). This soul-field may influence the brain. Once the brain dies, Hasker argues, the soul-field might become self-sustaining. Or, perhaps, God could arrange to sustain it by other means, perhaps by assigning it to a new body.

All of this is, of course, highly speculative. It is certainly not clear how the soul-field, derived from purely physical interactions, can itself be anything other than a purely physical entity. How does it become a personal, unifying self that feels, desires, and makes moral choices? Hasker gives no detailed argumentation as to how the soul-field can transcend physical properties. Nor does he give any rationale for the soul-field becoming self-sustaining at, or before, the death of the brain. Even if the soul-field could continue to exist, it would remain a purely physical entity. It would be incapable of leaving the earthly realm for the spiritual dwelling place of God, the place of the departed souls.

What about Hasker's suggestion that God sustains the soul-field by assigning it to a new body? The need for the continued existence of the soul demands that the new body would have to be assigned immediately when and where the old body dies. This has never been observed to happen.

In sum, semi-materialism offers no plausible account of the continued existence of the human soul after bodily death. Hence William Dembski finds it unsurprising that theologian John Stott, who had endorsed MacKay's materialist view on the soul, later promoted the notion that, at the end of the age, the unrighteous will not suffer eternal torment but, rather, will be simply annihilated. Dembski charges that Stott's annihilationism is a logical consequence of his semi-materialism (Dembski 1990:218).

Probing an Immaterial Mind

Interactive mind-body dualism is, we have argued, the view of both the Bible and common sense. Why, then, do so many Christian scholars today reject it? The main reason is that interactive dualism is widely thought to suffer from fatal deficiencies. Let us briefly look at some of the objections that have been voiced.

HOW DO MINDS OPERATE?

A common objection against mind-body dualism is that it is not clear how two distinct substances can possibly interact. How can mind and matter influence each other if they are two totally different substances? How can mental choices, governed by moral oughts, influence the physical body, governed by physical laws? Conversely, how can bodily activities generate conscious experiences?

We note, first, that this is no less a problem for materialism. In Chapter 6 we saw the great difficulty materialism had in accounting for conscious experiences and an active mind. As we already noted, physical properties cannot be merely different descriptions of mental properties, for physical laws are quite distinct from logical and moral laws.

Even if we were to consider mental properties to be of an ultimately physical nature, mental physical properties would still be so unlike non-mental physical properties that we would still be faced with the problem of how they interact. Hence, simply *calling* mind a special form or property of matter solves nothing. It just rephrases the question, rather than answering it.

A quite different resolution of the mind-body problem is to reduce matter to a property of mind. This is the *idealism* of the Irish philosopher George Berkeley (1685–1753). Berkeley, attacking the materialism of his day, denied the real existence of matter. He asserted that there exist only minds and ideas. All we really know about physical objects is the sense impressions they make on our minds. Berkeley argued that the physical universe existed not in itself, but only by its presence in the divine mind. God impresses the ideas of the physical world on to our minds. God ensures the consistency and uniformity of our ideas about the physical world. Thus Berkeley solved the mind-body interaction problem by reducing matter to a particular type of idea.

This ingenious philosophy seems contrary to our common experiences of the world. Our world seems to have a real, concrete existence. The English writer Samuel Johnson (1709–1784), upon learning of Berkeley's theory, is said to have kicked a rock along the street, saying as he did so, 'Thus I refute you!' But Berkeley's philosophy is not that easily refuted by either logic or experience. After all, Berkeley does not deny that we can have *experiences* of heartily booting solid stones. His point is that what we actually experience are only our mental sense impressions of rocks, never the actual rocks themselves.

Berkeley's philosophy has the merit of stressing the dependence of the material world on God for its continued existence. God indeed upholds all things 'by the word of his power' (*Heb.* 1:3). Perhaps the word 'word' does here convey the notion of an idea. Yet, if so, it must be a very special type of idea. God's creation of the world entails that, unlike other ideas, these are actualized ideas, existing in concrete form before the existence of man. We must then distinguish between *abstract* ideas and *actualized*, material ideas. This, however, brings us back to two different types of entities, or ideas, and the question of how they interact. Therefore, Berkeley's proposed solution, too, merely rephrases the problem.

It is not only mind-matter interactions that are puzzling. As we saw in earlier chapters, many matter-matter interactions are no less mysterious. Think of the action-at-a-distance of gravity or the unpredictability of atomic physics. We saw that, ultimately, physical laws are not *prescriptive* of what must happen but simply *descriptive* of what does happen. Why, then, should we not treat mind-body connections in the same manner? Our experienced mind-body interactions are no less descriptive of what does in fact happen, regardless of whether we can comprehend the underlying mechanism.

One might object that, unlike physical interactions, mind-body interactions involve two distinct substances that have nothing in common. However, even physical interactions can involve very different types of things. For example, the solid earth, with its specific shape and concrete properties, seems quite distinct from the invisible, all-pervasive gravitational field that it is thought to generate. Similarly, the probability wave of an electron differs greatly from the actual electron particle that eventually hits a photographic plate. Moreover, the principle of causality asserts only that every event has a sufficient cause. It does not insist that the cause be similar in substance to the effect. That is merely a materialist presupposition.

That spirit *can* influence matter is clear when we recall that God, a spirit, created the entire universe – matter and spirit – and continues to uphold it at each instant. He does so by his *Word* of power. Matter's very existence depends on a mind-matter causal relationship. Mind is therefore more fundamental than matter.

Could the God-world interaction serve as a model for the human mind-body interaction? The similarity between the two suggests a close link between theism and mind-body dualism. Indeed, many contemporary philosophers reject dualism precisely because of its perceived connection to theism. Nevertheless, this analogy should not be pressed too hard. Our mind is, at least in its present state, strongly dependent upon our body, whereas God is in no way dependent on the physical world.

Theism does, however, provide a possible mechanism for mind-body interaction. At each instant God, in his providence, upholds both our body and mind by his Word of power. Normally, barring miracles, the universe at the next instant will be in accordance with the properties God has assigned his creatures. One of these human properties is our mental control of our bodies. Hence, God, as the primary cause of all events, could cause our mental choices to be translated into physical effects. If God were to do this according to specific rules, it would be part of the normal functioning of his creation.

MINDING ENERGY

The most common objection against dualism is that it violates well-established physical laws, such as conservation of energy. This is often upheld as the decisive refutation of dualism. For example, materialist philosopher Mario Bunge asserts:

Dualism violates conservation of energy. If immaterial mind could move matter, then it would create energy; and if matter were to act on mind, then energy would disappear . . . Energy would fail to be conserved . . . and so physics, chemistry, biology, and economics would collapse. Faced with a choice between these 'hard' sciences and primitive superstition, we opt for the former . . . Dualism is consistent with creationism, not with evolutionism . . . A consistent evolutionist . . . will postulate that mental functions, no matter how exquisite, are neuro-physiological activities (Bunge 1980:17–18).

Similarly, philosopher Daniel Dennett writes:

Let us concentrate on the returned signals, the directives from mind to brain. These, *ex hypothesi*, are not physical . . . How, then, do they get to make a difference to what happens in the brain cells they must effect, if the mind is to have any influence on the body? A fundamental principle of physics is that any change in the trajectory of any physical entity is an acceleration requiring the expenditure of energy, and where is this energy to come from? It is this principle of conservation of energy that accounts for the impossibility of 'perpetual motion machines', and the same principle is apparently violated by dualism. This . . . is widely regarded as the inescapable and fatal flaw of dualism (1991:35).

How well-founded is this criticism of mind-body dualism? First of all, it is not clear that mental decisions do require any exchange of energy. For all we know, the implementation of a mental choice may be similar to opening or closing a frictionless switch in an electric circuit. This need not require any energy. Even if it did, chaotic effects might be used to amplify the initial mental signal, so that the initial energy required might be infinitesimally small or, at least, smaller than can be measured within quantum limits. A complicated mind-brain model, relying on quantum mechanics and obeying conservation of energy, has been developed by neuroscientist Sir John Eccles. Eccles optimistically concludes:

It is reassuring that all the richness and enjoyment of our experiences can now be accepted without any qualms of conscience that we may be infringing conservation laws (Eccles 1994:170).

It needs to be emphasized here that Eccles' model is very speculative and is by no means widely accepted. Nevertheless, Eccles'
model does suggest that energy concerns need not be a problem.

A further consideration is that the principle of conservation of
energy is thus far based on our observations of purely physical interactions. In the past, the definition of energy has been broadened
to accommodate new discoveries. For example, to balance the
energy equation, matter is now considered to be a form of energy.
In a similar fashion, it may be possible that our conception of
energy may have to be modified to accommodate mind-body
interactions. No sufficiently precise measurements have as yet been
made to determine whether or not conservation of energy applies
to mind-body interactions.

Finally, it must be kept in mind that the notion of conservation
of energy is itself a theoretical product of our mind. It is an extra-
polation of our limited experiences of purely physical interactions.
It presumes, for example, that induction is valid. The universality
of energy conservation is thus no more than a metaphysical assumption. Is it not absurd, then, that a product of our creative
mind should rule out the activity of the mind that constructed it
in the first place? The reality of mind-body interactions is one of
our most basic, direct conscious experiences. The task of our
scientific theories should be to *explain* these experiences, not to
dismiss them. Hence, were it to be the case that mind-body interactions *do* contravene energy conservation, we could infer from
this only that energy conservation is a limited physical concept
that does not apply to mind-body interactions.

WHERE IS YOUR MIND?

A further question raised by dualism is *where* the interaction takes
place. Where is the seat of the soul? Which part of the body turns
mental causes into physical effects?

The point of effective mind-body contact seems clearly to be
somewhere in the brain. But precisely where? Descartes thought
that the pineal gland was the place where the mind interacted

with the body. Other candidates that have been suggested are the pre-frontal lobe of the dominant hemisphere of the brain (Sir John Eccles), the upper brain stem (Wilder Penfield), and the hippocampus. Sir Francis Crick and Christof Koch (1992:158) suggest that consciousness is a process that is distributed over the neocortex.

We can answer only that, even if it were to remain a mystery *where* and *how* the mind interacts with the brain, *that* the mind *does* interact with the brain is undeniable.

WHO MADE YOUR SOUL?

One final puzzle is the question of where human souls come from. That Adam's soul came directly from God seems clear enough. But what about Adam's offspring?

This has been a subject of extensive debate among Christians. There are two basic views. The first is called *creationism*. It contends that the soul of each human being is directly created by God. Only the human body is transmitted from parents to their children. God unites the soul to the body at some point between conception and birth. Creationism is based on such texts as Genesis 2:7; Ecclesiastes 12:7; Isaiah 57:16 ('the souls that I have made'); and Zechariah 12:1 ('the LORD which . . . formeth the spirit of man within him'). This view is held by Roman Catholics and most Reformed theologians, including John Calvin and Louis Berkhof.

The opposing view is called *traducianism* (from the Latin *traducere*, which means 'to lead across' or 'propagate'). It holds that *both* body and soul are generated from human parents. Bible texts in its favour include Genesis 2:22 ('and the rib . . . made he into a woman'), which makes no mention of an extra soul added on by God; Romans 5:12 ('as by one man sin entered into the world, and death by sin; and so death passed upon all men, for that all have sinned'); and Hebrews 7:9–10 ('Levi also . . . payed tithes in Abraham. For he was yet in the loins of his father, when Melchisedec met him'). This view is supported, among many others, by Martin Luther, Gordon Clark, and Robert Reymond (1998:424).

One difficulty faced by creationism is that it allows for only a physical connection between Adam and his offspring. Yet elsewhere in Scripture it seems that parents transmit various aspects of character also. It is certainly our experience that children often have character traits that are remarkably similar to those of their parents. Yet, if God directly creates each human soul, how could mental or moral characteristics be propagated?

One particular problem for creationism is how Adam's sinful nature is passed on to his offspring. The Westminster Confession asserts that Adam's 'sin was imputed; and the same death in sin, and corrupted nature [were] conveyed to all [his] posterity descending from [him] by ordinary generation' (VI:3). Note the closing words *'by ordinary generation'*. This seems to favour traducianism. Creationism must postulate either that God immediately creates sinful souls or that the soul somehow becomes contaminated by the body.

Also, one wonders how animal souls are transmitted. It would seem plausible that the same general method of generation applies to both human and animal souls. Are we to believe, then, that God directly creates the soul of each dog, bird and bug? Or, if only human souls survive death, does this difference perhaps imply also a difference in the mode of generation?

One objection voiced against traducianism is that it seems to entail that Christ had a depraved human soul. However, this does not necessarily follow. Perhaps the sinful nature of the soul is passed on through only the father. In any case, the miraculous involvement of the Holy Spirit in Christ's conception adequately accounts for Christ's sinless soul.

Traducianism seems more plausible both with respect to the generation of animal souls and the transmission of human sinful nature. The biblical texts cited to support the divine creation of the human soul do not explicitly rule out secondary causes. Nevertheless, traducianism still leaves unanswered the question of *how* an immaterial soul can generate souls for its offspring.

Perhaps the solution is to be found in the same direction as that of mind-body interaction. If God can correlate our mental choices with our bodily actions, he can likewise assure, once specific physical conditions exist (*e.g.*, a fertilized egg), the creation of a soul with properties corresponding to those of its parents. Were this to occur according to specific rules, it would be part of the normal functioning of the world as decreed by God. In this manner souls could be directly created by God while, at the same time, transmitting hereditary properties.

Conclusions

In conclusion, the Bible teaches that we consist of body and spirit. Our spirit survives physical death and is re-united with its renewed body at the final judgment.

Materialist theories of soul are theologically objectionable because they cannot account for the soul's survival of physical death or for the continuance of our identity in a future embodied life. Objections against mind-body dualism, on the grounds that it violates causality and physical laws, were found to be unjustified.

As to questions of how and where the mind and body interact, or how new souls are generated, these remain largely unanswered.

14

A Christian View of Mathematics

CROSSFIRE

Whereas the quarrel about universals and ontology *had* its meaning and significance within the context of medieval Christian culture, it is an intellectual scandal that some philosophers of mathematics can still discuss whether whole numbers exist or not . . . No, there are no preordained, predetermined mathematical 'truths' that just lie out or up there. Evolutionary thinking teaches us otherwise.

YEHUDA RAV (*Math Worlds* 1993:81,100)

* * * * *

Doth not wisdom cry? . . . Unto you, O men, I call . . . For my mouth shall speak truth . . . I wisdom dwell with prudence, and find out knowledge of witty inventions . . . I am understanding . . . Those that seek me early shall find me . . . The LORD possessed me in the beginning of his way, before his works of old. I was set up from everlasting, from the beginning, or ever the earth was . . . When he prepared the heavens, I was there: when he set a compass upon the face of the depth . . . For whoso findeth me findeth life, and shall obtain favour of the LORD.

PROVERBS 8

What does mathematics have to do with God? A few years ago, when travelling through the Czech Republic, my wife and I lodged at an inn run by a local retired engineer. In the evening we joined him for a cup of coffee. He asked what my profession was. I told him I was a mathematics professor. Later the discussion turned towards religion. The engineer, like most Czechs we encountered, professed to be an atheist. When I related I was a Christian, he was amazed. 'How can you be a Christian if you are a mathematics professor?' he exclaimed. Evidently he thought that mathematics contradicted Christianity.

Most people probably believe that mathematics, if perhaps not hostile to Christianity, is at best neutral towards it. Even many Christians see little connection between God and mathematics. Indeed, mathematics is often considered to be the most difficult subject to integrate with Christianity.

Earlier, in Chapter 8, we saw, however, that mathematics needs God. The naturalist mathematician Yehuda Rav, in the opening quote, notes that within the context of Christianity it makes sense to talk about the objective existence of numbers and mathematical truths. However, once God is removed, there is nowhere to place abstract mathematical concepts and nobody to guarantee their truthfulness. Mathematics is then reduced to a mere human invention, which need not be true. Consequently, the erstwhile certainty of mathematics is forever shattered.

Against this, we supported the view called mathematical *realism*, which contends that mathematics does exist beyond mere human minds. Augustine, we saw, placed mathematics in the mind of God. This led to the classical Christian view of mathematics, which considered mathematics in terms of what an all-powerful, all-knowing God could do.

The goal of this chapter is to examine more closely the rich interplay between mathematics and Christianity. We shall consider in detail how mathematics fits within a Christian worldview. How does God relate to mathematics? Are mathematical laws *necessary* truths? If so, do they not present a challenge to God's sovereignty?

Can a Christian worldview provide a solid basis for believing that our current human mathematics is objectively true?

God and Math

How does God relate to mathematics? We consider first how God relates to logic. Note that the Bible frequently uses logical arguments. In fact, logic is indispensable in reading the Bible. The central biblical message, for example, is the good news of salvation – not its opposite. Furthermore, the Bible claims to be true ('Thy word is truth', *John* 17:17), not false. It follows that a major principle of biblical interpretation is that the Bible does not contradict itself. All of this presumes the validity of the laws of logic. Since the Bible is 'God-breathed' (*2 Tim.* 3:16) or 'inspired', this points to God as the guarantor of logic.

Further, the Bible contains numerous examples of elementary mathematics. It has many simple arithmetical calculations. The Bible depicts God as performing various mathematical operations. For example, 'He telleth the number of the stars; he calleth them all by their names' (*Psa.* 147:4) and, 'The very hairs of your head are all numbered' (*Matt.* 10:30). Further, Isaiah asks:

> Who hath measured the waters in the hollow of his hand, and meted out heaven with the span, and comprehended the dust of the earth in a measure, and weighed the mountains in scales, and the hills in a balance? (*Isa.* 40:12).

These passages, with their rich poetic metaphors, portray a God whose knowledge of his creation is very intimate and complete. It includes, as these passages indicate, detailed quantitative knowledge. *How* God knows such numerical things may well differ from how we acquire such knowledge. However, *that* the content of God's knowledge includes numerical data is indisputable.

Moreover, God has created the universe according to a rational plan that is, at least partially, comprehensible to man, God's steward. God has created the universe so that it has a mathematical structure. Thus God uses mathematics in both his spoken Word (*i.e.*, his works of creation) and his written Word.

The link between God and mathematics can be made stronger yet. It is evident that some aspects of God's character have a mathematical nature. Let's consider these.

God and Logic

Logic is closely related to God's character. The biblical God presents himself to us as a God of truth and faithfulness: 'God, that cannot lie' (*Titus* 1:2); 'The truth of the LORD endureth forever' (*Psa.* 117:2); 'Thy word is truth' (*John* 17:17). Since God's identity is eternally the same, the logical law of identity must be eternally valid. God is true, not false. God means what he says, not the opposite. Hence, the law of non-contradiction holds. Logic is not above God, but derives from God's constant and non-contradictory nature.

Reformed philosopher Gordon Clark notes, 'The law of contradiction is not to be taken as an axiom prior to or independent of God . . . the law is God thinking' (Clark 1968:67). Clark views truth and logic as attributes of God. Many other Christian thinkers concur. For example, philosopher Arthur Holmes states: 'A is not non-A . . . because God made it so, and because God Himself is God, and not non-God . . . It derives from God and his unchanging fidelity' (Holmes 1977:88).

In a similar vein, theologian John Frame writes:

> Does God, then, observe the law of non-contradiction? Not in the sense that this law is somehow higher than God himself. Rather, God is himself non-contradictory and is therefore himself the criterion of logical consistency and implication. Logic is an attribute of God, as are justice, mercy, wisdom, knowledge (Frame 1987: 253).

In short, the very nature of God implies the eternal validity of the basic laws of deductive logic (*i.e.*, the laws of non-contradiction, identity, and excluded middle).

Hence, in the Christian worldview, the laws of logic are universal because they reflect the nature and decree of the living God, who upholds the universe.

God and Number

Similar considerations hold regarding numbers. God's comprehensive knowledge includes all facts about the physical world, whether past, present or future. It includes also all human thoughts, all necessary truths, and even all possibilities. As such, God's knowledge surely embraces also all possible mathematical truths.

INFINITY

God's knowledge is infinite. This is proclaimed in such texts as, 'Great is our Lord, and of great power: his understanding is infinite' (*Psa.* 147:5). Here 'infinite' has the sense of 'boundless' or 'without number'. David exclaims: 'How precious also are thy thoughts unto me, O God! How great is the sum of them! If I should count them, they are more in number than the sand' (*Psa.* 139:17–18).

The concept of infinity is the key to the philosophy of mathematics. We can distinguish between *potential* infinity and *actual* infinity. *Potential* infinity is the notion of endlessness that arises from human counting. We soon realize that, given any large number, we can always obtain a yet larger one by adding 1 to it. There seems to be no largest number. Potentially, we can go on forever.

Actual infinity, on the other hand, is the notion that numbers exist as a totality, as a completed set. Plato believed in actual infinity; his student Aristotle held to only a potential infinity. Theological considerations led medieval philosophers to postulate an actual infinity. Today, however, humanism views actual infinity with suspicion.

Augustine considered actual infinity to be one of the mathematical entities that existed in God's mind. He wrote:

> Every number is known to him 'whose understanding cannot be numbered' (*Psalm* 147:5). Although the infinite series of numbers cannot be numbered, this infinity of numbers is not outside the comprehension of him 'whose understanding cannot be numbered'

... every infinity is, in a way we cannot express, made finite to God (Augustine, *City of God* xii, 19).

Since God knows all things possible, his knowledge must surely include also the totality of all possible numbers.

Note that an ideal, all-powerful and all-knowing mathematician would not need an eternity to count all the numbers. For example, at noon he starts with 'one', at 12:30 he counts 'two', at 12:40 'three', and so on. Number n is counted at time $1 - 1/n$. At 1 p.m. all the possible numbers would then be counted. The resultant set would contain an actual infinity of numbers. Of course, this is not how God acquires his knowledge of numbers. God's knowledge does not grow; it has always been complete. Yet this example shows that it is plausible for God to know the whole numbers as a completed, actual infinity.

Augustine's view regarding God's infinite knowledge was endorsed by the Russian-German mathematician Georg Cantor (1845–1918), one of the founders of modern set theory. Cantor believed that God's infinite knowledge implies an actual infinity of thoughts. It included, at the very least, the infinite set N of natural numbers $\{1, 2, 3 \dots\}$. Actual infinity could thus be considered to exist objectively as an actual, complete set in God's mind. Cantor believed that even larger transfinite numbers existed in God's mind (Dauben 1979:229).

The Trinity

Were numbers created by God? Many Christians believe that numbers were created either before, or along with, the physical universe. However, the role of number is much broader than its usage in the physical and mental worlds. Number is present not only in God's *knowledge* but also in his deepest being. The Bible presents God as consisting of *three* distinct Persons. Hence, as noted by mathematician-theologian Vern Poythress (1976:180), God's nature includes a *numerical* aspect. Since the three Persons of the Godhead – Father, Son, and Holy Spirit – are eternal, so is number.

It is sometimes alleged that the doctrine of the Trinity contradicts mathematics. Thus, for example, the engineer David Malcolm writes:

> No satisfactory proof has ever been devised to show that the basic number theory is universally true; rather, proofs have been put forward indicating that such a proof may be impossible. Thus mathematics cannot contradict Scriptural teaching that God exists as three persons in unity (Malcolm 1988: 56).

Malcolm seems to worry that, if mathematics were true, then the doctrine of the Trinity is undermined. Thus, appealing to Gödel's results (discussed in Chapter 8), he is ready to question the correctness of mathematics.

However, Gödel's theorem about the inability to prove consistency applies only to *full* arithmetic, which uses both addition and multiplication. The only mathematics needed here is that of adding positive integers (*i.e.*, 1+1+1 = 3, not 1). Such limited arithmetic, which uses only addition and not multiplication, *has* in fact been proven to be consistent. That being the case, Malcolm's reasoning implies that the doctrine of the Trinity is in serious trouble.

Christian astronomer Hugh Ross voices a similar concern. He writes, 'The Trinity is a mathematical absurdity in the context of just the four dimensions of length, width, height, and time' (Ross 1993:148). Ross seeks to rescue the Trinity from absurdity by placing God in multi-dimensional space. Consider, for example, an imaginary two-dimensional creature living on a flat plane. If a human were to stick three spread fingers through this plane the two-dimensional creature would experience this as three distinct, isolated circles. Yet, in the higher, three-dimensional world, these three fingers are actually connected to a single body. Ross conjectures that, in a similar fashion, God's three Persons might be unified into a single entity in a higher-dimensional space.

Now, it is true that God is Spirit and, as such, transcends our physical dimensions. Yet the Bible is quite clear that, even in this spiritual realm, God still consists of three distinct Persons. Thus the mystery is not resolved by merely referring to a single Being in a higher-dimensional space.

How, then, are we to view the Trinity? How can God be three and yet one? Here we must recall that the law of non-contradiction specifies that a proposition and its opposite cannot both be true *in the same sense at the same time*. Contradiction can be avoided by noting that the *Triune* God is three in *one* sense and one in *another* sense. God consists of three distinct *Persons*, each with his own subjective consciousness and particular characteristics. Yet, these three distinct Persons share the same divine *essence*, or nature, which consists of omniscience, omnipotence, goodness, and so on. The three Persons have the same objective knowledge of all things, including each other's thoughts. They are one in purpose.

Does this not imply tri-theism? Theologian Robert Reymond argues that it does not, because real tri-theism requires three *separable* gods, so that one could be eliminated without in any way impinging on the 'godness' of the others (Reymond 1998:323). But the three Persons of the Trinity are not three separable and distinguishable gods. Rather, they are eternally united. They have no separate existence. They exist only in relation to each other. Their dynamical interaction and communion constitutes an essential part of their being.

CONNECTING THE ONE TO THE MANY

The *triune* nature of God resolves the problem of the One and the Many, discussed in Chapter 4. As the Reformed scholar Rousas J. Rushdoony (1978:8) notes, the diversity and the unity of the Godhead are equally ultimate within the Trinity. They co-exist harmoniously throughout eternity. Because there is no tension between the divine One and Many, there is likewise no tension between the created One and Many. The harmonious co-existence of unity and diversity in the physical world is a reflection of the unity in diversity of its Creator. The plurality of this world – the works of God – finds its basis in the plurality of the fellowship of the Trinity. Similarly, the unity and inner consistency of the world derives from the oneness of God.

God and Necessary Truths

Orthodox Christianity maintains that only God is self-existent. He is the creator of everything else. How, then, are abstract, necessary objects related to God?

Philosopher Alvin Plantinga (1980) argues that, since God is necessarily all-knowing, necessary propositions (*e.g.*, 7+5 = 12) are necessarily always known to God, who thus affirms their exist-ence. The abstract objects of logic and mathematics exist as ideas in the mind of God. Although God has no control over these necessarily existing ideas, they pose no threat to God in any way. They are not agents that oppose God. On the contrary, they are merely inert ideas that depend on God for their existence. Plantinga writes:

> According to Kronecker God created the natural numbers and men created the rest . . . Kronecker was wrong on two counts. God hasn't created the numbers; a thing is created only if its existence has a beginning, and no number ever began to exist. And secondly, other mathematical entities (the reals, for example) stand in the same relation to God . . . as do the natural numbers. Sequences of numbers, for example, are necessary beings and have been created neither by God nor by anyone else. Still, each such sequence is such that it is part of God's nature to affirm its existence (Plantinga 1980: 142).

Here Plantinga refers to the German mathematician Leopold Kronecker (1823–91), who believed that, in mathematics, only the natural numbers had a real, objective existence. Plantinga believes that in exploring mathematics one is exploring the nature of God's rule over the universe . . . and the nature of God himself. He concludes, 'Mathematics thus takes its proper place as one of the loci of theology' (Plantinga 1980:144).

Some Christians have taken issue with such a high view of math-ematics. Christian philosopher Roy Clouser, for example, argues that God stands above logic and mathematics. Clouser contends that we cannot know anything about God's essential nature. He believes that God has taken on logical and numerical characteristics only for the sake of covenantal fellowship with us. Had God wanted to, he could have taken on quite different characteristics. According to Clouser (1991:183), God accommodates himself to our creaturely limitations. God's uncreated, unrevealed being is unknowable to us.

It is noteworthy that Plantinga and Clouser agree that God upholds the realm of objective mathematical laws. They differ on the question as to whether these laws are really necessary. If such laws are necessary, must they then not apply also to God? This raises deep, subtle questions pertaining to God's essential nature.

It is true that we cannot know anything about God other than that which he has revealed to us. Nevertheless, it seems implausible that God's unrevealed Being would be inconsistent with his revealed Being. Nowhere in his revealed Word does God give any hint of that. The Bible gives no indication that God's logic is any different from ours. Rather, genuine human wisdom appears to be part of the same wisdom that informs God (see Proverbs 8).

Moreover, it seems incoherent to claim that we can know nothing about God's essential nature and that normal logic does not apply to it. This implies that we *do* know something about God's essential nature, namely, that it is unknowable and above logic. But how do we know this to be true, if God has not revealed it to us?

Clouser aims to protect the sovereignty of God. He argues that only God is uncreated and necessary. Hence he should not be subject to anything, not even the laws of logic.

At this point it may be worthwhile to pause briefly to define our terms. A *possibility* is something that might conceivably be factually true. For example, it is possible that it will rain tomorrow or that I might some day be killed in a car accident. Something is *necessary* if it cannot be otherwise. Necessary truths include such things as logical truths (*e.g.*, the law of non-contradiction) and properties of numbers (*e.g.*, 2+3 = 5). A possibility may not contradict any necessary truth; necessary truths must hold in all possible worlds.

Mathematical truths include logical truths, as well as truths about numbers, shapes, and other mathematical systems. Mathematical truths are *universally true* in the sense that they hold independent of time, place or specific human cultures.

Some mathematical truths (*e.g.*, the laws of logic) are necessarily true in that they must hold in all possible worlds. However, not all mathematical truths are *necessary* truths in this sense. Out of all possible, potential worlds God has chosen one – the physical world we live in – to actualize from abstract potentiality to concrete actual form. Thus, for example, it is possible to have various geometric systems (*e.g.*, 5-dimensional Euclidean space) that are not necessarily actualized in all possible worlds. For such systems, the mathematical truths entailed in that system are necessarily true only in the sense that, for possible worlds containing that system, the theorems can be no other than what they are. So the theorems of 5-dimensional Euclidean geometry are universally true as mathematical truths but are not necessarily actualized in every possible world.

Returning to the Plantinga-Clouser dispute, it must be stressed that God is indeed the ground of all being. God upholds everything, even all possibilities. God establishes what is possible and what is necessary. Is it possible that God might have established other possibilities than those he did establish? In a deep sense, the answer is 'no'. Only those possibilities exist that God upholds. God has determined what is and what is not possible. He has set bounds on the possible.

Similarly, all necessary truths are ordained as such by him who determines all necessity. Hence, necessary truths by no means limit God's sovereignty. Rather, the omnipotence of God is most dramatically illustrated by the fact that God establishes and upholds even whatever is possible and whatever is necessary. Thus, whereas Plantinga seems to believe that God has no control over necessary laws, Clouser rightly stresses God's sovereignty over them. Even though they are eternal, they have been established as such by God.

In summary, mathematics has close ties with God. God created the world with a mathematical structure. God uses mathematics and logic in his Word. Some essential mathematical concepts, such as logic, numericity and unboundedness (infinity), are even reflected in God's own nature. God's sovereignty extends over mathematics, so that he establishes, upholds and knows all mathematical truths.

Justifying Math

How does our *human* mathematics compare to God's mathematics? How much of human mathematics can we accept as true? These questions will concern us for the remainder of this chapter.

How Do We Learn Math?

First, we must consider how finite, fallen man can come to know eternal mathematical truths. As the reader may recall, a prime objection to mathematical realism was the fact that abstract truths are beyond the grasp of our physical senses. How, then, can we gain access to the world of mathematics?

OUR INBORN ABILITIES

The Christian view of man, we noted in Chapter 10, is rooted in the biblical concept that man was made in the image of God (*Gen.* 1:26–30; *1 Cor.* 11:7). He was created with the ability to rule God's creation (*Gen.* 1:28). The divine image included not only righteousness but also rationality and creativity, involving the capacity for abstract thought, as well as the ability to reason, discern and symbolize. From the start, Adam had sophisticated linguistic ability. He could communicate with God (*Gen.* 2:16; 3:9–13). He could assign suitable names to the animals (*Gen.* 2:19–20).

Mathematical ability is closely linked to linguistic ability. Both involve abstraction, symbolic representation, and logical manipulation. The ability to do mathematics thus seems to be innate in human minds. Man was created with the potential to do mathematics, as part of his role as God's steward.

Unhappily, with Adam's fall into sin, man lost much of his original image. Yet, it is evident that, even after the Fall, man's ability to reason still functioned. He is still able to apply the laws of logic. He can still do valid mathematics. He may make logical and mathematical mistakes but these can be detected and corrected. The Reformer John Calvin comments on the work of unbelieving mathematicians:

> What shall we say of all the mathematics? Shall we esteem them the delirious ravings of madmen? On the contrary ... we shall admire them because we shall be constrained to acknowledge them to be truly excellent. And shall we esteem anything laudable or excellent which we do not recognize as proceeding from God? . . . Let us learn from such examples how many good qualities the Lord has left to the nature of man (Calvin *Institutes* II, ii, 15).

Thus mathematical ability must be seen as one of the good qualities still left to man after the Fall, even to unbelievers. 'Who hath put wisdom in the inward parts? or who hath given understanding to the heart?' (*Job* 38:36). God, in his mercy, still imparts wisdom and understanding to fallen man.

In practice, it seems that we are born with various basic, innate mathematical concepts such as:

The laws of deductive *logic*, for example, the law of non-contradiction.

The concept of *discreteness*, the ability to distinguish between objects. This is closely related to *counting*, involving the notion of natural numbers, and *collecting*, involving the notion of sets.

The concept of *continuity*, the ability to distinguish the sizes and shapes of spatial objects.

Perhaps a limited conception of *infinity*: 'He hath set the world (eternity) in their hearts' (*Eccles.* 3:11) – the word for *world* used here is *olam*, which the KJV elsewhere often translates as *eternal* or *everlasting*, and which other translations (*e.g.*, RSV, ESV) translate here as *eternity*.

These fundamental notions form the basis of logic, algebra, geometry, and analysis, respectively.

Whatever innate mathematics we may have, its potential is best developed through learning from others. Human mathematics has a strong cultural aspect, whereby mathematical knowledge is passed on through active interaction between teachers and students.

THE RULE OF LOGIC

How are mathematical truths established? Logic plays a major role in mathematics. We can demonstrate the correctness of a new theorem by proving that it can be logically derived from already known theorems. A prime goal of mathematics is to find all the true theorems that can be derived from a given set of axioms. Logical consistency is a crucial property of any mathematical system. Hence any mathematical conjecture must pass the test of logic.

THE LEAPS OF INTUITION

However, even in proving a theorem we need more than logic. Mathematics is not a purely deductive science. To prove a theorem from a set of axioms may require much experimentation using various approaches. Many dead ends may be encountered before a valid proof is found. What is needed is a well-developed insight as to what line of attack may or may not work.

Thus far we have just considered what goes into proving a theorem. But how was the theorem discovered in the first place? Often theorems are at first no more than lucky guesses. Logic alone can discover very little beyond some immediate consequences of known theorems. Many a profound theorem was postulated by an insightful mathematician who had no proof but who intuitively felt that the theorem must be true. Some outstanding mathematicians had an uncanny knack of conjecturing important theorems long before they were proven true. Progress in mathematics is largely due to the results of intuition.

Of course, our intuition is by no means infallible. Logic must step in to weed out those cases where intuition missed the mark. The main task of logic is to secure and confirm the gains made by intuition. Intuition must bow before logic.

What is mathematical intuition? It is a source of ideas and knowledge that transcends the senses and logic. It is closely related to imagination and creativity. Mathematical creativity involves the imagining of new ideas or novel combinations of old ideas. Unfortunately, relatively few new ideas lead to fruitful results. How can we avoid wasting our time exploring numerous dead-ends? Here is where intuition comes in. It guides us in choosing which new ideas to pursue.

Why do some people have a better mathematical intuition than others? Mathematical intuition has been likened to a sixth sense, whereby we 'see' the mathematical realm. Some people seem to be born with a strong natural mathematical intuition. This sense must, however, be further developed through training. Intuition seems to be connected also with long, sustained efforts of concentration.

The notion that some basic mathematical concepts are innate in man is granted also by naturalists. Naturalists consider the source of innate mathematics to be the evolution of human neural networks rather than the direct creation of God. However, a strongly developed mathematical intuition, needed for more advanced mathematics, is very difficult to explain from a naturalist perspective. It seems to require special, non-empirical knowledge of a non-physical realm.

Some mathematicians have claimed an even more direct contact with mathematical truth. On 10 November 1619, René Descartes claimed to have had a vision wherein he was visited by an Angel of Truth. This angel allegedly carried the message from God that mathematics was the conceptual key that unlocked the truths of physical reality. According to Descartes, this visit prompted him to discover analytical geometry, as well as the formulation of a new conception of metaphysical dualism. The discovery of analytical geometry was very significant for mathematics. It forged a link between abstract numbers and the form of concrete reality in space (see Kafatos and Nadeau 1990:119).

Similarly, Georg Cantor claimed that truths about transfinite numbers were directly revealed to him by God (Dauben:290). However, it has to be said that such 'revelations' are certainly not the common experience of most mathematicians.

How Can We Justify Math?

To be considered valid mathematical knowledge, the results of intuition must be proven to be derivable from the basic axioms of mathematics. The question then becomes, how can we demonstrate the soundness of our set of axioms? And what shall we accept as valid methods of proof?

A BIBLE-BASED MATH?

One possible approach is to try to ground the soundness of mathematics on the Bible. How feasible is this? As we already noted, the Bible frequently uses logical arguments (*e.g.*, *1 Cor.* 15:12–50 or *Matt.* 12:25–29). Many types of logical constructions can be found in the Bible, as is pointed out by Gordon Clark (1968:64–70). These include the laws of non-contradiction, identity, excluded middle, and rational inference.

Now, one may protest that what one finds are merely specific illustrations of such laws. Nevertheless, such illustrations are invariably in accordance with the basic laws of deductive logic. Further, the Bible contains the frequent usage of logical terms such as 'if . . . then', 'thus', 'therefore', 'so', and so on. These all presume the rationality of the reader and the general validity of logic. Moreover, it would seem that logic is necessarily involved in any communication of the 'logos' or 'Word' of God. The Bible proclaims God's will, rather than the opposite (*1 Tim.* 1:3–4; *2 Tim.* 4:2–4). So a strong case could be made for the thesis that the Bible itself entails the validity of logical laws.

In addition to logic, the Bible contains numerous instances of arithmetic operations – addition, subtraction, multiplication, and division. The physicist J. C. Keister (1982) claims that all the axioms of arithmetic are illustrated in Scripture. For example, he remarks that the text 'There shall be five in one house divided, three against two, and two against three' (*Luke* 12:52) states that '3+2 = 2+3'. This, he contends, illustrates the more general arithmetic axiom 'a+b = b+a'.

Such biblical examples certainly support the validity of our arithmetic and logic. Yet, one must be careful in drawing general conclusions from a limited number of specific cases. Moreover, even if this method were valid, it would justify only a very small subset of mathematics.

CLASSICAL MATH AND GOD

A better approach might be to ground the truth of mathematics on the attributes of the biblical God. These include his infinity, omniscience, and omnipotence, as well as the logical and numerical aspects of his nature. Classical mathematics, you may recall, is based on the ideal operations of such a God.

Mathematicians, we saw, differ about which mathematical concepts and methods are valid. The rejection of classical mathematics, on account of its implied theism, led to constructivism. Constructivism denies the law of excluded middle, proof by contradiction and numerous classical theorems based on these. This illustrates that worldview presuppositions, particularly those concerning God, can have dramatic implications for the contents of mathematics.

The Christian God, with his infinite knowledge, surely knows whether any proposition is true or false. Thus theism validates normal, two-valued logic. From this follows the soundness of both direct proofs and indirect proofs by contradiction. Theism validates also the existence of whole numbers and actual infinity, since these exist as eternal thoughts in God's mind.

Earlier, in Chapter 8, we noted that the quest of justifying mathematics boils down to finding a set of self-evident axioms that can be proven to be both *consistent* and *complete*. *Consistent*, so that they can never give rise to any contradiction; *complete*, so that all true mathematical theorems could be derived from them. Completeness and consistency have been proven for simple logic, Euclidean geometry, and simple arithmetic without multiplication. These, too, can thus be considered to be justified.

For any larger system, such as full arithmetic (with both addition and multiplication), Gödel proved (1) that the system is always incomplete and (2) that consistency cannot be proven by methods within that system.

We are thus faced with a number of problems. How can we prove the soundness of full arithmetic? How can we construct larger systems that include such things as calculus and more advanced mathematics?

Some Simple Set Theory

We consider first the problem of finding a basis for advanced mathematics. One possible approach is to use *set theory*. Set theory is very important for the foundations of mathematics. Remarkably, virtually all of modern mathematics can be derived from the few axioms of modern set theory. True, Gödel proved that all of mathematics can never be derived from a limited number of axioms. Yet, in practice, all of the mathematics that most mathematicians and physicists ever use can be derived from the few axioms of modern set theory. Those parts of mathematics that are not covered concern only some rather esoteric aspects of set theory that have little practical application.

What are *sets*? A set is a collection of objects. We can consider the set of all dogs, or the set of all even numbers, and so on. We use brackets {} to denote a set. Thus, for example, the set of even numbers is written {2, 4, 6, . . . }. Treating each set as an entity in its own right, we can then do various operations on these sets, such as adding sets, comparing their sizes, and so on.

Table 1. Axioms of Modern Set Theory

---

1. *Axiom of Extensionality*: two sets are identical if they contain the same members.
2. *Axiom of the Null Set*: there exists a set with no members, the empty set {}.
3. *Axiom of Pairing*: if A and B are sets, so is {A, B}.
4. *Axiom of the Sum-set*: for a set of sets, the members of all the sets form a set.
5. *Axiom of Infinity*: infinite sets exist (e.g., the set of all even numbers).
6. *Axiom of Replacement*: any formulated rule can be used to define a set.
7. *Axiom of the Power Set*: for any set S, the subsets of S form a set (the power set).
8. *Axiom of Regularity*: a set cannot be a member of itself.
9. *Axiom of Choice*: from any set of sets one can form a set consisting of one element from each set.

The axioms of modern set theory are shown in Table 1. The first eight axioms (called the *Zermelo-Fraenkel* or ZF axioms) plus the Axiom of Choice together yield what is called ZFC set theory. Note that Axiom 8 (*Regularity*) explicitly rules out self-reference. This avoids such paradoxes as the liar paradox. Axiom 7 (*Power Set*) refers to *subsets*. A *subset* of a set S is any set formed from members of S. Thus, if set S is the set {1, 2, 3}, the possible subsets of S are: {}, {1}, {2}, {3}, {1, 2}, {1, 3}, {2, 3} and {1, 2, 3}. The *power set* of S is the set of all possible subsets of S. In this example the power set of S has 8 members.

From these simple axioms, plus simple logic, almost all of mathematics can be derived.

So far no contradictions have been found. Can we be sure, however, that no contradictions will *ever* be found in this system? Taken individually, most of the ZFC axioms are very plausible – almost self-evident – when applied to *finite* sets. In that case constructive methods are adequate.

Difficulties arise, however, when the axioms are applied to *infinite* sets. Infinite sets are needed to get beyond number theory (which just concerns whole numbers) to real numbers (such as $\sqrt{2} = 1.414213\ldots$, which requires an infinite number of decimals to write out fully). Real numbers are needed for *calculus*, upon which physics heavily relies. The Axiom of Infinity is here of crucial importance. Further, we need the notion that certain operations on finite sets can be extended to infinite sets.

Constructivists, with their demand for constructive proofs and finite methods, do not accept the existence of infinite sets. Hence they do not consider the ZFC axioms to be a valid basis for mathematics.

The situation is quite different for the theist. Given an infinite, all-powerful and all-knowing Being, it is very plausible that the ZFC axioms hold for infinite, as well as finite, sets.

COUNTING BEYOND INFINITY

Consider, for example, the Power Set Axiom. Georg Cantor showed that, for any infinite set A, its power set is an order of infinity larger. By repeatedly applying this axiom we can generate an ever-increasing series of infinite sets. The set sizes correspond to ever-increasing transfinite numbers. The smallest order of infinity (symbolized by the first letter of the Hebrew alphabet, $\aleph_0$ or 'aleph null') corresponds to the set of whole numbers. Its power set, corresponding to the real numbers, has a size $\aleph_1$ ('aleph one'), which is the next largest known order of infinity. The power set of the real numbers would be $\aleph_2$, and so on. Most mathematicians do not use any infinities larger than $\aleph_2$.

The power set of an infinite set cannot be constructed by finite methods since mathematicians are unable to specify any sort of general procedure to list every possible subset of a given infinite set. Thus philosopher Christopher Menzel comments,

> In this sense, it is the Platonic axiom par excellence, declaring sets to exist even though humans lack the capacity to grasp or 'construct' them (Menzel 1990:218).

It is for this reason that constructivists reject the Power Set Axiom for infinite sets, as well as Cantor's transfinite numbers.

Cantor, on the other hand, justified his belief in infinite sets by his belief in an infinite God. He thought of sets in terms of what God could do with them. An infinite God would have no difficulty forming the power set of any given infinite set. Even today, almost every attempt to justify the principles of set theory relies on the notion of an ideal all-powerful and all-knowing Ideal Mathematician.

Alvin Plantinga claims that the theist has a distinct advantage when it comes to explaining sets and their properties. The existence of sets depends upon a certain sort of intellectual activity – a collecting or 'thinking together'. According to Plantinga:

> If the collecting or thinking together had to be done by human thinkers, or any finite thinkers, there wouldn't be nearly enough sets – not nearly as many as we think in fact there are. From a theistic point of view, the natural conclusion is that sets owe their existence to God's thinking things together . . . Christians, theists, ought to understand sets from a Christian and theistic point of view. What they believe as theists affords a resource for understanding sets not available to the non-theist (Plantinga 1990:35).

Thus Plantinga grounds set theory on God's infinite and comprehensive abilities.

THE AXIOM OF CHOICE

The Axiom of Choice states that, from every family of sets, it is always possible to form a new set containing exactly one element from each set. Thus, for example, if our set consisted of all the libraries in the world, a new set could be formed by taking one book from each library. The newly formed set, consisting of books, will have just as many members as the original set, consisting of libraries. This axiom plays a key role in modern mathematics. Many important theorems depend on it.

An important question that arises when applying the Axiom of Choice is how we are to choose the elements. In the above case we could, for example, specify that we choose that book whose title comes first alphabetically. This assumes that the books can be arranged in alphabetical order. But what happens if we have two or more copies of the first book? Which copy do we choose? Or, to take another example, what would be the rule for choosing balls from a set of boxes containing identical balls?

The Axiom of Choice asserts that, in principle, a suitable choice can always be made. The thinking behind the axiom is that we need not specify a definite rule as long as it is plausible that such a rule could in principle be established.

As long as we think in terms of an Ideal Mathematician, this poses no problem. Difficulties arise, however, if we are constrained to the finite methods of constructive mathematics. The axiom can be readily proven if the number of sets in the family is finite. For an infinite number of sets this is no longer so, particularly not if the sets are themselves infinite. In that case one cannot always specify exactly how a particular element is to be chosen from each set. Nor can one construct the new set in a finite number of steps. For these reasons constructivist mathematicians reject the Axiom of Choice.

The Axiom of Choice is equivalent to the *Well-Ordering Principle*, which asserts that any set can be re-arranged so that it has a definite first element. Once all the sets in question are well-ordered, one simply stipulates that the first element in each set be chosen to form the new set. Cantor believed that God could suitably re-arrange any set so that its elements would be well-ordered. Hence, for God, the Axiom of Choice would hold. Thus, this axiom, too, poses no problem for an all-knowing, all-powerful God.

Similarly, the Axiom of Replacement, which cannot be constructively confirmed for infinite sets, can be shown to present no difficulties for an Ideal Mathematician.

JUSTIFYING MATH AS A WHOLE

Thus far we have argued for the theistic justification of classical deductive logic, the natural numbers, and the Axioms of Infinity, Power Set, Choice, and Replacement. These latter axioms form the basis for ZFC set theory, from which almost all of modern mathematics can be derived. Most mathematicians never use axioms beyond ZFC.

One problem remains. Even if the above concepts and axioms were sufficient to serve as a basis for the bulk of contemporary mathematics, how can we be assured that this basis is *consistent*? Can we prove that this system can never give rise to any contradictions? How much of mathematics is guaranteed to be consistent?

As we already noted, consistency has been proven for simple logic, Euclidean geometry and arithmetic without multiplication. Gödel showed that, for any system large enough to include full arithmetic, the consistency of that system could not be proven within that system. To prove consistency for such systems one must necessarily appeal to axioms beyond that system.

In 1936 the German mathematician Gerhard Gentzen (1909–1945), a student of David Hilbert, proved the consistency of full arithmetic by using the equivalent of the Axiom of Choice. Hence, if one can accept the Axiom of Choice, arithmetic can be considered consistent. The above theistic justification for the Axiom of Choice thus validates the consistency of full arithmetic.

Alternatively, we could secure mathematics via ZFC set theory. Its most contentious axioms – the Axioms of Infinity, Power Set, Choice and Replacement – have all been validated by our theistic approach. Almost all of ordinary mathematics can be derived from ZFC set theory without the Axiom of Replacement. According to the American mathematician Paul Cohen (1966), this system can be proven to be consistent by applying the Axiom of Replacement. Hence almost all of contemporary mathematics can be proven consistent if one accepts the Axiom of Replacement, which we argued was justified by theism. A more detailed theistic justification of ZFC set theory has been developed by Christopher Menzel (1987).

Conclusions

In summary, the Christian worldview readily explains the intricate relations between mathematics, matter and mind. It supports mathematical realism, since God himself possesses logical and numerical attributes. Further, the infinite, omniscient, and omnipotent God ensures the validity of two-valued logic, proof by contradiction, actual infinite sets and the Axioms of Infinity, Power Set, Choice, and Replacement. These, in turn, provide a solid basis for modern mathematics.

Ultimately, the consistency and certainty of mathematics can be grounded upon the multi-faceted nature of God himself. Trust in God generates confidence in mathematics. It must be stressed that, although Christian theism may provide a solid foundation for mathematics, our limited human abilities will ensure that human mathematics will, of necessity, always be incomplete.

Finally, it must be kept in mind that God is, of course, much more than the foundation of mathematics. In this regard it is useful to recall Albert Einstein's conception of God. Einstein referred to God on various occasions, making statements such as, 'God does not play dice', 'God is not malicious', and so on. However, as we noted in Chapter 1, Einstein made it very clear that he did not believe in a personal God. Einstein elaborates,

> I have never imputed to Nature a purpose or a goal, or anything that could be understood as anthropomorphic. What I see in Nature is a magnificent structure that we can comprehend only very imperfectly, and that must fill a thinking person with a feeling of humility. This is a genuinely religious feeling that has nothing to do with mysticism (1981:39).

Einstein's God is no more than the personification of the mathematical structure found in nature.

It is thus important to stress that the biblical God, who upholds mathematics, upholds much more than just mathematics. He is the living, triune God who in his mercy saves sinners through Jesus Christ. Let me close this chapter with the astute words of Blaise Pascal:

> Even if someone were convinced that the proportions between numbers are nonmaterial, eternal truths, depending on a first truth in which they subsist that they call God, I would not think he had made much progress toward his salvation. The Christian's God does not merely consist of a God who is the Author of mathematical truths and the order of the elements. That is the notion of the heathen and the Epicureans . . . But the God of Abraham, the God of Isaac, the God of Jacob, the God of the Christians is a God of love and consolation. He is a God who fills the heart and soul of those he possesses. He is a God who makes them aware of their wretchedness while revealing his infinite mercy (Pascal 1989:149).

15

The Challenge Settled

CROSSFIRE

Even more purposeless, more void of meaning, is the world which science presents for our belief. Amid such a world, if anywhere, our ideals henceforward must find a home. That man is the product of causes which had no prevision of the end they were achieving; that his origin, his growth, his hopes and fears, his loves and his beliefs, are but the outcome of accidental collocations of atoms; that no fire, no heroism, no intensity of thought and feeling, can preserve an individual life beyond the grave; that all the labours of the ages, all the devotion, all the inspiration, all the noonday brightness of human genius, are destined to extinction in the vast death of the solar system, and that the whole temple of man's achievement must inevitably be buried beneath the debris of a universe in ruins – all these things, if not quite beyond dispute, are yet so nearly certain that no philosophy which rejects them can hope to stand. Only within the scaffolding of these truths, only on the firm foundation of unyielding despair, can the soul's salvation henceforth be safely built.

BERTRAND RUSSELL (*A Free Man's Worship* 1957:106)

* * * * *

And God shall wipe away all tears from their eyes; and there shall be no more death, neither sorrow, nor crying, neither shall there be any more pain: for the former things are passed away. And he that sat upon the throne said, Behold, I make all things new. And he said unto me, Write: for these words are true and faithful. And he said unto me, It is done. I am Alpha and Omega, the beginning and the end. I will give unto him that is athirst of the fountain of the water of life freely. He that overcometh shall inherit all things; and I will be his God, and he shall be my son.

Revelation 21:4–7

The time has come to settle the divine challenge. How has man fared in his ambitious quest for divinity? How well has he succeeded in explaining reality? In re-interpreting the universe in terms of human meaning and values? In establishing himself on the divine throne? Bertrand Russell's pessimistic words suggest that man's divine pursuit has failed miserably. Prideful man, upon rejecting God, ends up reducing himself to a meaningless accident, without purpose, joy or hope. Nevertheless, Russell, like other fallen men, is stubbornly determined to stick it out. He prefers to vainly seek his soul's salvation within the shaky scaffolding of unyielding despair, rather than to switch to the other path, the path that leads to life.

Our main goal was to compare how well Christianity, naturalism and post-modernity accounted for the three interacting worlds of matter, mind and mathematics. In this final chapter we shall briefly summarize the main conclusions reached and make a few final comments.

Brief Summary
The Nature of Worldviews

We stressed that the question was one of opposing worldviews. Everyone has a worldview, although most people may be unaware that they are viewing reality through the spectacles that a particular worldview provides.

All worldviews are based on presuppositions, on basic initial assumptions about reality that are rarely stated explicitly. Such worldview presuppositions set our standards for what we consider to be reasonable. Different worldviews may entail radically different views of rationality. Nevertheless, conflicting worldviews can usually be assessed in terms of quite general criteria such as consistency, experience, and livability. Any viable worldview must be able to accommodate the basic commonsense notions needed for normal conversation and scientific activity. In particular, we stressed the necessity of truth and logic, as well as the importance of the principle of sufficient reason.

Embracing a worldview is not a dry academic exercise. Our worldview sets the direction for our life. It determines the path we follow and the goals we seek. It guides us in deciding how to live our lives. Our answers to worldview questions are matters of life and death.

Naturalism and Relativism

The naturalist worldview was discussed extensively. Particular attention was paid to its most common, materialistic form. We found that naturalism has great difficulty explaining the universe's mathematical structure, the origin of life and mind, and our ability for rational thought. Naturalism cannot account for the ability of mind to cause physical effects. Naturalism fails to justify rational minds, immaterial norms and non-empirical knowledge. Its rational defence was found to be self-refuting.

Regarding advanced mathematics, we saw that naturalistic evolution cannot explain its origin, truthfulness, or applicability to the physical world. Naturalism has no place for moral or aesthetic values. It has no place for truth, meaning, love, goodness or beauty. It has no place for precisely those aspects of man that make him human and distinguish him from animals. By placing the ultimate reality in matter, naturalism has no place for the worlds of mind and mathematics.

Naturalistic attempts to bridge the gaps via promissory notes or emergence were found to be implausible. By undermining the reality of a purposeful self and the possibility of objective knowledge, naturalism entails relativism and scepticism.

Whereas naturalism stressed objective matter at the expense of the subjective self, post-modern relativism stresses the subjective self at the expense of objective truth and values. Post-modernity has in effect given up on explaining reality. Post-modern man no longer knows where he is, why he is, or who he is. The post-modern self, too, is reduced to meaninglessness. Furthermore, like naturalism, relativism is hard pressed to avoid self-refutation.

THE CHRISTIAN WORLDVIEW

The Christian worldview stresses the all-embracing sovereignty of God. God is the ultimate reality. The Christian worldview grounds its knowledge in the Bible, which it affirms to be the Word of God. As such, the Bible is our ultimate standard of truth.

The biblical God is a Spirit, personal, infinite, independent, omniscient, omnipotent, omnipresent and triune. He is distinct from everything else, which he has created and upholds. Everything unfolds according to his eternal plan.

Man was created in the image of God, fell into sin, and is redeemed through the atoning death of Christ. Man's divine image includes aspects of rationality. Man's senses and logic are generally reliable because God has created them to function properly. However, fallen man no longer uses them in the service of God. Hence, his speculative theorizing is often wrong. Man consists of body and spirit. Man's spirit survives physical death and is reunited with its renewed body at the final judgment.

God is the primary cause of all events. Although God normally works through secondary causes, sometimes God acts directly in miraculous ways. God's sovereignty rules out the existence of genuine chance. An indeterminist, libertarian view of human free will contradicts God's sovereignty. Indeterminism jeopardizes God's knowledge of the future, thus leading to open theism and process theology. Moreover, indeterminism destroys human freedom and undermines moral responsibility.

The Bible teaches that man is responsible for his thoughts, words and deeds, even though his will is enslaved by sin. The freedom that moral responsibility requires is freedom from *coercion*, not freedom from *causation*. Compatibilism is consistent with voluntary choice; it entails neither physical determinism nor fatalism. Although God is the primary cause of everything, he is not the *author* of sin, which is always directly and wilfully done by creatures. God has a morally sufficient reason for everything he foreordains, including sin.

Logic and number reflect, to a very limited degree, some particular aspects of God's multi-faceted nature. God establishes and upholds all necessary truths and universals. Theism validates full deductive logic, proof by contradiction, actual infinite sets, and various crucial axioms of modern set theory. Upon these, the vast bulk of modern mathematics can be grounded.

Thus God, the ultimate reality, upholds the three worlds of matter, mind and mathematics. He forges their links and ensures cohesion. He gives true meaning to everything.

Assessing Christianity

We have argued that the Christian worldview gives a coherent account of common sense, rationality and objective knowledge. The Christian worldview is internally consistent. It accounts for the full range of human experiences. It gives us a guide for our conduct, a purpose to our existence and the promise of future eternal joy with God.

Yet we saw that the Christian worldview does not fully resolve all mysteries. It does not completely answer all our questions. The Bible itself, however, explains this limitation. For one thing, God tells us that he has not (yet) revealed all his secrets: 'The secret things belong unto the LORD our God: but those things which are revealed belong unto us and to our children for ever' (*Deut.* 29:29). Our limited knowledge is, at least in part, an aspect of our present fallen state, to be broadened in our future life: 'For now we see through a glass darkly; but then face to face: now I know in part; but then shall I know even as also I am known' (*1 Cor.* 13:12).

The naturalist might object that grounding the links between matter, mind and mathematics in the nature and activity of God is no more of a solution than ascribing them to emergence. *Miracle* and *emergence*, it might be thought, are no more than empty words expressing our ignorance. Yet there is a difference. The Christian ascribes miracles to the purposeful work of a living, rational and omnipotent God. The naturalist, on the other hand, ascribes such miracles as the emergence of life, mind and mathematics to the purposeless complexity of dead, insensible and inert matter.

Defending the Faith

Much of our discussion is relevant to *apologetics*, which concerns our defence of our Christian faith. As the Apostle Peter admonishes, 'Be ready always to give an answer to every man that asketh you a reason of the hope that is in you, with meekness and fear' (*1 Pet.* 3:15).

Apologetics has both a positive and a negative aspect. Positively, apologetics involves the proclamation of the gospel, clearing up any misunderstandings, and responding to the objections of unbelief. One major task of apologetics is to outline how the biblical worldview offers a cohesive and comprehensive explanation of reality, particularly concerning man, with all his problems. This has been the burden of the last half of this book.

Apologetics has also a negative aspect. The unbeliever wilfully suppresses his knowledge of God. He builds his worldview on a treacherous foundation that rejects God's Word. Man pits his wisdom against that of God. The second major task of apologetics, therefore, is to expose worldly wisdom for the folly it is. We must unmask the foolishness of unbelief. Paul writes, 'For the preaching of the cross is to them that perish foolishness . . . I will destroy the wisdom of the wise' (*1 Cor.* 1:18–19). Hence, we must be busy with 'Casting down imaginations and every high thing that exalteth itself against the knowledge of God, and bringing into captivity every thought to the obedience of Christ' (*2 Cor.* 10:5).

The approach we have followed is that of *presuppositional* apologetics. We have stressed the large role presuppositions play in worldviews. This approach calls for a comparison between the merits of the Christian and non-Christian worldviews. The aim is to show that the Christian worldview gives a coherent explanation of man and his experiences, whereas the unbeliever's worldview makes nonsense out of history, science and even reasoning itself.

Along these lines the Reformed philosopher Cornelius van Til, in his book *The Defense of the Faith* (1967), developed his Transcendental Argument for Christianity. According to apologist Greg Bahnsen, a former student of van Til, this argument contends that 'only the truth of Christianity can rescue the meaningfulness and cogency of logic, science, and morality . . . only the Christian worldview provides the philosophical preconditions necessary for man's reasoning and knowledge in any field whatever' (Bahnsen 1998:5). The transcendental argument is primarily a *reductio ad absurdum* of the unbeliever's worldview.

A main thrust of the first portion of this book was to demonstrate that various non-Christian worldviews cannot be rationally defended. We have shown that the defence of extreme forms of naturalism and relativism are self-refuting. To avoid self-refutation, these worldviews must be modified to allow, at the very least, for the common-sense presuppositions implied in daily conversation and in scientific work. Viable worldviews must account for effective minds, universal norms and a means by which we can come to know these norms. Even then, the subjectivity of our beliefs is inescapable unless we have access to divine revelation. Making man, rather than God, the self-contained point of reference, inevitably leads to relativism and scepticism.

Our contention is *not* that the unbeliever cannot *know* anything or cannot *reason*. Thanks to God's mercy, the unbeliever still reflects, however dimly, the image of God. Hence, the unbeliever *can* still reason and acquire knowledge. His difficulty, rather, is that, within his unbelieving worldview, he cannot *justify* or *account for* his knowledge or reasoning abilities. Non-Christians are plagued by a fatally flawed theory of knowledge that undermines their philosophy.

Without belief in the absolute God of the Bible nothing in the world makes sense. The unbeliever's reasoning can be justified only on the basis of the Christian worldview. According to philosopher Robert Bishop, 'The belief that the universe is rational, and that we are able to express that rationality, finds its ground in the Christian view of creation' (1993:151). This conclusion is echoed by the physicist Paul Davies, who writes,

> Even the most atheistic scientist accepts as an act of faith that the universe is not absurd, that there is a rational basis to physical existence manifested by a law-like order in nature that is at least in part comprehensible to us. So science can proceed only if the scientist adopts an essentially theological worldview (Davies 1995:32).

Such sentiments confirm the judgment of Cornelius van Til that only Christianity gives a coherent explanation of our experiences. Only the Christian worldview provides an adequate basis for rationality and objective knowledge.

Why (Post-) Modernists Reject Christianity

The conclusion just reached provokes a question. If Christianity is in fact rationally superior to other worldviews, why is it not more widely accepted? Consider first of all naturalism. Given the lack of evidence for naturalism, its inability to explain the deeper mysteries of the universe, and its self-contradictory nature, why do so many scientists persist in their support of naturalism?

We note first that not all scientists are philosophically inclined. Perhaps many are simply not fully aware of the presuppositions underlying their worldview or the consequences of these. However, among those naturalist scientists who have thought things through more deeply, some are forthright enough to admit that their materialism is grounded in *faith*, rather than *evidence*. Thus, for example, Harvard biologist Richard Lewontin, a materialist, acknowledges:

Our willingness to accept scientific claims that are against common sense is the key to the understanding of the real struggle between science and the supernatural. We take the side of science – *in spite* of the patent absurdity of some of its constructs, *in spite* of its failure to fulfil many of its extravagant promises of health and life, *in spite* of the tolerance of the scientific community for unsubstantiated just-so stories, because we have a prior commitment to materialism. It is not that the methods and institutions of science somehow compel us to accept a material explanation of the phenomenal world, but, on the contrary, we are forced by our *a priori* adherence to material causes to create an apparatus of investigation and a set of concepts that produce material explanations, no matter how counter-intuitive, no matter how mystifying to the uninitiated (Lewontin 1997:31).

Lewontin is refreshingly candid about the weaknesses of (materialistic) science. He admits that it is primarily a question of presuppositions. Scientists are not neutral. They do not merely follow the evidence, regardless of where it might lead them. On the contrary, they interpret that evidence in terms of their adopted worldview.

Yet, knowing the shortcomings of materialism, why does Lewontin not reconsider his commitment to materialism? If it is primarily a matter of faith, why do materialists not weigh other, more viable options? Why do they cling so *tenaciously* to materialism? Materialists often retort that, whatever weaknesses materialism may have, it is the best we can do. There is, allegedly, no rational alternative.

In truth, however, any alternative is rejected from the start. This is clear from Lewontin when he adds:

Moreover, that materialism is absolute, for we cannot allow a Divine Foot in the door . . . To appeal to an omnipotent deity is to allow that at any moment the regularities of nature may be ruptured, that miracles may happen (Lewontin 1997:31).

In a similar vein, philosopher John Searle intimates that some philosophers and scientists deny mental causes because they fear what they see as the only alternative:

How is it that so many philosophers and cognitive scientists can say so many things that, to me at least, seem obviously false? . . . I believe one of the unstated assumptions behind the current batch of views is that they represent the only scientifically acceptable alternatives to the anti-scientism that went along with traditional dualism, the belief in the immortality of the soul, spiritualism, and so on. Acceptance of the current views is motivated not so much by an independent conviction of their truth as by a terror of what are apparently the only alternatives. That is, the choice we are tacitly left with is between a 'scientific' approach, as represented by one or another of the current versions of 'materialism', and an 'anti-scientific' approach, as represented by Cartesianism or some traditional religious conception of the mind (Searle 1992:3–4).

This suggests that, at heart, the commitment to materialism is driven by a deep, religious motivation.

The strong appeal of this irrational factor is voiced quite frankly by naturalist philosopher Thomas Nagel:

I am talking about . . . the fear of religion itself. I speak from experience, being strongly subject to this fear myself: I want atheism to be true and am made uneasy by the fact that some of the most intelligent and well-informed people I know are religious believers. It isn't just that I don't believe in God and, naturally, hope that I'm right in my belief. It's that I hope there is no God! I don't want there to be a God; I don't want the universe to be like that . . . My guess is that this cosmic authority problem is not a rare condition and that it is responsible for much of the scientism and reductionism of our time. One of the tendencies it supports is the ludicrous overuse of evolutionary biology to explain everything about life, including everything about the human mind (Nagel 1997:130–31).

The feared alternative is theism, particularly biblical theism. Thus, at bottom, at least some naturalists own up to being driven by a deeply entrenched desire to avoid God, even if that commits them to an irrational, self-refuting worldview.

What about post-modernity? Post-moderns, professing to attach little weight to rationality, might simply shrug off any charges of irrationality. The influential post-modern philosopher Richard Rorty, upon being interviewed on his views on religion, commented: 'I do not think that Christian theism is irrational. I entirely agree . . . that it is no more irrational than atheism. Irrationality is not the question but rather, desirability' (cited in Louthan 1996:178).

Post-modern man, like his modern predecessor, is propelled by the burning desire to avoid paying tribute to his Creator. Man wants to reinterpret the universe in terms of his own standards, no matter what the cost may be.

World Stories: Human and Divine

This brings us to the crux of the matter. Man's initial downfall was his desire to be like God. Prompted by Satan's seductive words, 'Ye shall be as gods, knowing good and evil' (*Gen.* 3:5), Adam and Eve disobeyed God. They ate from the tree of the knowledge of good and evil. Ever since, fallen man still wilfully rejects God and his Word. Man is still searching for metaphorical trees of knowledge of good and evil, magical shortcuts leading to divine knowledge and power.

The modern, naturalist worldview was based on the biblical worldview. The biblical worldview asserts that there is a real world beyond our senses. This world and its history have a purpose. There is an objective, true view of the world: God's view. As theologian Robert Jenson (1993) puts it, the biblical worldview has its own true *story* and *promise*. The *story* is the biblical story of creation, fall and redemption. The *promise* is the gospel of salvation in Jesus Christ and a future eternal life with God. The universe has a true story because there is a universal Historian.

Modernity took over the biblical notion of rational man in an orderly world but rejected the biblical God who created man and the world. In essence, it was just a continuation of man's war against God, begun in Eden. Modernity, Jenson notes, wanted to maintain a realist faith while denying the God who was that faith's object. It tried to live in a universal story of its own making, without a universal storyteller. Modernity's version of the gospel promise was its confidence in progress, in a future utopia where man would solve all his social problems.

Modernity is collapsing. In the modern world, human reason elevated itself above God and claimed sovereignty. This entailed that it could criticize all beliefs. Yet, once reason was given licence to criticize all things, it was inevitable that it must eventually criticize also itself. Then reason unmasks itself as unreasonable. Critical human reason, once uncorked, is an insatiable acid that dissolves *all* absolutes, whether in religion, ethics, science or logic. Eventually it erodes even its own foundation, causing modernity to self-destruct.

Modernity, having banished God, is now realizing that it is left with no sound basis for objective knowledge. Without a universal storyteller the universe can have no story. Meanwhile, modernity's hope in progress has been dashed by catastrophic World Wars, the fall of Marxism, the rise of international terrorism and the persistence of crime and violence that characterizes modern civilized society. Modernity has lost both its story and its promise.

Modernity has lived off the intellectual and moral wealth inherited from Christianity. This wealth is rapidly running out. Modernity cannot replenish it without denying itself and bringing back the biblical God it has banished.

In our *post*-modern era, many people have given up on formulating a coherent worldview. Whereas modernity asserted that the biblical story was wrong, post-modernity rejects the notion that there is a story at all. The post-modern world lacks any real meaning and substance. It is a hopeless, pointless absurdity.

The story of modernity and its demise into post-modernity reminds one of the story of the Tower of Babel, related in Genesis 11 (see the cover of this book). As Middleton and Walsh (1995:16–17) suggest, the tower built by modernity has human autonomy as its foundation. The first floor is science, which gives understanding. The second floor is technology, which gives power. The third floor is economics, which gives purpose for scientific and industrial progress. The fourth floor is consumerism, feeding superficial pleasures and driving the economy.

This modernist tower, with its pretensions of reaching into heaven, is, like its pagan predecessor, undermined by a confusion of language. This time, however, no divine intervention is needed. Post-modern man himself blows up his own tower by emptying his language of any meaningful content.

As Nietzsche had foreseen, the death of God inevitably entailed the death of truth. When man limits himself to unaided human reason, his search for truth must eventually undermine itself. Critical human reason, applied to itself, destroys the very possibility of finding truth. Consequently, ambitious modern man, instead of attaining god-like knowledge and wisdom, ends up with only the frustration of a hopeless quest.

The Return of the Pagans

The decline of modernity, with all its optimistic hopes of rational knowledge, and the advent of post-modernity, with its pessimistic denial of absolute truth and values, leaves a gaping void.

What will fill the vacuum? A major candidate is neo-paganism, the contemporary version of paganism. Paganism increases in popularity whenever rationality undergoes a crisis or when people lose confidence in their belief in an intelligent, transcendental God. Neo-paganism is *pantheistic*. Everything is inter-connected and divine. Nature and its parts – objects, persons, places, times, and events – can all be worshipped as sacred. Ultimately, however, all the gods of neo-paganism are only manifestations of the supreme divinity – the self.

The prime enemy of neo-paganism is Christianity. Christianity proclaims a God who insists that He alone is sacred, good and perfect. Christianity asserts that man receives his existence and values from God. Neo-pagans reject such a view of God and man. The pagan gods are imperfect and amoral. They impose no obligations on man. Hence, pagan man has no burden of sin and he is free to create his own values.

The pagan world is without any objective reality, without prior concepts and norms. The universe is a pointless flux wherein meaning can come only from humanity – not from God. Neo-pagans seek to create a new civilization with new values based on a non-Christian foundation. This requires that the world must first be emptied of Christian meaning. Thus, neo-pagans welcome the rehabilitation of non-Christian religions, art forms and social structures.

Neo-paganism is accompanied by the new occult. Humanity is to be transformed through a new kind of scientific super-magic. The modern magicians replace astrology and alchemy with sociology, technology and psycho-therapy. As philosopher Thomas Molnar (1995:35) comments, the goal is 'the transformation of man himself: his mind, body, genes, basic attitudes to others, orientations, and concepts of what is human, natural, and traditional'. Molnar concludes his analysis:

> Everybody may join, but the erasure of distinctions and rational judgments is precisely the factor that radically lowers the resisting capacity of prospective members. The magicians then move in . . . to teach the 'true doctrine', usually a caricature of monotheistic religion and with just enough 'spirituality' to put to sleep any suspicion. This spirituality is most ambiguous because it does not observe the balance between body and soul – our normal condition – but insists on 'raising our consciousness' and abolishing our sense perception and natural sensuality for the benefit of absolute immateriality. In other words, just as alchemy is supposed to accelerate the virtues inherent in minerals in view of a supernatural maturation, so this mental alchemy is supposed to produce a super-mankind. But this is no longer a community of wise men: it is a group of magical manipulators aspiring at naked power over the rest (Molnar 1995:35).

One is reminded here of the warnings of Jesus that, in the last days, 'There shall arise false Christs, and false prophets, and shall shew great signs and wonders; insomuch that, if it were possible, they shall deceive the very elect' (*Matt.* 24:24).

With the return of paganism we have a return also of the ancient heresies that sought to undermine Christianity. Theologian Peter

Jones, in his book *Spirit Wars* (1997), relates how gnosticism is, once again, attempting to subvert the Christian gospel. Gnosticism does so by adding gnostic books to the biblical canon, by advocating mystic interpretations of the Bible and by promoting homosexuality, feminism, goddess worship and witchcraft.

In sum, neo-paganism rejects the sterile rationalism of modernity. It advocates a return to a more mystical, man-made world of myth and magic. Neo-paganism is yet another phase in fallen man's long war against God.

Finale

Fallen man – whether modern, post-modern, or pagan – wants to dethrone God. Yet, having seized the divine throne, the self-made god does not experience the expected exhilaration. Instead, he encounters a depressing emptiness. Materialist Sir Francis Crick ended up reducing the self to a pitiful illusion. His co-believer William Provine (1988:70) laments, 'The universe cares nothing for us . . . there is no ultimate meaning for humans.'

Post-modernity is, if anything, even more pessimistic and disillusioned. The existentialist Jean-Paul Sartre (1957:22), we saw, was very distressed since, 'Everything is permissible if God does not exist, and as a result man is forlorn, because neither within him nor without does he find anything to cling to.'

The cost of eliminating God is immense. It entails spiritual, moral and philosophical bankruptcy.

Philosopher Roger Scruton, who is apparently an atheist, comments on post-modern culture:

> We know that we are animals, parts of the natural order, bound by laws which tie us to the material forces which govern everything. We believe that the gods are our invention and that death is exactly what it seems. Our world has been disenchanted and our illusions destroyed. At the same time we cannot live as though that were the whole truth of our condition. Even modern people are compelled to praise and blame, love and hate, reward and punish. Even modern people . . . are aware of self, as the centre of their being; and even modern people try to connect to other selves around them. We

therefore see others *as if* they were free beings, animated by a self or soul, and with more than a worldly destiny. If we abandon that perception, then human relations dwindle into a machine-like parody . . . the world is voided of love, duty and desire, and only the body remains (Scruton 1998:68).

The death of God entails the death of values, which, in turn, entails the death of humans as humans. Hence Scruton advocates that, although we know God is dead, we should still live *as if* God and his values still exist. Otherwise we cannot function properly. But this means that we must base our values on a lie. The resultant incoherent life that follows can hardly be expected to bring genuine satisfaction and fulfilment.

Man seems to be driven by an innate thirst for genuine truth, beauty and meaning. Man's inability to find these, on his own, is a source of great frustration. Bertrand Russell, who resolutely rejected God, nevertheless confessed in his autobiography, 'The centre of me is always and eternally a terrible pain – a curious wild pain – a searching for something beyond what the world contains, something transfigured and infinite' (1968:95–96).

This is a remarkable confession. Russell, we saw, was a full-blooded naturalist who insisted that there is nothing beyond this material world. Nevertheless, he is troubled by a great desire for something more. Where does this desire come from? It could hardly have come via naturalist evolution. A frustrated desire has little survival value. Nor does it seem plausible that material properties would give rise to transcendental quests.

A transcendental desire points to a transcendental Being. The Christian answer is that God, who created man in his image, created him with the need for divine fellowship. Augustine astutely noted:

Man is one of your creatures, Lord, and his instinct is to praise you . . . he cannot be content unless he praises you, and our hearts find no peace until they rest in you. (*Confessions* I,i)

Similarly, Blaise Pascal describes the human plight:

But what does all this restlessness and helplessness indicate, except that man was once in true happiness which has now left him? So he vainly searches, but finds nothing to help him, other than to see an infinite abyss that can only be filled by One who is Infinite and Immutable. In other words, it can only be filled by God himself (Pascal 1989:109).

Man has within his soul a God-shaped void that can be filled only by God himself. This echoes the earnest words of the Psalmist,

As the hart panteth after the water brooks, so panteth my soul after thee, O God; my soul thirsteth for God, for the living God' (*Psa.* 42:1–2).

Man's apt punishment for rejecting God is to be left with an unquenchable thirst for the transcendental Absolute.

Even Nietzsche could not forget the God he had so vigorously rejected. In his last set of poems, *Dionysus Dithyrambs*, Nietzsche sadly acknowledges the weariness and loneliness of life without God. Through the mouth of Ariadne, a character in one of his poems, Nietzsche begs for God's return:

> No! Come back,
> With all your torments!
> All the streams of my tears
> Run their course to you!
> And the last flame of my heart –
> It burns up to you!
> Oh, come back,
> My unknown God! My pain!
> My last . . . happiness!
> (Nietzsche 1961:267)

Shortly after Nietzsche wrote these heartrending words he met his tragic end. He suffered a nervous breakdown. During the remaining eleven years of his life he never regained his sanity.

If God alone can satisfy man's deepest needs, why does man not turn to God? Man is hindered by his fallen nature, which is marked by its self-delusion and pride. Adam and Eve's desire to be wise like God led them to disobey God's command. Their just punishment included, among other things, a darkened mind. This became the common plight of all their rebellious, fallen offspring. As the apostle Paul writes: 'And even as they did not like to retain God in their knowledge, God gave them over to a reprobate mind' (*Rom.* 1:28). Man, seeking to become divinely wise, becomes enslaved by the empty illusions of his own fertile imagination. In the end times, man's depraved condition becomes even worse: 'God shall send them strong delusion, that they should believe a lie: that they all might be damned who believed not the truth, but had pleasure in unrighteousness' (*2 Thess.* 2:11–12).

In all of this we must not forget the leading role of Satan, the father of all lies (*John* 8:44). He is the arch-enemy of God, first and foremost among those who covet God's throne. He was the one who incited Adam and Eve to rebel. Yet, Satan's downfall, too, is inevitable. The just reward of Satan and his fellow would-be gods is to be cast into the lake of fire, there to be tormented for ever and ever (*Rev.* 20:10).

So much, then, for Nietzsche's claim, 'God is dead.' Whatever Nietzsche might have hoped, the Christian God is no mere figment of the human imagination. He is the living God, the only true God. It is impossible that he should die. Indeed, all else depends on the living God of the Bible for its continued existence. The death of this indestructible God is the mere wishful thinking of wicked creatures, would-be murderers of God who cannot exist without him.

The gods that die are the fake gods created by God's scheming creatures. As the prophet Jeremiah declares,

> But the LORD is the true God, he is the living God, and an everlasting king: at his wrath the earth shall tremble, and the nations shall not be able to abide his indignation. Thus shall ye say unto them, The gods that have not made the heavens and the earth, even they shall perish from the earth, and from under these heavens (*Jer.* 10:10–11).

The only true God will decisively settle the challenge by utterly vanquishing his challengers.

Thus, in assessing man's attempts to answer God's challenge, the inevitable conclusion is that given by God himself:

> For I beheld, and there was no man; even among them, and there was no counsellor, that, when I asked of them, could answer a word. Behold, they are all vanity; their works are nothing: their molten images are wind and confusion (*Isa.* 41:28–29).

The only hope for man is to repent of his unbelief and to embrace the salvation offered in Jesus Christ. But this requires him to swallow his pride. Rebellion against God is, after all, founded on pride. Pride hinders the ability of apologetic arguments – no matter how rationally sound – to convert unbelievers. As Thomas Molnar (1980:180) notes, 'Atheism is essentially *pride* – the pride of the creature setting himself over against the Creator – and the proud man is proud of his being proud. He would lose his self-respect, he would be humiliated, if he renounced his pride.'

The day will come, however, when all human pride will be humbled:

> For the day of the LORD of hosts shall be upon every one that is proud and lofty . . . And the loftiness of man shall be bowed down, and the haughtiness of men shall be made low: and the LORD alone shall be exalted in that day (*Isa.* 2:12,17).

Hence the Bible urges us to relinquish our pride and to embrace humility:

> God resisteth the proud, but giveth grace unto the humble. Submit yourselves therefore to God. Resist the devil, and he will flee from you. Draw nigh to God and he will draw nigh to you. Cleanse your hands, ye sinners; and purify your hearts, ye double minded . . . Humble yourselves in the sight of the Lord, and he shall lift you up (*James* 4:6–10).

Yet, the unbeliever so stubbornly clings to his pride and resists God's gracious gospel offer that it requires the special intervention of the Holy Spirit to transform hardened hearts and darkened minds.

In sum, we can make proper sense of reality only if we abandon our vain pretensions of human wisdom and recognize it for the foolishness it is. True wisdom consists of humble submission to the revealed Word of our sovereign Creator. Only God, through his written Word, can endow our lives with genuine purpose, meaning and direction. Only thus can we look forward with firm confidence towards a glorious future, when all things will culminate in 'good to them that love God, to them who are called according to his purpose' (*Rom.* 8:28).

* * * * *

The four and twenty elders fall down before him that [sits]
on the throne, and worship him that liveth for
ever and ever, and cast their crowns
before the throne, saying,

Thou art worthy, O Lord, to receive glory
and honour and power: for thou
hast created all things, and
for thy pleasure they are
and were created

(REVELATION 4:10–11).

Bibliography

ALSTON, WILLIAM P. 'Divine Action, Human Freedom, and the Laws of Nature', In Russell, R. J., Murphy, N., Isham, C. J. (eds.) *Quantum Cosmology and the Laws of Nature* (2nd ed.), Vatican City: Vatican Observatory Publications (1996).

ARISTOTLE 1952. *The Works of Aristotle, Vol. 1. [Great Books of the Western World, Vol. 8]*. Robert M. Hutchins (ed.). Chicago, IL: Encyclopaedia Britannica.

ATKINS, PETER 1994. *Creation Revisited*. Harmondsworth: Penguin.
——— 1998. 'Awesome versus Adipose', *Free Inquiry Magazine* Vol. 18, No. 2 (1998).

AUGUSTINE 1972. *The City of God*. David Knowles (ed.). New York: Penguin Books.

AYER, A. J. 1936. *Language, Truth and Logic*. New York: Dover [1947].
——— (ed.) 1959. *Logical Positivism*. Glencoe, IL: Free Press.

BAHNSEN, GREG L. 1998. *Van Til's Apologetics: Readings and Analysis*. Phillipsburg, NJ: Presbyterian & Reformed.

BARTHOLOMEW, D. J. 1984. *God of Chance*. London: SCM Press.

BARROW, JOHN 1992. *Pi in the Sky*. Oxford: Oxford University Press.

BAVINCK, HERMAN 1999. *In the Beginning: Foundations of Creation Theology*. Edited by John Bolt, translated by John Vriend. Grand Rapids, MI: Baker Books.

BENACERRAF, PAUL 1983. 'Mathematical Truth' in Paul Benacerraf & Hilary Putnam (eds.) *Philosophy of Mathematics* (2nd ed.). Cambridge: The University Press.

BISHOP, ERRETT 1967. *Foundations of Constructive Analysis*. New York: McGraw-Hill.

—— 1985. 'Schizophrenia in Contemporary Mathematics', in E. Bishop: *Reflections on Him and His Research*, Murray Rosenblatt (ed.), American Mathematical Society, Providence, pp.1–32.

BISHOP, ROBERT C. 1993. 'Science and Theology: A Methodological Comparison'. *Journal of Interdisciplinary Studies* V (1/2): 141–62.

BLACKMORE, S. J. 2000. *The Meme Machine.* Oxford: The University Press.

—— 2002. 'The Grand Illusion', *New Scientist*, 22 June 2002: 26–29.

BOYD, GREG 2000. *God of the Possible: A Biblical Introduction to the Open View of God.* Grand Rapids, MI: Baker Book House.

BULTMANN, RUDOLF 1964. *Kerygma and Myth.* 2nd edition. Edited by H. W. Bartsch, translated by R. H. Fuller. London: SPCK.

BUNGE, MARIO 1980. *The Mind-Body Problem.* Toronto: Pergamon.

BYL, JOHN 2001. *God and Cosmos: A Christian View of Time, Space and the Universe.* Edinburgh: Banner of Truth.

CALVIN, JOHN 1949. *Institutes of the Christian Religion*, John Allen (ed.). Grand Rapids, MI: Eerdmans.

CHOMSKY, NOAM 1972. *Language and Mind.* Cambridge, MA: MIT Press.

—— 1980. *Rules and Representations.* New York: Columbia University Press.

CHURCHLAND, PAUL M. 1984. *Matter and Consciousness.* Cambridge, MA: MIT Press.

—— 1988. 'The Ontological Status of Intentional States', *Behavioural and Brain Sciences* 11/3: 507-508.

—— & PATRICIA S. CHURCHLAND 1999. *On the Contrary: Critical Essays, 1987-1997.* Bradford: MIT Press.

CLARK, GORDON 1968. *The Philosophy of Gordon Clark: A Festschrift*, Ronald H. Nash (ed.), P & R, Philadelphia, pp. 64–70.

CLARKE, W. NORRIS 1987. 'Christian Theism and Whiteheadian Process Philosophy' in Ronald Nash (ed.) *Process Theology.* Grand Rapids: Baker.

CLOUSER, ROY A. 1991. *The Myth of Religious Neutrality*, Notre Dame: University of Notre Dame Press.

COHEN, I. B. (ed.) 1978. *Isaac Newton's Papers & Letters on Natural Philosophy*, 2nd edition. Cambridge, MA: Harvard University Press.

COHEN, PAUL J. 1966. *Set Theory and the Continuum Hypothesis*. New York: W. A. Benjamin.

COOPER, JOHN W. 1989. *Body, Soul & Life Everlasting*. Grand Rapids: Eerdmans.

CRAIG, WILLIAM L. 1987. *The Only Wise God: The Compatibility of Divine Foreknowledge and Human Freedom*. Grand Rapids, MI: Baker.

CRICK, FRANCIS 1981. *Life Itself*. New York: Simon and Schuster.

———— 1994. *The Astonishing Hypothesis*. New York: Touchstone.

———— & C. KOCH 1992. 'The problem of consciousness'. *Scientific American* 267(3):153–9.

DARWIN, CHARLES 1881. *The Autobiography of Charles Darwin and Selected Letters*. Ed. Francis Darwin. New York: Dover [1958 repr.].

DAUBEN, JOSEPH W. 1979. *Georg Cantor: His Mathematics and Philosophy of the Infinite*. Princeton, NJ: Princeton University Press.

DAVIES, PAUL 1983. *God and the New Physics*. New York: Simon & Schuster.

———— 1988. *The Cosmic Blueprint*. New York: Simon & Schuster.

———— 1992. *The Mind of God*. London: Penguin.

———— 1995. 'Physics and the Mind of God'. *First Things* (August/Sept.): 31–5.

———— 1995. *Are We Alone?* New York: Basic Books.

DAVIS, JOHN JEFFERSON 'Quantum Indeterminacy and the Omniscience of God', *Science & Christian Belief* (1997) 9: 129–44.

DAWKINS, RICHARD 1976. *The Selfish Gene*. Oxford: Oxford University Press.

———— 1991. *The Blind Watchmaker*. Harmondsworth, UK: Penguin.

———— 1995. *River Out of Eden*. New York.

DEHAENE, STANISLAS 1997. *The Number Sense: How the Mind Creates Mathematics*. Oxford: The University Press.

DEMBSKI, WILLIAM A. 1990. 'Converting Matter into Mind'. *Perspectives on Science & Christian Faith* 42 (No. 4): 202–26.

———— 1999. *Intelligent Design: The Bridge Between Science and Theology*. Downers Grove, IL: InterVarsity Press.

DENBIGH, KENNETH 1975. *The Inventive Universe*. London: Hutchinson.

DENNETT, DANIEL C. 1991. *Consciousness Explained*. London: Penguin.

───── 1995. *Darwin's Dangerous Idea*. New York: Simon & Schuster.

DERRIDA, JACQUES 1976. *Of Grammatology*. Trans. Gayatri Spivak. Baltimore, MD: Johns Hopkins University Press.

DREES, WILLEM B. 1996. *Religion, Science and Naturalism*. Cambridge, The University Press.

ECCLES, JOHN C. 1994. *How the Self Controls Its Brain*. New York: Springer-Verlag.

EINSTEIN, ALBERT 1954. 'Science and Religion II'. *Ideas and Opinions*. New York: Crown Publishers, Inc. 1954, pp.41–9.

───── 1956. *Lettres à Maurice Solovine*. Paris: Gauthier-Villars.

───── 1981. *Einstein: the Human Side*. Helen Dukas and Banesh Hoffman (eds.). Princeton, NJ: Princeton University Press.

───── 1999. *The World as I See It*. Secaucus, NJ: The Citadel Press.

FEINBERG, JOHN S. 2001. *No One Like Him*. Wheaton, IL: Crossway.

FOUCAULT, MICHEL 1977. *Discipline and Punishment: Birth of the Prison*. Trans. Alan Sheridan. New York: Random House.

FRAME, JOHN M. 1987. *The Doctrine of the Knowledge of God*. Phillipsburg, N.J: Presbyterian & Reformed.

GEISLER, NORMAN 1999. *Chosen But Free*. Minneapolis: Bethany House.

───── & WINFRIED CORDUAN 1988. *Philosophy of Religion* 2nd ed. Grand Rapids, MI: Baker Book House.

GENTZEN, GERHARD 1936. 'Die Widerspruchsfreiheit der reinen Zahlentheorie', *Mathematischen Annalen* 112:493–565.

GITT, WERNER 2001. *In the Beginning Was Information* (3rd ed.). Bielefeld, Germany: Christliche Literatur-Verbreitung.

GÖDEL, KURT 1931. 'Über formal unentschedbare Sätze der Principia mathematica und verwandter Systeme I.' *Monatshefte für Mathematik und Physik* 38: 173-198.

GRIFFIN, DAVID R. 2000. *Religion and Scientific Naturalism: Overcoming the Conflicts*. Albany, NY: SUNY Press.

───── 2002. 'Naturalism: Scientific and Religious', *Zygon* 37 (No.2): 361–80.

HABERMAS, JÜRGEN 1990. *Moral Consciousness and Communicative Action*. Trans. Christian Lenhardt & Shierry W. Nicholsen. Cambridge, MA: MIT Press.

HARDY, G. H. 1967. *A Mathematician's Apology*, Cambridge: The University Press, pp.123–4.

HASKER, WILLIAM 1983. *Metaphysics: Constructing a Worldview*. Downers Grove, IL: InterVarsity Press.

HAWKING, STEPHEN W. 1988. *A Brief History of Time*. New York: Bantam Books.

HELLMAN, G. 1993. 'Constructive Mathematics and Quantum Mechanics: Unbounded Operators and the Spectral Theorem', *Journal of Philosophical Logic* 23: 221–8.

——— 1997. 'Quantum Mechanical Unbounded Operators and Constructive Mathematics – A Rejoinder to Bridges'. *Journal of Philosophical Logic* 26:121–7.

HERBERT, NICK 1993. *Elemental Mind: Human Consciousness and the New Physics*. New York: Penguin.

HERSCH, REUBEN 1997. *What Is Mathematics, Really?* Oxford, UK: The University Press.

HIGHFIELD, RON 2002. 'The Function of Divine Self-Limitation in Open Theism.' *Journal of the Evangelical Theological Society.*

HILBERT, DAVID 1927. 'The Foundations of Mathematics' in Jean van Heijenoort 1967, *From Frege to Gödel*. Cambridge, MA: Harvard University Press.

HOFSTADTER, D. R. 1979. *Gödel, Escher, Bach*. New York: Basic Books.

HOLMES, ARTHUR 1977. *All Truth is God's Truth*. Grand Rapids: Eerdmans.

HUME, DAVID 1777. *An Enquiry concerning Human Understanding*. La Salle: Open Court (1958 reprint).

——— 1969. *A Treatise of Human Nature*. Harmondsworth: Penguin Books.

JAKI, STANLEY L. 1989. *God and the Cosmologists*. Washington, DC: Regnery Gateway.

JAUNCEY, JAMES 1971. *Science Returns to God*. Grand Rapids: Zondervan.

JENSON, ROBERT W. 1993. 'How the World Lost Its Story'. *First Things* 36:19–24.

JOHNSON, PHILLIP E. 1995. *Reason in the Balance*. Downer's Grove, IL: InterVarsity.

———— 2000. *The Wedge of Truth*. Downer's Grove, IL: InterVarsity.

JONES, PETER 1997. *Spirit Wars: Pagan Revival in Christian America*. Mulkilteo, WA: WinePress Publishing.

JORDAN, JAMES B. 1999. *Through New Eyes: Developing a Biblical Worldview*. Eugene, OR: Wipf and Stock.

KAFATOS, MENAS & NADEAU, ROBERT 1990. *The Conscious Universe*. New York: Springer-Verlag.

KEISTER, J. C. 1982. 'Math and the Bible', *The Trinity Review* No. 27, pp.1–3.

KIM, JAEGWON 1993. *Supervenience and the Mind*. Cambridge: The University Press.

———— 1994. What is 'Naturalized Epistemology'? In Hilary Kornblith, ed. *Naturalizing Epistemology*. 2nd ed. Cambridge, MA: MIT Press: 33–55.

LAKOFF, GEORGE & RAFAEL NUNEZ 2000. *Where Mathematics Comes From*. New York: Basic Books.

LARMORE, CHARLES 1996. *The Morals of Modernity*. Cambridge: The University Press.

LARSON, EDWARD J. & LARRY WITHAM 1999. 'Scientists and Religion in America', *Scientific American* (September 1999): 88–93.

LAVINE, SHAUGHAN 1994. *Understanding the Infinite*. Cambridge, MA: Harvard University Press.

LEARY, CHRISTOPHER C. 2000. *A Friendly Introduction to Mathematical Logic*. Upper Saddle River, NJ: Prentice Hall.

LEWIS, C. S. 1947. *Miracles*. New York: Macmillan [1978 reprint].

LEWONTIN, RICHARD C. 1992. 'The Dream of the Human Genome'. *New York Review of Books* XXXIX (28 May, 1992): 31–3.

LOUTHAN, STEPHEN 1996. 'On Religion – A Discussion with Richard Rorty, Alvin Plantinga and Nicholas Wolterstorff', *Christian Scholar's Review* XXVI (2): 177–83.

LUTHER, MARTIN 1525. *The Bondage of the Will* (trans. by Henry Cole). 1976 reprint. Grand Rapids, MI: Baker Book House.

LYOTARD, JEAN-FRANCOIS 1992. *The Postmodern Explained*. Minneapolis, MN: University of Minnesota Press.

MACKAY, D. M. 1979. *Human Science and Human Dignity*. Downers Grove, IL: InterVarsity Press.

MACKIE, J. L. 1982. *The Miracle of Theism*. Oxford: Clarendon Press.

——— 1979. *Ethics: Inventing Right and Wrong*. Harmondsworth: Penguin.

MADDY, PENELOPE 1993. *Realism in Mathematics*. Oxford: The University Press.

MALCOLM, DAVID 1988. 'Humanism and Modern Mathematics'. *Ex Nihilo Technical Journal* 3:49–58.

MARLIN, GEORGE J., RICHARD P. RABATIN, & JOHN L. SWAN, eds. 1987. *The Quotable Chesterton*. Garden City, NY: Image.

MAYNARD-SMITH, JOHN 1969. 'The Status of neo-Darwinism' in *Towards a Theoretical Biology*. C. H. Waddington (ed.), Vol.2. Edinburgh: The University Press.

McGINN, COLIN 1991. *The Problem of Consciousness: Essays Toward a Resolution*. Oxford: Oxford University Press.

——— 1999a. 'Can we ever understand consciousness?' *The New York Review of Books* (June 10, 1999).

——— 1999b. *The Mysterious Flame: Conscious Minds in a Material World*. New York: Basic Books.

MENZEL, CHRISTOPHER 1987. 'An Activist Model of the Metaphysics of Mathematics' in *Sixth Conference on Mathematics from a Christian Perspective*, Robert L. Brabenec (ed.).

——— 1990. 'Theism, Platonism, and the Metaphysics of Mathematics'. *Christian Theism and the Problems of Philosophy*, Michael D. Beaty (ed.), University of Notre Dame Press.

MEYER, STEPHEN C. 1999. The Return of the God Hypothesis. *Journal of Interdisciplinary Studies* XI (1/2): 1–38.

MIDDLETON, J. RICHARD & WALSH, BRIAN J. 1995. *Truth is Stranger than It Used to Be*. Downers Grove, IL: InterVarsity Press.

MOLNAR, THOMAS 1973. *God and the Knowledge of Reality*. New York: Basic Books.

——— 1980. *Theists and Atheists: A Typology of Non-Belief*. The Hague: Mouton Publishers.

——— 1995. 'Paganism and Its Renewal'. *The Intercollegiate Review* Fall 1995:28–35.

MONK, J. 1976. *Mathematical Logic*. Heidelberg: Springer-Verlag.

MONOD, JACQUES 1972. *Chance and Necessity*. London: Collins.

MOORE, GEORGE E. 1953. *Some Main Problems in Philosophy*. New York: Collier.

MORELAND, J. P. 1989. *Christianity and the Nature of Science*. Grand Rapids, MI: Baker.

———— & SCOTT B. RAE 2000. *Body & Soul*. Downers Grove, IL: InterVarsity Press.

———— 2000. 'Naturalism and the Ontological Status of Properties.' In William L. Craig & James P. Moreland, eds. *Naturalism: A Critical Analysis*. London: Routledge: 67–109.

MURPHY, NANCEY 'Divine Action in the Natural Order: Buridan's Ass and Schrodinger's Cat', In Russell, R. J., Murphy, Nancey, & Peacocke, Arthur (eds.) *Chaos and Complexity: Scientific Perspectives on Divine Action*. Vatican City: Vatican Observatory (1995), pp. 325–57.

NAGEL, THOMAS 1997. *The Last Word*. New York: Oxford U.P.

NASH, RONALD 1999 *Life's Ultimate Questions*. Grand Rapids: Zondervan,

NIETZSCHE, FRIEDRICH 1920. *The Antichrist* (trans. H. L. Mencken). New York: Knopf.

———— 1961. *Thus Spoke Zarathustra* (trans. R. J. Hollingdale). New York: Penguin.

———— 1974. *The Gay Science* (trans. W. Kaufmann). New York: Vintage Books.

O'HEAR, ANTHONY 1997. *Beyond Evolution: Human Nature and the Limits of Evolutionary Explanation*. Oxford: The University Press.

PAGELS, HEINZ R. 1982. *The Cosmic Code: Quantum Physics as the Language of Nature*. New York: Simon and Schuster.

PASCAL, BLAISE 1989. *The Mind on Fire: An Anthology of the Writings of Blaise Pascal*. Edited by James M. Houston. Portland, OR: Multnomah Press.

PEACOCKE, ARTHUR 1993. *Theology for a Scientific Age* (Enlarged ed.), London: SCM Press.

———— 1997. 'Response to Davis', *Science & Christian Belief* 9:145–7.

PENROSE, ROGER 1990. *The Emperor's New Mind*, London: Vintage Books.

———— 1994. *Shadows of the Mind*. London: Vintage.

PEREBOOM, DERK 2001. *Living without Free Will*. Cambridge: The University Press.

PINKER, STEPHEN 1994. *The Language Instinct*. New York: William Morrow.

PIPER, JOHN 2000. *The Pleasures of God*. Sisters, OR: Multnomah.

PLANTINGA, ALVIN 1980. *Does God Have a Nature?* Marquette University Press, Milwaukee.

———— 1990. 'Prologue: Advice to Christian Philosophers'. *Christian Theism and the Problems of Philosophy*, Michael D. Beaty (ed.). Notre Dame: University of Notre Dame Press.

———— 1993. *Warrant and Proper Function*. New York: Oxford University Press.

POLKINGHORNE, JOHN 1998. *Belief in God in an Age of Science*, New Haven: Yale University Press.

POLLARD, WILLIAM *Chance and Providence: God's Action in a World Governed by Scientific Law*. New York: Scribner (1958).

POPPER, KARL R. 1972. *Objective Knowledge: An Evolutionary Approach*. Oxford, UK: Clarendon.

———— & JOHN C. ECCLES 1977. *The Self and Its Brain*. New York: Springer International.

POYTHRESS, VERN 1976. 'A Biblical View of Mathematics', *Foundations of Christian Scholarship*, Gary North (ed.). Vallecito, CA: Ross House Books.

PROVINE, WILLIAM 1988. 'Progress in Evolution and Meaning in Life'. In *Evolutionary Progress* (ed. Matthew H. Nitecki) Chicago: University of Chicago Press, 47–74.

———— 1994. 'Darwinism: Science or Naturalistic Philosophy?', *Origins Research* 16(1/2), 9.

PUTNAM, HILARY 1983. *Realism and Reason*. New York: Cambridge University Press.

QUINE, WILLARD V. O. 1981. *Theories and Things*. Cambridge: Harvard University Press.

RAV, YEHUDA 1993. 'Philosophical Problems in the Light of Evolutionary Epistemology.' In *Math Worlds*, Sal Restivo (ed.). Albany, NY: State University of New York Press: 80–109.

REYMOND, ROBERT L. 1998. *A New Systematic Theology of the Christian Faith*, Nashville: Thomas Nelson.

RORTY, RICHARD 1991. *Objectivity, Relativism and Truth, Philosophical Papers 1*. Cambridge, UK: The University Press.

———— 1995. 'Untruth and Consequences.' *The New Republic* (31 July): 32–6.

ROSS, HUGH 1993. *The Creator and the Cosmos*. Colorado Springs, CO: NavPress.

RUSE, MICHAEL 1998. *Taking Darwin Seriously*. Amherst, NY: Prometheus Books.

———— 1995. *Evolutionary Naturalism: Selected Essays*. London: Routledge.

———— & WILSON, E. O. 1986. 'Moral philosophy as applied science', *Philosophy* 61: 173–92.

RUSHDOONY, R. J. 1978. *The One and the Many*. Fairfax, Va: Thoburn P.

RUSSELL, BERTRAND 1945. *A History of Western Philosophy*. New York: Simon & Schuster.

———— 1956. *Portraits from Memory*. London: George Allen & Unwin.

———— 1957. *Why I am Not a Christian and Other Essays on Religion and Related Subjects*. New York: Simon & Schuster.

———— 1959. *The Problems of Philosophy*. New York: Oxford U. P.

———— 1968. *The Autobiography of Bertrand Russell, Vol. 2*. Boston: Little Brown & Co.

———— 1975. *My Philosophical Development*. London: George Allen and Unwin.

SARTRE, JEAN-PAUL 1957. *Existentialism and Human Emotions*, Secaucus, NJ: The Citadel Press.

SCRUTON, ROGER 1998. *An Intelligent Person's Guide to Modern Culture*. London: Duckworth.

SEARLE, JOHN R. 1992. *The Rediscovery of the Mind*. Cambridge, MA: MIT Press.

SEGAL, ROBERT 1989. *Explaining and Interpreting Religion*. Atlanta: Scholars Press.

SIRE, JAMES W. 1997. *The Universe Next Door* (3rd edition). Downers Grove, IL: InterVarsity.

SMITH, BABARA HERRNSTEIN 1997. *Belief and Resistance: Dynamics of Contemporary Intellectual Controversy*. Cambridge, MA: Harvard University Press.

SQUIRES, EUAN 1990. *Conscious Mind in the Physical World*. New York: Hilger.

STAPP, HENRY P. 1993. *Mind, Matter, and Quantum Mechanics*, Berlin: Springer-Verlag.

STEINER, MARK 1998. *The Applicability of Mathematics as a Philosophical Problem*. Cambridge, MA: Harvard University Press.

STOB, HENRY 1978. *Ethical Reflection*. Grand Rapids, MI: Eerdmans.

TAYLOR, RICHARD 1974. *Metaphysics* (2nd ed.). Englewood Cliffs, NJ: Prentice-Hall.

TIESSEN, TERRANCE L. 2000. *Providence and Prayer: How Does God Work in the World?* Downers Grove, IL: InterVarsity Press.

VAN TIL, CORNELIUS 1967. *The Defense of the Faith* (3rd ed.). Philadelphia: Presbyterian & Reformed.

WAGNER, JOSEPH 1991. 'The Revolt Against Reason: Mistaken Assumptions in Post-Positivist Relativism.' In Wendy Oxman-Michelli & Mark Weinstein, eds. *Critical Thinking: Focus on Social and Cultural Inquiry.* Upper Montclair: Institute for Critical Thinking: 61–87.

WARD, KEITH 1996. *God, Chance and Necessity.* Oxford: One World.
——— 1999. 'Why God Must Exist', *Science & Christian Belief* 11:5–13.

WEINBERG, STEVEN 1992. *Dreams of a Final Theory.* New York: Pantheon Books.

WIGNER, EUGENE 1960. 'The Unreasonable Effectiveness of Mathematics', *Communications on Pure and Applied Mathematics* 13:1-14.

WILLARD, DALLAS 2000. 'Knowledge and Naturalism.' In William L. Craig & James P. Moreland, eds. *Naturalism: A Critical Analysis.* London: Routledge: 26–48.

WILSON, EDWARD O. 1979. *On Human Nature.* New York: Bantam Books.
——— 1998. *Consilience: The Unity of Knowledge.* New York: Vintage.

WRIGHT, R. K. MCGREGOR 1996. *No Place For Sovereignty: What's Wrong with Freewill Theism.* Downers Grove. IL: InterVarsity Press.

WRIGHT, SEWALL 1977. 'Panpsychism and Science.' In John B. Cobb Jr. & David Ray Griffen, eds. *Mind in Nature: Essays on the Interface of Science and Philosophy.* Washington, DC: The University Press of America: 77–88.

Index

Adam, 185–6, 229, 232–3, 241, 265–6, 289, 296
Affirming the consequent, 30–1
Alston, William P., 204
Apologetics, 284–6
Aristotle, 13, 64, 73, 174–5, 239, 258
Arithmetic, 121, 129, 139–43, 148
Atkins, Peter, 44, 46, 57
Augustine, 121, 136, 168, 239–41, 258–9, 294
Axiom of choice, 272, 274–6
Axiomatic method, 138–40
Ayer, A. J., 123

Bahnsen, Greg, 285
Barrow, John, 142–3
Bartholomew, D. J., 72, 203–5, 211, 214, 217
Bavinck, Herman, 198
Beauty, 102, 129–31, 281
Beliefs, 106–8, 285
Benacerraf, Paul, 125–6
Bible, 172–3, 187, 195, 221, 227–31, 256, 269–70, 282–3, 293, 297
Bishop, Errett, 144
Bishop, Robert C., 286
Blackmore, S. J., 97, 100–1, 103–5

Bohm, David, 76–7, 79–80
Bohr, Niels, 74–5, 79
Boyd, Greg, 202
Brain, 80–1, 96–9 103, 107–8, 116, 147–8
Buddhism, 34, 61, 172
Bultmann, Rudolf, 196–7
Bunge, Mario, 248–9
Butterfly effect, 67, 208

Calvin, John, 233, 266
Cantor, Georg, 149, 259, 268, 273–4
Causality, principle of, 27, 64–81
Causation – efficient, final, 116
Cause – primary, secondary, 199–203, 218, 282
Cells, 83–9
Challenge, 2–4, 280–98
Chance, 64–81, 92, 201–9, 211–2, 216–7, 282
Chaos, chaotic systems, 48–9, 66–8, 90, 110, 135, 208
Chesterton, G. K., 163
Chomsky, Noam, 127–9
Christ
  his miracles, 201
  redemption through, 186–7, 229, 278, 282, 289
  resurrection of, 197

Churchland, Paul M., 100–1, 105
Clark, Gordon, 252, 256, 269
Clarke, W. Norris, 171
Clouser, Roy A., 262–5
Cohen, I. B., 65
Cohen, Paul J., 276
Common sense, 21–3, 159, 167,
    174, 243, 283
Compatibilism, 213–4, 221–7,
    234, 236, 283
Completeness, 139–43, 152, 271
Complex specified information,
    91–3
Complexity, 84–7, 90–4, 98, 110
Comprehensibility of the world,
    53–4, 197–8
Concurrence, 199–200, 204
Consciousness, 77–8, 80–1,
    95–110, 158–9
Consistency, 20, 139–43, 154, 161,
    165, 193, 271, 276–7, 283
Constructive mathematics, 144–7,
    154, 270, 273–6
Contingency, 47–8, 58, 91–2
Cooper, John W., 243
Copenhagen interpretation,
    quantum mechanics, 61, 74, 80
Craig, William L., 218
Creation, 183–9, 197–8
Creationism (of souls), 251–3
Crick, Sir Francis, 7, 18, 92, 102,
    106–7, 159, 222, 251, 293
Criteria, for testing worldviews,
    19–21

Darwin, Charles, 39, 83–5, 113
Dauben, Joseph W., 259, 269
Davies, Paul, 49, 85, 92, 94, 130,
    148, 286
Davis, John J., 206–7
Dawkins, Richard, 82–4, 87,

103–4, 109, 115
Death, 238, 241–3, 253
Dehaene, Stanislas, 147
Dembski, William A., 91–2, 244–5
Denbigh, Kenneth, 158
Dennett, Daniel C., 105, 249
Denying the antecedent, 31
Derrida, Jacques, 161–2
Descartes, René, 37–9, 64–5, 95,
    160, 239–40, 250, 268–9
Determinism – hard, soft, 68,
    72–6, 81, 107, 202–6, 212–236,
    283
Divine revelation, 42, 168, 171,
    179, 285
DNA, 85–90, 92, 110, 157
Double slit experiment, 68–70
Drees, Willem B., 124–5
Dualism, see Mind-body dualism
Duality – mind/body, see Mind-
    body dualism
Duality – wave/particle, 68–71

Eccles, Sir John, 100, 103, 107,
    109, 215, 249–51
Einstein, Albert, 1, 2, 4, 13, 53, 75,
    277–8
Election, 230–1, 234
Emergence, 94, 98–100, 157–9,
    281, 284
Empiricism, 38, 42, 60, 122–5, 132
Energy conservation, 248–50
Epiphenomenon, 108
Epistemology, 14, 79, 112–32
Euclidean geometry, 138–9, 264,
    271
Everett, Hugh, 78
Evil, problem of, 231–5
Evolution, 39, 41, 83–4, 90, 103,
    109, 114, 128–131, 147–9,
    154, 166–7

Existentialism, 155–6, 172

Fatalism, 223–4, 283
Feinberg, John S., 38
Foreknowledge, 206–9, 218–9, 223–4
Formalisms, 56
Foucault, Michel, 162–3
Frame, John M., 257
Freedom – of spontaneity, of indifference, see Compatibilism, Libertarianism
Free will, 159, 202, 212–236

Geisler, Norman, 136, 214
Genes, 87–9, 103–4
Gentzen, Gerhard, 276
Gitt, Werner, 90–1
Gnosticism, 35
God, the ultimate reality, 179–82, 282
Gödel, Kurt, 140–3, 148, 152, 154, 166, 271, 276
Goldbach conjecture, 145
Gravity, 64–6, 81, 247
Griffin, David R., 115–6, 118, 125–6, 159, 168–71
Group theory, 54–5

Habermas, Jürgen, 164
Hardy, G. H., 149, 151
Hasker, William, 224–6, 244–5
Hawking, Stephen W., 58
Heisenberg, Werner, 70–1
Heisenberg uncertainty principle, 70–1, 74
Hellman, G., 146
Herbert, Nick, 68, 77–8
Hermeticism, 35, 37
Hersch, Reuben, 121–2, 126
Highfield, Ron, 217–8

Hilbert, David, 133–4, 139–40
Hinduism, 34, 61, 172
Hofstadter, Douglas R., 89
Holmes, Arthur, 257
Holy Spirit, work of the, 230, 298
Hume, David, 18, 38, 51–3, 73, 108, 124, 173, 215, 227
Huygens, Christiaan, 68

Idealism, 245–7
Indeterminism, 72, 79, 282
Induction, problem of, 51–3, 199
Infinity, 258–9, 266–7, 273–4
Information, 85–7, 90–3, 110, 157
Innate abilities, 127–9, 147–8, 168, 265–8
Intelligent design, 91–3, 110
Intentionality, 97–9
Interactive dualism, 243–53
Intuition, 148, 153, 168, 171, 267–9
Irreducible complexity, 92–3
Islam, 172

Jaki, Stanley L., 73
Jauncey, James, 200
Jenson, Robert W., 289
Johnson, Phillip E., 105
Jones, Peter, 292–3
Jordan, James, B., 36

Kafatos, Menas, 269
Kant, Immanuel, 13, 38
Keister, J. C., 270
Kepler, Johannes, 8, 37, 54–5
Kim, Jaegwon, 109, 124
Knowledge, objective, 112–32, 154, 160–8, 173–7, 187–9, 283, 290
Kronecker, Leopold, 133, 262

Lakoff, George, 147
Language, 97, 104, 112, 126–9
Laplace, Pierre Simon de, 67
Larmore, Charles, 120–1
Larson, Edward J., 19
Law of excluded middle, 29, 145–7
Law of non-contradiction, 29, 106, 119
Leary, Christopher C., 142
Leibniz, Gottfried, 65
Lewis, C. S., 106
Lewontin, Richard C., 89, 286–7
Liar paradox, 140, 143
Libertarianism, 214–221, 224–5, 235, 283
Life, 83–95
Livability, 21, 165, 175–7, 193–4
Locality, 76
Locke, John, 38, 66, 109
Logic, laws of, 24–31, 117–9, 145–7, 256–7, 263–4, 266, 269
Logical positivism, 123–4
Lotka, Alfred, 68
Louthan, Stephen, 289
Luther, Martin, 219–20, 252
Lyotard, Jean-François, 162

MacKay, D. M., 244–5
Mackie, J. L., 48, 119–20, 125
Maddy, Penelope, 147–8
Magic, 34–5, 37
Malcolm, David, 260
Mandelbrot set, 149–51
Many-worlds interpretation, quantum mechanics, 78
Marlin, George J., 163
Materialism, 10, 18, 39–40, 78, 93–110, 246, 253, 281–2, 287–8
Mathematical objects, 118, 125, 134–7

Mathematical realism, 122, 136–7, 149–54, 255, 265, 277
Mathematical structure of universe, 134, 152–3, 167, 256, 281
Mathematics, 8, 54–9, 118, 121–2, 133–54, 254–78, 283
Matter, 7, 40, 44–62, 95–100, 109
Maynard-Smith, John, 90
McGinn, Colin, 96, 99, 158–9
Memes, 103–6
Mental causation, 108–9, 243, 248–50, 287–8
Menzel, Christopher, 274, 277
Meta-narratives, 162–3, 165–6
Middle knowledge, 206–7, 218–9
Middleton, J. Richard, 165
Mind, 95–110, 113–6, 168, 170, 173–4, 243
Mind-body dualism, 38–9, 243–53
Mind-body problem, 245–53
Miracles, 5, 52–3, 137, 196–201, 282
Misplaced concreteness, fallacy of, 57, 79–80
Models, 30, 56–8, 137
Modernity, 289–91
Modus ponens, 30
Modus tollens, 30
Molina, Luis, 206, 218
Molnar, Thomas, 33–4, 292, 297
Monod, Jacques, 93–4
Moore, George E., 174–5
Morality, 102, 119–21, 124–5, 189–90, 227–8
Moral responsibility, 213–216, 224–31, 282–3
Moreland, J. P., 99, 117, 239, 243
Murphy, Nancey, 205–6, 212, 218
Myth, 6, 34–6

Nagel, Thomas, 176, 288
Nash, Ronald, 15
Natural selection, 83–4, 87, 93, 103, 113–4, 128–30, 148
Naturalism, 17–18, 32–43, 61–2 113–32, 156–60, 168–73, 281–2, 284, 286–8, 289–91
Necessary truths, 136, 262–5, 283
Necessity, 47, 58
Neo-paganism, 291–3
Neo-realism, 76,79
Newton, Isaac, 8, 37, 65–6, 68
Nietzsche, Friedrich, 4–7, 178–9, 291, 295–6
Norms, 118–25, 156, 169, 171, 285
Number theory, 139–43

O'Hear, Anthony, 130–1
One and the Many, problem of the, 13, 59–61, 171, 261–2
Open theism, 202, 208, 217–8, 220, 282
Order, 48–51

Paganism, 33–6, 291–3
Pagels, H., 63–4
Pan-psychism, 41, 95, 99–100, 168–71
Pantheism, 34, 169
Panentheism, 169
Pascal, Blaise, 238, 215, 278, 294–5
Peacocke, Arthur, 24, 34, 202, 204–7, 212
Penrose, Roger, 8, 10, 13, 57, 60, 149, 152, 167–8
Pereboom, Derk, 210, 225–6
Performative contradiction, 159, 165
Philo, 136
Physical determinism, 212–3, 222

Physics-ism, 41, 96, 157
Pilot wave, 76–7, 80
Pinker, Stephen, 111–2, 126–9
Piper, John, 234
Plantinga, Alvin, 114, 117, 232, 262–4, 274
Plato, 73, 121, 135–6, 258
Platonism, 121–2, 125–6, 135–7, 148
Polkinghorne, John, 79
Pollard, William G., 205
Popper, Karl R., 107
Possibility, 263–4
Post-modernity, 6, 160–7, 282, 288–9, 290–1
Power set, 272–4
Poythress, Vern, 259
Presburger arithmetic, 139
Presuppositions, 15, 43, 48, 52, 174, 280–1, 285–7
Pride, 3, 233, 280, 296–7
Process theology, 95, 168–71, 220, 232, 282
Proof by contradiction, 145–7, 270–1
Providence, 198–209, 217
Provine, William, 39–40, 237–8, 293
Purpose, 42–3, 93–5, 113, 115–6
Putnam, Hilary, 118–9, 123–4
Pyrrho, 173, 175–6
Pythagoras, 135, 147

Quantum effects, 68–81,166, 202–8, 211, 215
Quine, Willard V. O., 118, 126

Rationalism, 38
Rationality, 112–32, 137, 281–3, 286
Rav, Yehuda, 122, 254–5

Realism, 40, 57, 75–6, 152–3

Reductio ad absurdum, 21, 25, 101, 103, 109, 174, 285

Reductionism, 96, 106, 108, 157

Relativism, 18–19, 160–7, 281–2, 285

Representation, 97, 117, 126

Responsibility, see Moral Responsibility

Resurrection, 197, 244

Reymond, Robert L., 234, 252, 261

Rorty, Richard, 18, 113–4, 160–2, 289

Ross, Hugh, 260

Ruse, Michael, 102, 114, 117, 119

Rushdoony, R. J., 61, 261

Russell, Bertrand, 12–13, 52, 135, 143, 279–80, 294

Salvation, 186–7, 220, 229–30

Sartre, Jean-Paul, 155–6, 171–2, 293

Satan, 200–1, 229, 233, 296

Schrödinger's wave equation, 71

Science, 5–7, 19, 23–4

Scientific revolution, 36–40

Scruton, Roger, 293–4

Searle, John R., 98–9, 101, 287–8

Second law of thermodynamics,

Segal, Robert, 43

Self, the, 102–4, 112–3, 160, 166, 173, 222, 282

Self-refutation, 25, 101, 106, 108, 159–60, 164–6, 175, 281–2, 285

Semi-materialism, 244–5

Set theory, 148, 271–4

Sin, 185–6, 188–9, 228–9, 232, 282–3

Sire, James W., 15

Scepticism, 173–7

Smith, Babara Herrnstein, 18, 162

Soul, 38–9, 239–53, 282

Sovereignty of God, 180, 208, 211–2, 216–21, 232, 264–5, 282

Spirits, 196–7, 200–1, 240, 248

Stapp, Henry P., 72–3, 216

Steiner, Mark, 55–7

Stob, Henry, 229

Sufficient reason, principle of, 27, 48, 73, 80, 206, 221, 236, 281

Taylor, Richard, 48, 98, 115, 216

Theism, 17, 48, 79, 114, 125–6, 131, 137, 144, 147, 153–4, 168–71, 270–1, 274–8, 283, 288–9

Tiessen, Terrance, 216, 224

Tower of Babel, 127, 290–1

Traducianism, 251–3

Transfinite numbers, 269, 273–4

Transcendental argument for Christianity, 285

Trinity, the, 181, 204, 259–61

Truth – correspondence, coherence, pragmatic, relativistic theories, 26–7, 113–122, 160–7, 176

Two-valued logic, 144–7, 270, 277

Uniformity, 23, 51–3

Unity of the self, 7, 102–4, 112–3

Universals, 121, 167–9, 171, 283

Van Til, Cornelius, 285

Von Neumann, John, 77, 79

Wagner, Joseph, 164

Ward, Keith, 47, 57, 72, 106, 167, 212

Wave function, 70–1, 77–8, 80

Weinberg, Steven, 55

Wigner, Eugene, 54–5, 153
Willard, Dallas, 117
Wilson, Edward O., 18, 32–3, 39, 85, 102–4, 157
World stories, 163, 165–6, 289–91
Worldviews, 13–28, 167–8, 173–7, 190–5, 280–5, 287

Wright, R. K. McGregor, 215–6, 220
Wright, Sewall, 99

Zermelo-Fraenkel (ZF) axioms, 272
ZFC set theory, 272–3, 276–7

—◦◦◦—

ALSO AVAILABLE FROM THE BANNER OF TRUTH TRUST

From the author of
The Divine Challenge:

God and Cosmos

A Christian View of Time,
Space and the Universe

In his best-selling book *A Brief History of Time*, the famous Cambridge cosmologist Stephen Hawking held out the prospect of a complete theory of the universe, by means of which we should know 'why it is that we and the universe exist . . . then we should know the mind of God'. Christian mathematician John Byl disagrees. 'Hawking overestimates the value of a Theory-of-Everything, while underestimating the content of God's mind.'

We already have in Scripture a source of knowledge superior to all other sources and already know 'the mind of God', so far as He has been pleased to reveal it to us. On this basis, Byl questions much of modern cosmology, including the Big-Bang theory of origins. He deals with the limitations of human knowledge, biblical teaching relevant to cosmology, the quest for extra-terrestrial intelligence, the existence of the spiritual realm, heaven, angels, life after death, and much else. Byl's approach is a refreshing counter to the dreary and ultimately meaningless outlook of modern cosmology.

DR JOHN BYL is Professor of Mathematics and Head of the Department of Mathematical Sciences at Trinity Western University, Langley, British Columbia, Canada. He gained his Ph.D. in Astronomy at the University of British Columbia and is the author of numerous published papers

From unsolicited reviews of God and Cosmos
on the World Wide Web:

'I include this book on my small "must-read" list for Christians, "Essentials for a balanced Christian faith and world view", for two reasons. (a) Dr Byl presents a valid framework for how we know what we know . . . This framework is sorely needed; too often professing Christians base their thought on explicitly non-Christian assumptions. (b) Cosmology has taken a place of exaggerated importance in "pop science" . . . In the debate over origins, Christians and non-Christians alike build their arguments on a non-Christian epistemology; anyone who understands this work by Byl should be free from this.'

'Points out a number of problems in big-bang cosmology. A good introduction that makes a number of very good points and conducts good critiques . . . a solid introduction into the world of cosmology.'

'Perhaps the best young-earth creationist book ever. Byl has written a fascinating and sure-footed work on the subject of Christianity and astronomy . . . being theologically and philosophically astute [Byl] does a very credible job. Anyone interested in science and religion from a conservative religious theistic perspective should read the book, which should be the definitive work on astronomy from a young-earth perspective for decades . . . Byl's Reformed flavour of Christianity plays a role in his case.'

Two of the above reviewers on Amazon.com gave the book five stars out of five.

ISBN 0 85151 800 1
256 pp., large paperback

For free illustrated catalogue please write to
THE BANNER OF TRUTH TRUST

3 Murrayfield Road,   P O Box 621, Carlisle,
Edinburgh EH12 6EL   Philadelphia 17013,
UK   USA

www.banneroftruth.co.uk